THE LIFE OF
DAVID DUDLEY FIELD

David Dudley Field

THE LIFE

OF

DAVID DUDLEY FIELD

BY

HENRY M. FIELD

It was the boast of Augustus that he found Rome of brick and left it of marble. But how much nobler shall be the sovereign's boast, when he shall have it to say, that he found law dear and left it cheap; found it a sealed book, left it a living letter; found it the patrimony of the rich, left it the inheritance of the poor; found it the two-edged sword of craft and oppression, left it the staff of honesty and the shield of innocence.

—LORD BROUGHAM.

Fred B. Rothman & Co.
Littleton, Colorado
1995

Library of Congress Cataloging-in-Publication Data

Field, Henry M. (Henry Martyn), 1822-1907.
The life of David Dudley Field / by Henry M. Field.
p. cm.
Originally published: New York : C. Scribner's, 1898.
ISBN 0-8377-2140-7
1. Field, David Dudley, 1805-1894. 2. Lawyers--New York (N.Y.)--Biography. 3. Law reform--United States--History--19th century. I. Title.
KF368.F5F525 1995
340'.092--dc20
[B]
95-6814
CIP

Printed in United States of America

The paper used in this publication meets the minimum requirements of American National Standard for Information Sciences—Permanence of Paper for Printed Library Materials, ANSI Z39.48-1984.

THE LIFE

OF

DAVID DUDLEY FIELD

BY

HENRY M. FIELD

It was the boast of Augustus that he found Rome of brick and left it of marble. But how much nobler shall be the sovereign's boast, when he shall have it to say, that he found law dear and left it cheap; found it a sealed book, left it a living letter; found it the patrimony of the rich, left it the inheritance of the poor; found it the two-edged sword of craft and oppression, left it the staff of honesty and the shield of innocence.

—LORD BROUGHAM.

NEW YORK

CHARLES SCRIBNER'S SONS

1898

PRESS OF J. J. LITTLE & CO.
ASTOR PLACE, NEW YORK

TO STEPHEN J. FIELD

JUSTICE OF THE SUPREME COURT OF THE UNITED STATES.

We are all that are left! One by one, father, mother, brothers, sisters, have passed on till we are standing alone! When, last of all, our eldest brother left us, it would have fallen to you to write the story of his busy life, but that you were so engrossed with your duties on the bench as to forbid any other labor.* Hence the task has fallen to me, who can only write as a layman. But if the picture be wanting in some professional details, it will at least be drawn by a loving hand. And yet it is not from mere personal regard that we cherish the memory of our beloved dead, but that he was a great figure in his generation. We who were nearest to him felt the inspiration most, and now that he is gone, we recognize more than ever what we owe to him, as next to what we owe to those who gave us being, and it is our highest ambition to be not unworthy of such a brother, and of such a father and mother.

---

*The preparation of this volume was begun soon after the death of Mr. Field, and has occupied all the time that the writer could give to it for three years. It is a singular coincidence that as he closes his work upon it, his brother retires from the Supreme Court of the United States after a service of thirty-four years and six months—a longer time than that of any other man who ever sat upon the bench since the foundation of the Government, not excepting the great Chief Justice Marshall.

PREFACE

"For at least a third of a century," said the late Mr. Austin Abbott, "David Dudley Field was the most commanding figure at the American bar." This alone would justify, if it did not demand, some record of his long and splendid career, while the traditions of his great arguments still linger in the memories of the survivors of his generation. But he was not merely "a figure at the bar," however "commanding"; he was a reformer and reconstructor of the law itself; in which the work that he did cannot be appreciated without some knowledge of the unsatisfactory state of the law when he entered upon the practice of his profession.

In the colonial period of American history, our law was the common law of England, that dates back to the time of Alfred the Great, and was overlaid with the accumulations of a thousand years. The Acts of Parliament were scattered through hundreds of volumes. There were whole libraries of decisions of the courts—decisions that were often so contradictory as to create hopeless confusion. And even more confusing than the law itself, was the administration of the law, as there were two Forms of Procedure: in Law and in Equity;

whereby what was decided in one might be reversed in the other. Was there any necessity for this roundabout way to secure simple justice? Was it not possible to reduce somewhat the enormous bulk of the English law; to gather up the mighty fragments that were scattered all along the centuries, and frame them into fixed codes? Such were the questions that a young lawyer asked himself more than fifty years ago. He believed that, even where chaos reigned, it was within the power of man to restore order: to cut a passage through the jungle, and "cast up an highway" that should lead straight to the Temple of Justice. But the very suggestion was so presumptuous as to seem to be almost sacrilege. It was a want of respect to the traditions of the most conservative of professions. The Reform and the Reformer were attacked with argument and ridicule: by lawyers and judges; in courts and legislatures. But he was in that stage of early manhood when one is inspired by high ideals. The very idea of justice was sacred to him. God was the Great Lawgiver, and human justice should be framed as far as possible on the foundation of eternal justice. That was the only thing that could hold the world together. If, as Mr. Webster tells us, "Justice is the great interest of man upon earth," there can be no greater service to humanity than to establish justice by law. The union of Justice and Power is the only solid foundation for human society. Inspired by such a conviction, the Reform of the Law was to its projector a holy crusade. Brought up in the old Puritan faith that the law of God was not only for the wise but for the simple, he would have the law of man brought down to the intelligence of all who were under it. No foreign phrases should obscure its meaning. Every word should be in the dear old English tongue wherein we were born. If all men could not understand the intricacies of the law, they could at least understand justice, as they felt the stings and wrongs of injustice. He would have the pressure of the law like the pressure of the atmosphere, resting alike upon all, yet not as a burden, but as the very breath of life, the inspiration of freedom as well as of justice, that makes men strong and nations great. Thus the law should be "of the people, by the people, and for the people."

Such was the dream of the young Reformer. But how far did he achieve what he undertook? A Lord Chancellor of England, the late Lord Cairns, said that he "had done more for the reform of the law than any other man living;" and expressed his amazement that he could undertake the enormous labor it involved, while at the same time carrying on a large professional practice. This was indeed the wonder of all who knew him. The work of the student and the codifier alone was more than enough to absorb the undivided labor of the longest life. But the Reformer was not a recluse, shut up within the walls of libraries, which no sound from the outer world could invade. He was a soldier who was always in the thick of the fight, as must be one who was a "commanding figure at the bar." Nor was this all. No man was more deeply interested in the political questions of the day. A Democrat by principle, he was one of the first to break with his party on the point of the extension of slavery, which he fought in conventions, when he stood almost alone—a movement that took form in the old Free Soil party, which was the nucleus of the Republican party, that at last won its victory in the election of Lincoln, and kept possession of the government for a whole generation after the war.

But above all professional or political ambitions was the Reform which he undertook in his early manhood, and which filled up the measure of his days till he breathed his last in his ninetieth year, a purpose thus briefly recorded on his tomb:

HE DEVOTED HIS LIFE TO THE REFORM OF THE LAW:
TO CODIFY THE COMMON LAW;
TO SIMPLIFY LEGAL PROCEDURE;
TO SUBSTITUTE ARBITRATION FOR WAR;
TO BRING JUSTICE WITHIN THE REACH OF ALL MEN.

Did any man, living or dead, ever aim higher than this? Is it possible to conceive of anything more noble than "to bring justice within the reach of all men"? How far he succeeded is another question, which the writer, after telling the story in a simple narrative, leaves to the reader, asking only that his opinion, whatever it may be, should be formed entirely apart from personal considerations. The character here portrayed was a very positive one, and roused strong antagonisms. The Reformer—like other Reformers—was a man of war from his youth, and gave, as well as received, tremendous blows. But all this is over now. He has gone to the grave, and in that grave should be buried all the passions of the hour. But though he is gone, his work remains, an inheritance to future generations, and may safely be left to the verdict of posterity. His name has passed into history, and by history let it be judged.

CONTENTS

PORTRAITS

CHAPTER I.

FROM THE STOCK OF THE PILGRIM FATHERS.

The history of New England dates from Plymouth Rock. But the Mayflower was from the beginning a sort of forlorn hope. Of the hundred pilgrims that it had on board, the greater part were so worn out with the three months' voyage, and the winter's cold, that when the spring came one half were in their graves; so that the brave little ship is but a picturesque figurehead in the great drama of American history, and has its place of honor chiefly as the pioneer of larger emigrations that had in them more of the seeds of empire. Ten years later came John Winthrop with an expedition a thousand strong, and founded the Colony of Massachusetts Bay. About the same time another pilgrim ship had among its passengers a grandson of John Field, the astronomer, who, a hundred years before Isaac Newton, introduced into England the Copernican Astronomy. That he was a Puritan of the Puritans may be inferred from his very name, the good old Scriptural name of Zachariah. But Puritan as he was, he was none the less a man of affairs, of the energy and enterprise that are needed in the making of a new country.

Some historical critics, to whom nothing is sacred, would take from us the heroism of our Pilgrim fathers, by telling us that they were not seeking "freedom to worship God" so much as to better their worldly fortunes. But the two things were not inconsistent in the Puritan any more than in the "canny Scot," whose psalm-singing and long prayers did not prevent his being thrifty at a bargain, or a tremendous fighter on the field of battle. The men who landed on the rock-bound coast of New England, had first of all to fight for existence; to find homes for their wives and children. But wherever they went in the wilderness, they carried the ark of God with them, and

> "The sounding aisles of the dim woods rang
> To the anthem of the free."

Full of the life of the New World, Zachariah Field remained but a few years near Boston, when he pushed into the interior over a hundred miles to the valley of the Connecticut. The old records of Hartford show that he was one of the original proprietors, who bought the land from the Indians, part of which was held as the property of the town, and part was assigned to individuals in proportion to the amount contributed to the purchase. As he was still in the vigor of manhood he was one of the forty-two men furnished by

Hartford to take part in the Pequot war. He was afterwards one of a company that bought from the Indians nine miles square of land lying north of Mount Holyoke, and moved up the valley of the Connecticut, living first in Northampton, and then in Hatfield, where he died in 1666.

In venturing thus far towards the frontier he exposed his family to great dangers from the savages that were lurking near the settlements. A few years later King Philip's war stirred up the Indians from one end of Massachusetts to the other. The massacre of Bloody Brook (a part of Deerfield), in which a whole company of soldiers were killed, sent a thrill of horror through the new settlements, that were soon deserted, the people fleeing to Northampton for safety. But a few months later the whites turned the tide in the battle of Turner's Falls, which gave them rest for some years, till the Indians were stirred up again by the French, and attacking Deerfield at night, set fire to the town, and massacred part of the inhabitants, and made prisoners of the rest. In all these terrible scenes few families suffered more than the Fields, of whom some were killed and others, including women, were carried off as captives to Canada.

But in spite of all dangers the brave settlers held the fort, or rather held the frontier, and became the ancestors of families who have kept the name in honor in Northwestern Massachusetts for six generations.

Among their descendants are not only ministers and lawyers and judges, but men of business, whose vast interests require as much financial ability as to be Secretary of the Treasury of the United States; so that we may be pardoned if we claim it as another proof that blood will tell, that Mr. Marshall Field, of Chicago, is a direct descendant of the old Puritan, Zachariah Field.

But, though this tribe of Israel was of a fighting race, the bravest of men do not care to be wakened too often by the war-whoop of the savage: and a grandson of Zachariah, "Ebenezer," signifying "Thus far hath the Lord helped us," thought it more for his peace of mind to go back to the land from which his forefather came out, and returned to Connecticut. Nor did he stop at Hartford, but went on to the shore of Long Island Sound and took up his home in Guilford, in the eastern part of the town, now called Madison, where he married Mary Dudley, (a descendant of two governors of the Colony of New Haven) through whom the name of Dudley came into the family. Here he and those that came after him abode for more than a hundred years. In the old burying ground where

"The rude forefathers of the hamlet sleep."

may still be seen side by side three low headstones which mark the heads of three generations: for after Ebenezer came his eldest son, David, who settled in the north part of Madison, probably as early as 1720, in a district which, as it was yet uncleared, was called "The Woods," where he soon after erected a frame house of two stories, that was literally founded on a rock, and is standing to this day.

After David came Timothy, who lived on the old homestead, which he inherited from his father. He was a man of great vigor and resolution, which led his fellow-townsmen to look to him as a leader in troublous times. When he was in the prime of manhood—a little over thirty years of age—the War of the Revolution broke out, and he entered the army. In 1776 he joined the seventh regiment raised in Connecticut for the defence of the State, and served under Washington, when the great leader, rallying his forces after the disastrous defeat on Long Island, took a position of defence on the upper part of New York Island, between Fort Washington and the East River, to watch the British troops which then held the city, and took part in the battle of White Plains. He was afterward in command of a coast guard organized for protection against expeditions that might attack towns along the shore of Long Island Sound, in which he once saved Guilford from a raid of Tories who landed June 17th, 1781, and had begun to burn the town, when, mustering the farmers with their muskets, he attacked them with such spirit that he drove them to their boats, leaving their dead and wounded behind them.

Captain Field lived many years after the war, and

was a fine specimen of the old "Continentals," who united the character of the farmer and the soldier. The older inhabitants of the town still remember his striking figure. One who says "he can see him now," describes him as "a large, broad-breasted, well-built man." Even while engaged in peaceful pursuits he kept up the military style of dress of other days. "He always wore a cocked hat, short breeches, long stockings, and bright, silver shoe-buckles; and I never saw him, either on the farm or abroad, that he was not dressed in this manner."

This revolutionary veteran had eight children, of whom six were daughters. The sons were both ministers. The elder, who bore his father's name of Timothy, was one of the early pioneers of Western New York, and was settled in Canandaigua, where are still many of his kindred. He afterward returned to New England, and became a pastor in Westminster, Vermont, where he died in 1844, leaving a name that is held by the old residents in loving remembrance. The other son was the Rev. David Dudley Field, the father of the subject of this biography.

It would be a very imperfect narrative that did not pause before the figure of the venerable patriarch who forms the link between past generations and the present, and whom all who survive hold in tenderest love and reverence. He was descended, as we have seen, from a race of brave and God-fearing men, who in times of danger defended the frontier settlements against the savages, and fought for their country's independence. But it was a small world into which he came. Yet not so small as it seemed. Those days had their excitements as well as ours. It was just after the Revolutionary war. Indeed he was born before the contest was decided. The last gun was fired while he was in his cradle. Such great events left their impression far behind them. The agitation remained long after the conflict was over, and the mind of the country was still rocked and tossed, like the ocean after a storm. Every hamlet in New England was full of tales of the great struggle. The actors in those scenes were still upon the stage. There were men who had fought behind the entrenchments on Bunker Hill; who had followed Washington in all the vicissitudes of the long conflict; who had camped with him at Valley Forge; who had witnessed the surrender at Yorktown. From a child he was familiar with these heroic traditions, for at his father's fireside he heard stories of the camp and the field. Nor were such things altogether of the past, for now and then, like distant thunder, came the sound of wars and revolutions beyond the sea.

With all this, there was an intellectual life in New England at the close of the last century and the beginning of this, perhaps as great as at the present day. In every town there were men of education and learning. Yale College exerted a powerful influence in Connecticut, as Harvard did in Massachusetts. It raised up a body of educated men—ministers, physicians, lawyers, and judges—who were scattered through the State, filling positions of influence, and forming an educated class. The town of Guilford had as its minister Rev. John Elliott, a man of high classical attainments, whose discourses—a few of which are still preserved—show him to have possessed uncommon ability and eloquence.

Like his older brother, this son of Captain Field chose the profession of the ministry, for which indeed he had such a natural taste, as might be interpreted as a Divine call. A schoolmate used afterwards to relate how, when boys, they would go off into the woods, where "David" would mount a rock, and "preach" at him as long as his youthful listener would hear. As he walked on the sea-shore, he shouted to the waves, which seemed like answering voices, as they came rolling up the beach. The late Dr. John Todd, who spent a part of his early life in Madison, said: "In my boyhood I used to hear about 'Mr. Field,' the young man who had gone to college. I walked on the hard sands of the beach where he had walked, I stood on the same fishing-rocks on which he had stood, and I listened to the same surf-roar of the sea to which he had listened."

Bent on an education, he applied to his minister, who had the pleasure of a scholar in reviewing his old studies, and fitted him for college along with two of his class-mates, Erastus Scranton and Jeremiah Evarts, the father of William M. Evarts, the late Secretary of

State. They entered Yale together in 1798. Field and Evarts were room-mates during their college course, and always entertained for each other the warmest affection. The class of 1802 numbered among its members others whose names became honorably distinguished in after life—Isaac C. Bates, Senator from Massachusetts; Judge Hubbard of Boston, William Maxwell of Virginia, Governors Tomlinson and Pond of Connecticut, Junius Smith, who has been called the father of ocean steam navigation, and Pelatiah Perit, an eminent merchant of New York. But perhaps the best that Yale College gave to its students then, came from the personal influence of President Dwight, a man of such noble presence, combined with such intellect and such eloquence, as gave him a great ascendancy over the minds of his pupils, who looked up to him as a king of men. No one felt his influence more than Field, and the impression remained to the end of his life. While in college, and for some time after, the intervals of study were occupied in teaching school, by which he obtained means to complete his education.

Graduating with high honors in 1802, he had next to prepare for his profession. At that time there were no theological seminaries in the country, and students of divinity pursued a course of study with some eminent minister. Among these was Dr. Charles Backus of Somers, to whom the young graduate went, and found something better than theology in his future wife, a young lady who bore the name of Dickinson, the daughter of Captain Noah Dickinson, who had served as an officer under General Putnam in the old French war, and afterwards was in the army in the war of the Revolution, and at the return of peace settled down to the quiet life of a farmer. One who knew him only in the last years of his life describes him as a man of commanding appearance, nearly, if not quite, six feet high, with an intellectual head and face, that made him a fine type of "the gentleman of the Old School."

The daughter of this old soldier was long remembered by those who knew her in her youth as having great personal beauty, a light graceful figure, and a very animated countenance. It was the fashion of those times to give to daughters the names of the Christian graces, which of course they were expected to exemplify, such as Faith, Hope, Patience, and Charity. One of her sisters was named Love, and upon this daughter of the Puritans was bestowed the meek name of Submit. In after years her children sometimes playfully told her that the appellation was not the most appropriate, since she had a due share (but not a whit too much) of true womanly spirit. As she was born on the first day of October, 1782, she had but just reached the age of twenty-one when she was married in 1803. And truly, if a good wife is from the Lord, no one ever had more reason to recognize a special Providence in the gift than this young minister. From that day she was for nearly fifty-eight years the light and joy of his home. Whoever in all those years shared her hospitality, will not forget what brightness and sunshine she shed around her. Whatever of success or prosperity has attended the family, has been due in a great measure to her unselfish spirit, which made every sacrifice for the education of her children—to her perpetual buoyancy of temper, to her womanly patience, courage, and hope.

These are tender memories that stand out in touching relief against the dark background of those early times of struggle and of war, while the figures of grandsires who perilled their lives for their country is not only a matter of pride for the past, but an inspiration for the future. Nobody felt this more than the Law-Reformer, whose life was one long battle. In the days when he had to stand almost alone against a host of opponents, he was always able to strengthen his courage by remembering that he had the blood of these old soldiers in his veins.

CHAPTER II.

BIRTH AND BOYHOOD. REMOVAL TO STOCKBRIDGE.

It is hard to transport ourselves back nearly a hundred years, so as to enter into the life in New England at the beginning of this century. It was very primitive as compared with the life of to-day. There were no railroads and no steamboats. Locomotion was slow and difficult. If a country minister wished to visit his brother in the next town to discusss the hard points of Calvinism, he could not be whirled to the spot in an electric car, but had to jog over the hills in his "one-hoss shay." But after all the slower gait furnished the more time to think and "ruminate" by the way, and many a minister has preached a sermon to his horse before he preached it to his people. Perhaps there was as much general intelligence, as much true manliness and womanliness, and as much real happiness, in those simple days of our fathers as in these eager and rushing days of ours. Happiness belongs to no place or time. Love brings heaven down to earth, and makes all things new, and no painter or poet could have pictured a sweeter idyll than that of the home-coming of the young minister with his young bride; as they rode over the hills that autumn day, when the woods were aflame with purple and gold, and down the valley of the Connecticut to the village that was to be their home for many years to come. Every step of the way brought him nearer to the home of his childhood, to the place where he was born, and to the College where he was educated. What a joy it would be to drive down to the seaside, where he used to walk upon the beach, or to the City of Elms, to meet his old classmates on Commencement day, when they would exchange their experiences, their hopes and fears, as they ventured out upon the scenes of active life. Apart from these imagings the new parish might not have seemed quite so inviting, for Haddam is a rough and rocky town, its chief source of wealth being its quarries of granite. Nor was there any beauty in the long, straggling village. The old meeting house was a huge barn-like structure, which answered not only for a place of worship, but for town meetings, and now and then for the court, if some poor wretch was to be tried for murder, when the eagerness "to be in at the death" was such that no other roof could cover the multitude. But after all nature had been kindly to the old town, which was framed in between the rocky hills and the majestic river that wound its way among them on its course to the sea.

The parsonage was not after the pattern of an English rectory, with its Gothic doors and windows covered with vines, nor of any modern architecture. No Quaker dwelling could be plainer than the two-story frame house, that stood so close upon the street as to leave but a few feet for a bit of green grass. Nor was the salary oppressive. If he was not, like the preacher in Goldsmith's Deserted Village, "passing rich on forty pounds a year," his stipend amounted to but little more, though nominally it was more than twice as much—a hundred pounds, or five hundred dollars! This was riches indeed had it all been paid in money, but in those days there was very little money in the country. There was no question between gold and silver as legal tender, for it was not often that the people saw the glitter of either coin, and those who could not pay in cash paid "in kind." A farmer brought a load of wood, and received credit for so much toward the minister's salary.* I have heard him say that in all these years he never had at one time so much as a hundred dollars! But what cared the young minister and his wife so long as they had health, and heart, and hope? If their dwelling was plain without, it was bright within, as the young mistress filled it with the sunshine of her presence; and never was it so warm and bright as on

* When Jonathan Edwards was settled in Stockbridge in 1750, the town voted him a salary of six pounds, thirteen shillings and fourpence, lawful money, and a hundred sleigh-loads of fire-wood—of which twenty were furnished by the white settlers and eighty by the Indians!

a winter day, February 13th, 1805, when they welcomed into the world their first-born son, to whom they gave his father's name of David Dudley Field.

Hardly was the little creature out of his cradle before he began to show signs of a will of his own. An old dame who was employed in the family, and in after years used to boast that she had administered to him necessary domestic discipline, gave as a reason for it that "he was a most determined little fellow." She found it hard to break his will. In this the child was father of the man. Many found the same difficulty in the later stages of his career.

A boy so full of life could not but be fond of sports, though under a little restraint, as he was the minister's son! But outdoor exercise of any kind exhilarated him, whether it was skating on the ice-bound river, or being whirled at full speed over the crisp and glittering snow.

Still keener was the enjoyment to sit on a winter night before a blazing fire, and hear old men tell tales of old times! Their next-door neighbor had been a seafaring man. On a winter evening he and his boys were commonly occupied in knitting nets for the shad fishery. Then was the time for the old seaman's yarns, to which young David would listen with infinite delight.

As soon as he was old enough he had been sent to school. But from all his schooling he gathered only the rudiments of knowledge, for while he was still a mere boy, his father took him in hand, to teach him something better than learning by rote, to think for himself, as he would study out his sums in arithmetic. If in after years he showed a remarkable power of reasoning, he owed it largely to the mental discipline that he had in his father's study.

Then came a passion for reading. But where to find the books! In those days there were no circulating libraries. Indeed there was not a library of any kind in the town except his father's, and that was composed chiefly of books of divinity! "Of tales and romances there were none; of the English classics little; and of poetry just three books—Milton's Paradise Lost, Young's Night Thoughts, and Watts' Psalms and Hymns!" The Night Thoughts suggested doleful meditations, and Watts' Psalms and Hymns were meant to be sung, and as he was not a singer, he would not presume to devote himself to them; but the sonorous lines of Milton caught his ear. He committed pages of them to memory, and was constantly repeating them to himself as he was wandering about among the rocks and hills.

With this love of poetry and of nature, nothing so captivated him as the broad bosom of the Connecticut, divided by a long and narrow island, which he in his youthful enthusiasm thought "one of the prettiest spots in the world." Of all things in nature that speak not and hear not, there is not one that can become so real a companion as a river. Soft and still may be its flow, yet in its gentle murmurs it whispers to the heart, if it does not speak loudly, while it lulls the too sensitive nature. It is not a dead thing, like yonder cliffs of granite, that change not with the passing centuries. It is alive, and the very image and reflection of our own life, as it is ever in motion and always in one direction, never turning back, but flowing on and on, forever and forever! Those who in after years were accustomed to see the great advocate at the bar, in the contests of professional life, could not imagine how full his mind was of poetry and of the love of nature. But those who knew him intimately can see him in his boyhood, sitting for hours at the window of his father's house, or in the summer time on the grassy slope, or under the trees, in that silent communion with nature, which to him was one of the most exquisite delights to the last hour of his life.

And now, as he looks at the river, there go the ships! Even in those early days there was a considerable inland commerce on the Connecticut as on the Hudson. Sloops and schooners went down the river, bound to New York, or it might be to the West Indies, and now and then came a full-rigged ship, with broad wings outspread to fly across the sea! All this excited the boy's imagination, till he was seized with a passion for the life that thus passed before him, and went to his father and begged him to let him go to sea!—a passion that grew stronger when there was a prospect of something more exciting than a seaman's life, however full it might be of novelty and adventure, as all along the coast was heard the sound of war, for among the recollections of his boyhood, he recalled distinctly the breaking out of the war of 1812. Once, talking of the old times, he said: "I remember when a boy seven years of age, as I was riding with father over the hills to Killingworth, a man met us on the road, and told us that war was declared with England! My father was startled by the news. The country had been expecting it, and yet it caused a shock when it came. It was a strange coincidence, that at that moment there came up a thunder storm. The sky grew black, the lightnings flashed, and the thunder rolled from one end of the heavens to the other, as if the elements were in sympathy with the storm of war that was to burst upon the country. I remember two privateers going down the Connecticut river; and once at New Haven I saw English ships-of-war sailing up the Sound. I remember also a playmate running up the hill behind the village to tell us the great news that Bonaparte had been beaten at Waterloo."

Life in a country village in those days was not very eventful. There was not even the sensation of evil, as it was a very peaceable community, where every man dwelt in safety, with none to molest or make him afraid. The farmers did not lock their doors at night, for there was nothing to tempt a thief or a robber. The very infrequency of crime made it more startling when it came, an illustration of which may show the gravity and the solemnity with which the people of New England administered justice as under the authority, not only of the State, but of God, who had commanded that they should not bear the sword in vain.

In 1815 a man by the name of Peter Lung, living in Middletown, of violent temper, and maddened by intoxication, murdered his wife. He was arrested, and taken to Haddam, the county seat, and confined in jail. When the time for trial came, such was the excitement of the people, and the eagerness to witness it, that the court house did not suffice, and the trial was transferred to the meeting house, whose wide floor and deep galleries held a crowd, that looked on the scene with awe and wonder. The venerable Judge Trumbull presided, taking his seat in front of the pulpit, in his ruffled shirt sleeves and bosom, and his short-clothes. The trial was conducted with due deliberation, but the case was clear, and could have but one issue.

After receiving sentence the prisoner was taken back to his place of confinement, where the village pastor was constant in his ministrations till the day of his execution, which was to be accompanied by a service such as we know not if it could be found anywhere else in Christendom, though it once existed in Scotland, and is described by Scott in The Heart of Midlothian. It was that a sermon should be preached at the execution:

and this not only to the spectators of the scene, that they might profit by the lesson which it conveyed, but *in presence of the condemned*, who was brought into the church, and sat in the aisle in front of the pulpit, and whom the preacher addressed in person. As the prisoner had become attached to his spiritual adviser, he desired him to be with him on his last day, to strengthen him for the moment that he was to suffer, and to preach the sermon ! The execution took place in Middletown, and drew an immense concourse of people from all the surrounding country. Mr. Field took with him his son, but ten years old, whose eyes were ready to burst when the soldiers brought in the prisoner, and fifty years after he said: "I can see them now, and hear the clang as they grounded their arms!" The sermon, as was fitting in view of the cause of the crime, was a warning against drunkenness, from Luke xxi. 34: "Take heed to yourselves, lest at any time your hearts be overcharged with surfeiting and drunkenness, and cares of this life, and so that day come upon you unawares;" from which the preacher denounced that which is the cause of so many acts of violence and blood. As he drew near the close, he turned to the unhappy man before him, who rose and stood (as he had done when receiving sentence from the judge), to hear these last words before he was launched into eternity. The preacher then addressed him as follows:

"PETER LUNG: By your confessions, intemperate

drinking has been the cause of the calamities which have come upon you. This inflamed your passions, naturally violent and impetuous; filled your tongue with profaneness and threatening, and your hands with frequent acts of violence, even upon her who was the wife of your covenant. In a fit of intoxication you inflicted upon her wounds, marks of which she carried to the grave. What you have done, as it has been judged by the proper tribunals, subjects you to an ignominious execution. From this there is no escape. But men who forfeit their lives to the laws of their country, may upon repentance receive a pardon from God. During your long confinement, as your life has drawn nigh unto the grave; as you have been counted with them that go down into the pit; have you cried day and night before God? . . Pray God to search your heart, to see if there be any wicked way in you, and to lead you in the way everlasting. Whatever you do, you must do speedily: for this day thou shalt die. Before yonder sun shall set in the west, your probationary state will be closed forever. If in any doubt about your preparation, you may yet find mercy. He who pardoned the penitent thief on the cross, may pardon you in the place of execution. Pray God, then, if perhaps your sins may be forgiven you. Cry to Him, God be merciful to me, a sinner! and continue those cries till death shall remove you hence. May the Lord Almighty support you in the trying scene before you, and through infinite grace have mercy on your soul!"

When this solemn service was over, the mournful procession took up its line of march, the soldiers leading the way to the place of execution. Young David, who followed in the throng, remembered how the wretched man, dressed in a long white robe, that was to be his winding-sheet, stood upon the scaffold, which was guarded by a body of troopers, who closed up around it, and cut the fatal cord with their swords. When this last act was over, all turned away, and as the people from the country round rode back over the hills, they talked together of a scene the like of which, at least in the feature here described, has perhaps not since been witnessed in New England.

While these years passed on, the parsonage was being filled with a little group of children. Seven were born in Haddam, of whom one died in infancy, and six were living, with ages from two to thirteen years. There were so many little mouths to be fed, little bodies to be clothed, and the older ones to be sent to school. How this problem was solved, is the secret of the mysterious power that lies in a woman's heart and hand. With a salary of five hundred dollars, and six children, there was no time for idleness. In those days there were no Irish servants, and indeed hardly servants of any kind, except a few colored people kept in old families. Almost every woman in the country did her own work with such "help" as she could now and then find from the assistance of a farmer's daughter. Yet such tasks did not daunt this gentle mother with her delicate and slender frame. She did not count it hardship or self-denial, for the passion of her life was devotion to her husband and her children, and she moved about the house with a light step, singing as she went. All day long was the parsonage kept alive by her busy hands and feet. But now she was to be left alone for five months together, which was their first, and—except a visit to Europe thirty years later—their last separation.

This was an episode in his ministerial life that at once separated and linked together his two places of settlement. The people of New England had begun to wake up to the idea of the Great West, which then included Western New York, a large part of which was still covered by the primeval forest. He read about the emigrants from Connecticut and Massachusetts going out into the wilderness. Why should he not go and preach to them? He was just in his prime, but thirty-seven years old! Who could endure hardship better than he? Whereupon he resigned his quiet parish on the river side, and accepted an appointment under the old Missionary Society of Connecticut, to the new settlements on the southern shore of Lake Ontario and on the banks of the Oswego River. The country was then a wilderness, through which he rode on horseback, preaching in log-houses and under the shade of trees. This frontier had been the scene of constant fighting during the then recent war, and as he rode along he visited several of the fields of battle. Buffalo had been burnt by the British, and was still but a small straggling village, in which there was not a single church, and he preached in the court house !

This absence continued for five months, during which the young mother was left alone with her little flock, to watch over them, and keep them safely within the fold. In after years she often told us of the anxieties of those days : how at night, when the little ones were in their nests, she would go round the house to see that all was quiet, and then lie down and sleep beside her children, feeling that they were safe under the eye of God.

During this period she had a great comfort in her oldest boy, who, though he was but thirteen years of age, at once took in the situation, and felt that a certain responsibility rested upon him to be in the place of the absent father, as the protector of his young mother, and of his only sister, and the four little boys, the youngest of whom was but just out of his cradle. This feeling of an older brother, as being the natural guardian of the younger, remained through life : a care that was rewarded in after years, when he lived to see the youngest of those little brothers, and a son of that sister, meet on the bench of the Supreme Court of the United States.

But at last the father was coming home! On his return he passed through Stockbridge, Mass., where the old minister, Dr. Stephen West, past his eightieth year, was no longer able to preach, and Mr. Field was asked to supply the pulpit for several weeks, and soon after was called to be the pastor, and settled the following year, August 25, 1819, then beginning a ministry that was to continue nearly eighteen years.

The removal was no small affair. Teams were sent to Connecticut to bring the furniture—a week's journey to go and return. There were beds and bureaus, tables and chairs, and most weighty of all, boxes piled with books, for the minister had accumulated a large library. Nearly fifty years after, the subject of this biography and the writer of it, both of whom lived in New York, had their summer homes in Stockbridge, and took their exercise on horseback together. One morning as they were riding over the hills, they passed bv a farmer's door, who told them that he had in his possession one of the teamster's waggons that had done service in this memorable exodus, and they rode into the yard to see it. There it was, looking like an old army waggon, that had been through the wars. It required but little imagination to picture it piled with all the treasures of the household, while on the top, riding high in air, were perched half a dozen children; and thus bearing "Cæsar and his fortunes," it rumbled over the mountains to the new home among the Berkshire Hills.

CHAPTER III.

THE NEW HOME. GOING TO COLLEGE.

The removal of the family to Stockbridge was an event to all concerned, and a turning-point in their history. It is with men as with trees, that the best of them may be improved by transplanting. True, the Housatonic was not as large as the Connecticut, but it has a beauty all its own as it winds its way through the Berkshire Hills. At this point the valley widens, stretching away in meadows, that rise gently into hills covered with forests, till the horizon is shut in by an amphitheatre of mountains. The village is on a plateau near the river, and is laid out in one long street, arched with elms, underneath which were the residences of families some of which bore the names, as they retained the manners, of the old Colonial aristocracy.

The town had a history, which, if not more notable than that of many other New England towns, gave it a local distinction. The fertility of the valley had attracted a tribe of Indians, who gave their name of Housatonic to the river, and it was to plant a mission among them that the first white men came from Eastern Massachusetts. What John Eliot had been a hundred years before, John Sergeant was now, an apostle to the Indians, by whom he was so beloved that when he was laid to rest, they wished to be buried beside him that they might rise with him in the resurrection. After him appeared the stately form of Jonathan Edwards, who found the quiet of the wilderness a fit seclusion in which to revolve the ever vexed questions of

> "Fate, free will, foreknowledge absolute."

Then came one who was pastor of the church for sixty years, that spanned the whole period from the time of the old French war through the Revolution and the second war with Great Britain. This was Stephen West, who, though a man of small stature, was full of patriotic fire, as he showed when the tidings came of the battle of Lexington, and the minute men were mustered on the village green, and he addressed them, telling them to do their duty to God and their country! He lived to a good old age, and was always a notable figure in the town when he walked abroad arrayed in his three-cornered hat, his silver knee buckles, and his gold-headed cane, and all stood aside and uncovered their heads with a deference that is too much forgotten in these democratic, not to say degenerate, days.

In the line of this apostolic succession came the new minister in the autumn of 1819. Among the special attractions for the young student was an excellent Academy under the instruction of a famous teacher, Mr. Jared Curtis, who had a reputation for turning out thorough scholars. And what was even more important than the "head-master," he met here for the first time three young men of similar tastes, with whom he formed an intimacy that ripened into the closest friendship, that continued to the end of their lives. These were the brothers Mark and Albert Hopkins, the first of whom afterwards became the President of Williams College, and the other Professor of Astronomy; while the third was John Morgan, who became a Professor at Oberlin, Ohio, where his name is held in honor, as are the two others in the heart of every man who has been a student at Williams within the past generation.*

From the Academy the next step was to the College. Had his father continued to reside in Connecticut, the son would have gone, as his father did, to Yale. But Western Massachusetts had a College of its own, which bore the name of a gallant soldier, Colonel Ephraim Williams, who went from Stockbridge, and fell in the old French war. And so to Williams he went with the other students from Stockbridge. Those were among the

* Mr. Field survived them all. It was while he was in Europe, in the summer of 1887, that President Hopkins died: but on his return he prepared, at the request of the Trustees of the College, a fitting tribute to the memory of his life-long friend. It was delivered at the following Commencement, and is published in Volume III of his Miscellaneous Addresses.

happiest days of his life. He loved study, and the harder the subject the more he loved it for the very fact that it taxed his intellectual ability. No matter what the study was, Latin or Greek, or the problems of geometry, he attacked them all with a fierce determination. In those days scientific explorers in Europe and America were beginning to make their discoveries, and his eager mind was greatly excited by the mysteries which they revealed. Long years after he said: "I remember, as of yesterday, my feeling at my first lesson in chemistry. The world had changed. Instead of a cold, inanimate nature, I saw that everything was alive. The trees seemed nodding to me as I passed; the air whispered in my ears; every blade of grass, every green leaf, opened its wonderful structure. The ground moved beneath my feet; the rain, the light, and the clouds brought messages; and even the solid rocks stood full of affinities, ready to dissolve and form again in new combinations of their elements." But what fascinated him more than all was the starry heavens, even though it was before the modest Observatory had arisen, with its dome and its telescope. It was his interest in this study, together with his personal regard for Albert Hopkins, which led him in after years to give $25,000 to endow the professorship of astronomy.

How he ranked as a scholar compared with his classmates, I cannot speak from personal knowledge, as I did not enter College for many years after: but even then there was a tradition of a race of giants that had gone before us: among whom stood the four Stockbridge boys. I heard a great deal about them from an "Old Mortality," the "Professor of Dust and Ashes," who was the collector and purveyor of all the College gossip, and as such the most copious, if not the most credible, chronicler of his time. He used to say to me, perhaps to exalt my family pride, "They all said that Field was the best scholar that they had had in the College in ten years!"

And yet, though his standing was so high, he did not graduate. "The reason why I cannot tell." Something had given offence to the President, Dr. Griffin, who was somewhat tenacious of his dignity, and so the young man left the College a year before the end of his course, without waiting for the valedictory, that his classmates said was sure to be his. But whatever the petty irritation, it was soon after removed, and from that time to the hour of his death, Williams College had no more loyal son than he. The very ground on which it stood was sacred. How he loved this "Mother," he showed by coming back almost every year to the old home, to meet his classmates, the companions of other days, and recall their common associations. At the Commencement in 1875—fifty years after the graduation of his class—he delivered the Address before the Literary Societies, in which he christened his Alma Mater

"Williams the Beautiful." A few passages will show the spirit of the whole:

"We, who have returned to this beloved teacher of our youth, have come to recall and commemorate the past. We are thinking less of the new than of the old. We lay aside for the day whatever thoughts of the busy world outside might disturb the place or the time, while we revisit the scenes of college life, call up again the memories of those early years, take one another by the hand, look into one another's faces, listen to one another's voices, and rekindle sympathies dormant or forgotten. However long or short be the time since we went forth from the gates of this valley, however divergent our paths of life, we stand here as brethren. The youngest among us is the comrade of the oldest, as the recruit of to-day in a regiment that bears upon its colors the names of a hundred fights, looks upon the veteran as his comrade, and himself as one of a line of soldiers, inheritor and partaker of their fame. Here as there the files are continuous despite the changes in the ranks. Once a year we have our muster, and though each roll-call, like that of the morning after battle, bears many a name to which there is no answer, our lines, however thinned, are never broken.

"The sight of these faces, of these old roofs and halls, of these meadows and streams, and of these encircling hills, so quickens the inward sense that it sees forms that have vanished and hears voices that are silent forever. I behold my classmates as I beheld them then filing into the chapel, or gathered at recitations, or sauntering along the walks, or resting beneath the trees. I mark their gait; I hear their earnest debate, their hearty laugh, and I recall the strifes, the friendships, the greetings and the partings of those far-off days. I look into the sky —it is the sky of my boyhood; the stars clear and silent shine upon me as they shone fifty years ago.

"We came as boys; we studied and contended with one another. No doubt of the future gave us disquietude. The hereafter was the land of promise, bright with the dew of morning. The collegian is a dreamer, and, for the most part, a dreaming boy. He comes full of energy, incited by hope. He lays his hand upon the book of knowledge and opens it. What a revelation! The curtain is lifted and a new world is spread before him. He finds in every lesson something new; the past opens its treasures and Nature reveals herself; the rocks become histories; the clods grow instinct with life; the streams pouring from the hills have something to tell.

"Was it not a great thing for us that, while we were shut from the outer world by these mountain barriers, we were shut within this valley? I shall never cease to congratulate myself that my sense of beauty was trained within the circle of these mountains; that the morning light gilded for my eyes the sides of Greylock; that I saw the sun at noon standing over this endless variety of wood, meadow, and stream; that the evening twilight heightened while it softened the beauty of noon; and that when I looked from my window into the moonlight, it lay like a transparent celestial robe upon the sleeping valley and the watchful hills.

"So we passed our days. We formed a little community by ourselves. Our cares were few, our hopes many, and our friendships eternal. Factitious distinctions take no root in college ground. Nowhere else is character more truly measured; nowhere more than here is a sham found out. The words 'college-mate, class-mate, room-mate' signify a great deal beyond ordinary fellowship. Two students sitting under the trees at evening, or walking in the moonlight, confide to each other their inmost thoughts. The heart is too fresh to doubt, too young to betray.

"College life, though short reckoned by years, is long reckoned by impressions. These impressions are as ineradicable as the heart, whose pulsations begin and end with life. Go where you will—take the wings of morning and seek the uttermost parts of the earth; lose yourself in African jungles or South Sea islands—the memories of college days will go and abide with you. I have strolled along the Meles with a college-mate, and while we talked of Homer, who sang upon its banks, and of many other things, new and old, our thoughts reverted to the walks along the Hoosac, and we laughed as boys laugh over college anecdotes. I have stood on the slopes of Lebanon by the side of an American missionary, and as we looked over the sea into the West, our thoughts outran our sight, and lighted on 'Williams the Beautiful,' its historic Haystack and its Mission Park."

This feeling continued as long as he lived. Seldom did a Commencement pass that, if he was this side the Atlantic, he did not return to the old beloved spot, which had to him a peculiar fascination. The mountains about it were like the mountains roundabout Jerusalem to the pious Jew. Every walk along the riverside or among the hills had its associations, so that he went about as in a happy dream, recalling times long past, with loving memories of the living and the dead. On the College grounds no figure was more familiar than his, nor in the meetings of the Alumni, where he will long be remembered with sorrow that they shall see his face no more.

CHAPTER IV.

STUDIES LAW AND ENTERS PRACTICE IN NEW YORK. MARRIAGE : DEATH OF HIS WIFE : A YEAR ABROAD.

The young student had now come to the parting of the ways. He had finished his College course, and was to choose his profession. On that depended his future. The character of his mind, his habit of questioning, and his ardor in debate—what some would call his combativeness—drew him to the profession in which there were great battles to be fought and victories to be won, and he decided in favor of the law.

But where and how was he to get his education? There were no law schools in those days, and a student was fortunate who was so favored as to have a chair in the office of some lawyer of repute, where, in the intervals of such services as he could render, he had the freedom of the meagre library, from which, as well as from observing the practice in the courts, he could pick up the rudiments of his profession.

Such an opportunity came to him through a family resident in Stockbridge, but that might have been said to belong to the country, that of Judge Sedgwick, a veteran of Revolutionary times: who had been a member of the old Continental Congress; and, after the adoption of the Constitution, a member of the House of Representatives; from which Washington invited him to enter his Cabinet as Secretary of the Treasury; but who seems to have felt himself more at home in Congress, where he served in both houses, being three years in the Senate, and again in the House, where he was Speaker of the Sixth Congress. After these long years of service to his country, he retired from political life, and returned to the law as Judge of the Supreme Court of Massachusetts. When he passed off the stage he left three sons as the inheritors of his profession, as well as of his honored name. The eldest of these, Mr. Theodore Sedgwick, had long practised law in Albany, where he was the contemporary and friend of Martin Van Buren and of others second only to him. On retiring from practice he returned to Stockbridge and lived in the old ancestral home. But his former partner, a gentleman of Dutch descent, Mr. Harmanus Bleecker, still continued in Albany, to whom he gave Mr. Field an introduction, that at once opened his door to the new candidate for the bar.

The day was fixed for his departure. His mother's heart was very full, and yet with the courage that is combined with the tenderness of woman, she would have bid him go, if duty called him, like the Roman mother, if it were to return upon his shield ! His father always found strength for any crisis in his religious faith, and taking his son into his study, he knelt down and commended his first-born son to the protection of Almighty God, and then gave him for his only capital, ten dollars and a little Bible, which he kept to his dying day. Thus he went forth from under the paternal roof with ten dollars, a Bible, and his father's prayers ! As they came out of the door, the old-fashioned stage-coach rolled up and took him away. His home was behind him and the world was before him !

It was a long drive across the country, and the day was far spent when he came in sight of Albany, and crossing the river in a ferryboat, walked up the hill that was crowned by the Capitol in which he was in the future to make so many arguments before Courts and Legislatures. If "the heart of the stranger" was at first very lonely, the feeling was soon removed by the kindness of Mr. Bleecker, who, with true Dutch cordiality, made him welcome, not only to his office, but to his home, so that he wrote to his father: "My situation is quite pleasant. Mr. Bleecker is very polite and very kind. I have every facility for study which I can wish, and I endeavor to improve them. I feel in good spirits. Stockbridge is indeed pleasanter, but when our situation is not the best, it may be the next to it" —a bit of practical philosophy, to make the best of everything, that he carried through life.

It was not long before he began to feel at home in the dear old Dutch city, for which he had a kindly feeling ever after; but still his thoughts would turn to New York as offering a larger field for his activity. And then what prizes there were in the line of his profession! He knew of a young man who realized from it five hundred dollars a year! "Could he ever attain to such greatness as that!"

Here again the way was opened for him by the Sedgwicks, for while the eldest of the family had been in the practice of law at Albany, his two brothers, Henry and Robert, were in the front rank of their profession in New York, and showed the same readiness to forward the interests of one who came from dear old Stockbridge, who, thus invited, transferred his place of study to the city that was to be his home for more than sixty years.

While referring to this act of kindness, I cannot refrain from mentioning another instance of the same which was told me by the person concerned, the late William C. Bryant, who, like Mr. Field, had studied at Williams College, and afterwards entered on the practice of law in Great Barrington. But as the shy temperament of the poet did not promise great success at the bar, Mr. Henry D. Sedgwick invited him to come to New York, with the kind assurance that he "would see what he could do for him," and showed his friendship by introducing him to literary occupation that ended in his connection with the Evening Post, which brought both fame and fortune, an obligation that he was always ready to acknowledge, even when he had risen to such eminence that there was no man in all the city who was held in higher respect. Mr. Bryant and Mr. Field came to New York about the same time, and boarded in the same house, and thus began an intimacy and friendship which continued through life.

The change to New York was altogether to his taste, as he was more in the current of life, with everything to stimulate his ardor in his profession. His first business was to make himself master of the law, to which he applied his mind with such intensity as excluded everything beside. Day and night he thought of nothing else. By this devotion he so approved himself to the Messrs. Sedgwick, that when the elder brother, Henry, was obliged by ill health to retire from practice, the younger, Robert, invited Mr. Field to become his partner, a promotion which not only gratified his youthful ambition, but enabled him to take another step that was needed to complete his happiness. In the year 1829 (October 26th), when he was but twenty-four years old, he was married to Jane Lucinda Hopkins, a cousin of Mark Hopkins, who united such grace of person with such refinement of manner, so much sweetness with so much character, that he was the happiest of men in the thought that he should always have that gentle figure at his side; and when a year later he took in his arms his first-born, a son, it seemed as if there was nothing more that he could ask of God. And yet there was one thing more—a daughter, as a companion to the little brother, which was also his three years later.

But all this brightness was too much to last. After but little more than six years, the bride of his youth was taken from him, to be followed a few months later by a last child, not a year old, who, even in the grave, was laid to sleep on her mother's breast. Thus in a few months all of joy that the world had given him, had vanished out of sight, and sick of heart, he left—not his home, for home he had none—but his city and his country, and crossed the sea.

In after years Mr. Field repeated the voyage so often that Europe became almost as familiar to him as his own country. And yet there is never but one *first* view, when all impressions are fresh and new. A few dates recall his first glimpses of England and the Continent:

"On the 3d of May, 1836, I took passage in the packet Westminster for London. There were no steamers on the Atlantic in those days. Among the passengers were Horace Binney, Professor Hare, and John Hare Powell. On the 28th of May we arrived off the coast of Cornwall where the ship was becalmed, and most of the passengers, including myself, went ashore at Falmouth. The beauty of England at that season was enchanting. The hawthorn hedges were in blossom. I took the mail coach for Exeter, and from there posted to Bath, and from Bath rode on the outside of a coach, the most delightful way of seeing the country, to London. I remember well my sensations at seeing Windsor Castle, with the royal standard flying, as we drove past in the valley below. The sights of London were of course very attractive to me, as I had read of them all my life. My eyes devoured Westminster Abbey, Westminster Hall, Temple Bar, the Tower, and the other historical places. I witnessed the parade in Hyde Park on the anniversary of Waterloo, when the Duke of Wellington received the salute of the troops, and I remember the people going in and out of Apsley House, to see the tables set for the Waterloo Banquet. In the House of Lords I heard the Duke of Wellington, Lord Holland, Earl Gray, and the Lord Chancellor. I remember the Duke presenting a petition in which the petitioners asked that the Lords should not yield to intimidation, 'That, my Lords,' said the Duke, as he laid down the petition, in the tone of one accustomed to give orders, 'is also my opinion.' In the House of Commons I heard O'Connell, who in the course of his speech, referring to the upholders of Irish grievances, said 'They are men of blood!' at which there was a loud cry of 'No! No!' and the Speaker drawled out, 'Order! Order!'

"After a few days' stay in London I went to Paris by the Malle-Post, taking a seat in the coupé. From Paris, where I spent a week or two, I returned to London through Belgium, and soon set out for a tour on the Continent, visiting Holland, Germany, Denmark, Sweden, Finland, Russia, Poland, Bohemia, Austria, and Italy."

Of this first year in Europe he wrote on his return a number of sketches full of the life and spirit of a young American abroad for the first time, under the title of "Sketches over the Sea," that appeared in the Democratic Review.

This absence from his country was for more than a year and at a very critical time. When he returned in July, 1837, it was to find the country in a financial collapse. A panic had swept all the cities, and there was a frightful state of alarm in all directions. But such was the very time when men needed the counsel of the ablest and most trusted legal advisers. Mr. Field entered at once on the duties of his profession, and soon found his practice larger than ever. If success at the bar had been his sole ambition, he had as much of it as any man of his age in the country. But there was something connected with the law that attracted him still more: not the law as it was, but as it should be—an ideal of the law, which now rose like a star above the horizon, towards which he was to direct his course during the remainder of his long and eventful career.

CHAPTER V.

THE REFORM OF THE LAW. THE CODES OF CIVIL AND CRIMINAL PROCEDURE.

When David Dudley Field began the study of law, it was with a feeling of reverence amounting almost to awe. The libraries were filled with books giving the laws of England and of all European states, illustrated by thousands of cases, which showed how the law was applied, not only in the familiar relations of life, but in almost every case that was possible or conceivable in human society. These mighty tomes, dark with age, embodied the wisdom of past generations—the wisdom of all countries and all times—the priceless inheritance from all the past to the present and to the future *in secula seculorum*—an inheritance which it was almost sacrilege to touch.

Such was the feeling with which this seeker after knowledge and wisdom entered upon the study of the law. Nor was it a feeling that he ever fully got over. He was never, as some have supposed, an iconoclast who would break down all ancient traditions. On the contrary, he would conserve, not only "with judicious care," but with religious care, all the treasures of wisdom and of learning that have come down from the past. Beginning the study of the law with this feeling, the first thing which he attempted was to make himself master of the practice, and so hard did he work that he had reason to say that "if ever there was anything which he understood, it was the practice at common law and in equity as then established in the Courts of New York." But he had not gone very far in his studies before he began to have misgivings as to whether the law as "received from the fathers" was absolutely ideal in its perfection. The more he studied it, the more did it seem to him a very artificial structure—complicated by a multitude of legal technicalities that made of it almost an occult science, to be understood only by the initiated. In this opinion he was confirmed by Mr. Henry D. Sedgwick, who had begun the practice of law in Massachusetts, and found it much less embarrassed by these technical details than in New York, where an excess of forms made the progress of a case through the courts very slow. This might serve the purpose of legal practitioners, as it made their services the more necessary, or indeed indispensable, but did it serve the purpose of those who appealed to the law for protection? Was there no way to hasten the laggard steps of justice?

While he was thus groping towards the light, he was confirmed in his doubts by a couple of opinions from high authorities. One was Livingston's Report of a Code for Louisiana; the other a Discourse on the History and Nature of the Common Law, delivered before the New York Historical Society by William Sampson in 1823, and republished with other papers under the title "On Codes and Common Law."

Out of all this reading and thinking came into the mind of the young student at law a vague and misty dream of something better, which slowly crystallized into a conception of a Reform, and then into a purpose of attempting it, even if he should have to undertake it single-handed and alone. But what could he do? As long as he was but the junior partner of an eminent lawyer, it was not his business to make the law, but to practise it. But afterward, when he opened an office for himself, he was more free to indulge his dreams. Now that he was his own master, was there anything that he could do? The ideal was plain enough: it could be stated in a sentence, for it had but two elements: first, that the law, as enacted by human governments, should be founded in natural justice; and second, that it should be set forth in the simplest and clearest language, so that it should be "understanded of the people." These two points comprised the whole vast question of law reform.

Reform of the Law! It was a high-sounding phrase, that must carry in it something that is vital to the State: something which goes down to the very foundations of government—to the granite base on which rests the mighty fabric of human society. That the reform might be complete, it must combine the substance of the law with the modes of procedure in the courts whereby justice is administered. In the natural order of division we should begin with the substance of the law. But in taking down a mighty structure which has been the work of ages, to rebuild it, it is more convenient to begin at the top, and dismantle it by degrees, taking away stone by stone, and replacing the old by the new. Following this toilsome but solid method of reconstruction, the first step in Law Reform was in the Codes of Procedure.

Mr. Field had long felt that the great impediment to justice was that the way was made wearisome by the double mode of Procedure in Law and Equity, which was a sort of double-tracked road, on which a man travelled the distance twice over—first being ushered into a luxurious carriage, where he reclined on soft cushions, and was carried swiftly and smoothly over the ground for a hundred miles; at the end of which he was received most graciously, and assisted across the track to another drawing-room car fitted up in the same gorgeous style, and in a few hours was whirled back to the place from which he started! On alighting, his impressions were somewhat divided. It was certainly the poetry of motion, but as to progress toward his final destination, really he might as well have stayed at home!

Such was the system of procedure in the Courts when he returned to this country in the summer of 1837, and he began to consider what he could do for its improvement. His first public effort was a Letter to Gulian C. Verplanck, published in 1839, on the Reform of our Judicial System. After this he went to Albany, and addressed a Committee of the Legislature on the subject. Two years later, at the general election in November, 1841, he sought and obtained a nomination from the Democratic party for the Assembly of New York, with the view of introducing law reform measures into the Legislature. Being defeated through the interference of Bishop Hughes in his opposition to the Public School system, then prevailing in New York, which he wished to subvert, he contented himself with preparing the draft of three Bills to be introduced by Mr. O'Sullivan, his colleague in the candidacy, accompanied by a long Letter in explanation of their provisions. These Bills were introduced; but the Judiciary Committee, to which they were referred, did not adopt or recommend them. They were printed, however, with the Letter, in the Journal of the Assembly.

The calling of the Constitutional Convention, pursuant to an act of the Legislature of 1845, gave him a new opportunity. Before the delegates were elected, and in January, 1846, he wrote and published in the Evening Post a series of articles on "The Reorganization of the Judiciary," which were collected in a pamphlet and widely circulated. He wished to obtain a seat in the Convention, with a view to promoting law reform; but the unpopularity to which he had subjected himself by his hostility to the annexation of Texas and the extension of slavery, made it impossible for him to obtain a nomination from the Democratic party, then the only one from which he could expect an election. But if he was not permitted to influence the Convention by his voice within its walls, he could influence it from without, and he did so to the utmost of his power, by conversation and correspondence with the members, and by articles in the newspapers. The Convention met on the first of June, and during the whole summer he kept at work. The Evening Post alone had nine or ten articles from him, relating to different parts of the Constitution. The instrument which the Convention offered to the people was adopted at the general election in November. It contained two law reforming provisions—one in the first article, aiming at a general Code; and the other in the sixth article, aiming at the Reform of the Practice; both to be set in motion by appointments of the Legislature. Both of these provisions owed their existence very much to his voice and pen.

In anticipation of the action of the Legislature, he published on the first of January, 1847, a little treatise of thirty-five pages, entitled "What shall be done with the Practice of the Courts? Shall it be wholly reformed? Questions addressed to lawyers." This he followed up by a Memorial to the Legislature before the passage of any act by that body, to which he procured the signatures of Vice Chancellor McCoun, Charles O'Conor, E. P. Hurlbut, F. B. Cutting, Theodore Sedgwick, James J. Roosevelt, Joseph S. Bosworth, Erastus C. Benedict, and forty-three other lawyers of New York. It was in these words:

"*To the Senate and Assembly of the State of New York:*

"The memorial of the undersigned members of the Bar in the City of New York respectfully represents that they look with great solicitude for the action of your honorable bodies in respect to the revision, reform, simplification and abridgment of the rules and practice, pleadings, forms and proceedings of the courts of record. They are persuaded that a radical reform of legal procedure in all its departments is demanded by the interests of justice and by the voice of the people; that a uniform course of proceeding in all cases legal and equitable is entirely practicable, and no less expedient; and that a radical reform should aim at such uniformity, and at the abolition of all useless forms and proceedings.

"Your memorialists, therefore, pray your honorable bodies to declare by the Act appointing Commissioners, that it shall be their duty to provide for the abolition of the present forms of action and pleadings in cases at common law, for a uniform course of proceeding in all cases, whether of legal or equitable cognizance, and for the abandonment of every form or proceeding not necessary to ascertain or preserve the rights of the parties." *

* This was presented to the Legislature, and a section introduced into the pending Bill in accordance with the Memorial, except that the word which Mr. Field wrote "every" was by mistake made to read "any."

Mr. Field's name was naturally brought forward in connection with the appointment of Commissioner; but the conservative feeling was too strong, he was too radical, and Mr. Nicholas Hill was appointed in his stead. The Commission, consisting of Mr. Hill, Mr. David Graham, and Mr. Arphaxad Loomis, was established by a law passed April 8th, 1847. The Commissioners could not agree, however, in carrying out this provision, and Mr. Hill resigned in September. By that time the feeling in favor of radical reform had been strengthened, and Mr. Field was appointed in Mr. Hill's place by a resolution of the two Houses passed on the 29th of that month. Meantime he had published "Some suggestions respecting the rules to be established by the Supreme Court," designed to effect a considerable reform in the pleadings and practice. Upon the reorganization of the Commission, it went to work in earnest, and on the 29th of February, 1848, reported to the Legislature the first instalment of the Code of Civil Procedure. This was enacted on the 12th of April following, with very little change, and went into effect on the first of July. It was, however, but an instalment of the whole work contemplated, and the residue was reported from time to time in four different Reports, until the first of January, 1850, when completed Codes of Civil and Criminal Procedure were submitted to the Legislature. These two works covered the whole ground of remedial law.

"The whole ground of remedial law!" Only six words! Yet it is not easy to take in the vast territory they cover, and the labor they involve! This fell most upon Mr. Field, for though he had two associates on the Commission, they recognized the movement for reform as begun by him, and to him, as the gallant leader, they left the chief burden, which he in his eagerness for the cause was not unwilling to bear. The labor involved was almost incredible. Of this I can speak from personal observation. In the year 1847 I went abroad, and spent the following winter in Paris, where I was a witness of the Revolution of 1848, which upturned all Europe. Returning in the autumn, I passed the winter of 1848-9 in New York, and under Mr. Field's roof. He was then in the midst of his work on the Commission, and I looked on with amazement at the amount of labor that he did in every twenty-four hours, for he was at the same time carrying on a professional practice which had grown to be one of the largest in the city. No man stood higher at the bar, or was engaged in more important cases both in the State and the Federal Courts. It was at such a time, when he was already doing the work of half a dozen men, that this additional burden was put upon his shoulders.

But he did not shrink from the double duty, though he could not have borne it but by the most careful economy of his strength. As he was "called to be a soldier," he divided the hours of the day with military precision. He rose early, and, taking a cup of tea, mounted his horse, which was standing at the door, unless it was a bitter winter day, and rode up one of the avenues towards what is now the Central Park. This morning ride was never intermitted except in the severest weather. After breakfast, if he was not required to be at the opening of the courts, he shut himself up for two or three hours in his library on the work of the Commission, and then walked rapidly down town. Everybody knew him, for he was tall and straight as a grenadier, and he passed down Broadway with rapid strides, like a soldier marching to battle. From his office he went to the courts, where he remained till a late hour of the afternoon, when he walked home again. The hour of dinner was one of perfect abandon, into which no word of business was allowed to intrude: the hour belonged to his family, and he gave himself up to the enjoyment of their society. When the last good story was told, and the last laugh went round the table, he threw himself upon a sofa for a half hour's rest, from which he rose like a giant refreshed with wine, and ready for his *magnum opus!* Now the deck was cleared, and he gave himself to that which was at once the task and the joy of his life, the reconstruction of the Codes, the fascination of which often kept him at his work till long after midnight.

A life like this, kept up month after month, year

in and year out, would kill most men: it would have killed him, but for the one "saving clause" that nature had put into his iron frame. After the day's "fitful fever" he slept well. He had not only the power of continuous labor such as I never saw in any other man, but when the work was done, he could put his hand on the machine and stop it in an instant. He would work all day and all night, and for days and nights together, with only the briefest snatches of sleep; but when all was over, he could lie down and fall asleep like a child. By this heroic discipline, and the alternation of work and rest, he kept the fire in his bones, and the blood in his veins, till he breathed his last in his ninetieth year.

There was also another restorative that he found in his voyages to Europe. He loved the sea. He was a good sailor, never yielding to the roughest storm, and so in his later life he went abroad almost every year. The fame of his codes went before him, so that his reputation was as great in England as in America, perhaps greater, as he had not been there, as here, in such fierce antagonism with his opponents. In August, 1850, he went abroad with his family and left them in Rome, returning to New York in December. In England he found a small but determined party of reform grappling with the double-headed monster of Law and Equity. At a meeting of the Law Amendment Society, at which he was present by invitation, Sir Richard Bethel, afterward Lord Chancellor Westbury, made a speech in which he said that he thought it "a burning shame that a party could recover a judgment on one side of Westminster Hall, and on the other side be branded as a fraudulent rogue for having recovered it!" And yet in presence of this monstrous absurdity all the legal wisdom of England seemed insufficient to devise a remedy. Even Lord Brougham, who had taken up the cause of Law Reform with his accustomed energy, while he commended the efforts for the fusion of Law and Equity in America, doubted if it could be effected in England. Perhaps, however, the long interview that he had with Mr. Field may have removed his doubts, for only a few months after he wrote from Cannes that sooner or later it was sure to be adopted.

How new life was put into the movement for Law Reform appears from the following in the London Spectator :

"The visit of Mr. Dudley Field to England, and his interesting statements to the members of our Law Amendment Society this week, are real events in the progress of law reform in this country. The injustice which the English people submit to in the revered name of Law, and in the sacred, but in their case profaned, name of Equity, is more enormous than the future historian will be able remotely to conceive. The keystone of the barbarous Gothic portal to Justice in our common-law procedure was struck out some twenty years ago, when the logical forms of legal contest were reduced to their now moderate number; other heavy blows have further undermined the ruin, and almost cleared away whatever was feudal in that portion of their edifice; and then came the raising of the new and noble portal of the County Courts. Still, in all but the most trivial litigation the delay and expense are such that justice can only be had at a per centage utterly disgraceful to a nation either honest or merely clear-handed and commercial. We still preserve a diversity of tribunals, to administer laws that ought not to be inharmonious; and we are prevented from making the laws harmonious by the difficulties of finding tribunals able to rule the concord and administer the whole field of law as a single empire. In this case, as in a multitude of others, our young relations across the Atlantic have done that which we only longed to do. In this rivalry of nations, so far above all other rivalries, they have pushed development of institutions which they received from forefathers common to us both, to a more rapid perfection than we. Mr. Dudley Field is one of three men who framed a constitutional law for the State of New York, under which the courts of legal and equitable jurisdiction have been successfully merged; the enactment has succeeded in practical working; and the spectacle of 'Equity swallowing up Law' has been so edifying to the citizens of his State that three other States of the Union have resolved to enact, and four further States have appointed conferences to deliberate upon, a similar procedure. It is impossible—however narrow-minded lawyers may object—that what Americans find practicable and beneficial should be either impracticable or disadvantageous to Englishmen."

Returning to New York in December, Mr. Field published in the Evening Post five articles on "The Completion of the Code," designed to secure the immediate adoption by the Legislature of the two Codes of Procedure which had been reported complete. But they had still several years to wait. In May, 1851, he rejoined his family in Europe, and travelled with them over a great portion of the Continent, and into Egypt and Palestine. While in England, on his return home, a dinner was given him at the London Tavern by the members of the Law Amendment Society, an account of which was published in the Morning Chronicle of the next day, December 22, 1851. Among the speakers was Robert Lowe, afterwards Lord Sherbrooke, who was Chancellor of the Exchequer under Mr. Gladstone. He had lived for some years in Australia, and knew how wise laws, whether framed in England or America, affected legislation at the very extremities of the British empire. In his speech he paid a tribute to Mr. Field such as has seldom been paid to any legislator, living or dead. He said:

"He trusted that his honorable friend, Mr. Field, would go down to posterity with this glory—that he had not only essentially served one of the greatest countries in the States of America, but that he had also provided a cheap and satisfactory code of law for every colony that bore the English name. Mr. Field, indeed, had not squared the circle; he had not found out any solid which answered to more than three denominations; he had not discovered any power more subtle than electricity, nor one that would bow with more docility to the service of man than steam. But he had done greater things: he had laid the foundations of peace, happiness, and tranquillity, in the establishment of a system which would make law a blessing instead of a scourge to mankind. He believed that no acquisition of modern times—if he rightly understood what had been done in the State of New York—he believed that no achievement of the intellect was to be compared to that by which Mr. Field had removed the absurdities and the technicalities under which New York, in common with this country and the colonies, had so long groaned." And again: "As to the colonies, he could only repeat that he trusted the example of New York would not be lost upon them. While England was debating upon the propriety of some small and paltry reforms in the administration of law, a great master in the art of administrative reform had risen there in the person of his distinguished friend, Mr. Field, and had solved the problem which they in England were timidly debating. America had a great future before her, in the establishment and diffusion of the arts of peace. Let them leave to others—to absolute governments—to have their subjects shot down in the street, rather than wait even for the headlong injustice of a court-martial; but let it be the lot of England, hand in hand with America, to lead the way in the arts of Jurisprudence as well as in other arts—let them aim at being the legislators and the pacificators of the world."

CHAPTER VI.

A DOMESTIC EPISODE. THE GOLDEN WEDDING.

When a man has fought a long and hard battle—or rather a three years' campaign—with the prospect of another trial of strength still longer and harder—he may be excused if now and then he should retire from the scene of action to enjoy a brief interval of rest. Amid all the contests of the bar Mr. Field never forgot the old home, nor the dear Father and Mother, whose gray hairs gave them an added beauty, and whose faces, filled with a sweet serenity, seemed to reflect the peace of that better world which they were approaching.

Not that there had been anything very notable in the years that had passed beyond the ordinary life in a country parsonage. In the earlier days of New England the minister did not migrate from church to church so often as now. Not infrequently a young man was settled over a parish, and there remained for life, while children and grandchildren grew up around him.

Not so with the Stockbridge pastor, whose experience was peculiar, in that, while he had but two parishes, he had one of them twice over, swinging as it were, like a pendulum, between the old and the new. The people of Haddam, who in 1819 had let him go, afterwards got into a divided state, which it seemed as if no one but their old minister could heal, and called him back again; and he, the good man that he was, who always thought more of others than of himself, accepted, and for seven years preached in the old barrack as before, though to another congregation, for the sons had come in the place of the fathers, after which the long and straggling parish was cut in twain, and he took the Northern division of Higganum, where he preached for seven years more. It was during this period, in 1848, the year of the Revolutions in Europe, that he went abroad with his son Stephen, and spent several months in England and on the Continent.

In 1851 he completed his seventieth year; when his children, who had grown to manhood and womanhood, felt that he had served his generation so faithfully that his working days should come to an end; and asking the privilege of providing for his wants, they begged him to return to Stockbridge, the dearest spot on earth, and there abide till the going down of the sun. This loving request could not be refused, and so he made his last pilgrimage across the mountains, to the sweet home in which he was to spend the remnant of his days.

Here it was that the autumn of 1853 recalled an anniversary that was of interest to us all, as it completed fifty years since our father and mother had begun the journey of life together; and now, as they had come back to the old home, what more fitting than that children and grandchildren should gather round the patriarch and his faithful companion for half a century, and celebrate their Golden Wedding !

The family was not only a large one, but a very united one: both from affection, and from the necessity that was upon them to help one another. This mutual helpfulness comes out most under an humble roof. Love flourishes in a small interior. The arena is not large enough for combats. It is the great and princely halls that resound with fratricidal war. Where parents and children sit round one table, or one fireplace, the instinct of nature draws them together. If for once I sketch a domestic scene, it is not so much to show the beautiful family life in the old home, as to throw a strong side-light on the central figure which it is my purpose to portray. Thanks to our dear parents, who never had an idle day in their lives, we were all educated to the habit of taking care of ourselves, and then of one another. In this, as in many other things, the eldest of us set an example which we all recognized with grateful affection: and never did the heart of the son and the brother come out more strongly than at this family reunion. There was a light in his face, that never shone so brightly as on this happy day.

Every man has two lives: the outward and the inward; which may exist quite apart, even if they be not contrary one to the other. A man's public life is not his whole life, but only half of it, and perhaps not the more interesting or attractive half, which may be hidden out of sight by his public career. It is a delicate matter to draw aside the veil that hides that interior life, but in the case of a strong personality, it may be necessary in order to understand the real character of the man. The soldier who is bravest in battle may be the gentlest when he returns to his little cottage under the hill; and he who is by his very profession placed in antagonism to other men, and has to strike heavy blows, may be quite another man when he returns to the relations of domestic life. It is this "other man" that I desire to disclose to those who thought they knew him, but are just beginning to find out his true character now that he is gone to the grave.

Few men in our great commercial city were better known in one sense and less known in another. He lived in New York for more than sixty years: no figure was more familiar to the public eye; and yet no man was so little understood. Of those who knew him in professional life, probably nine out of ten thought him to be a man of iron, cold, stern and severe, all of which he may have been in those contests of the bar which were a part of his daily life. But at the same time he was a man of the strongest personal attachments. True, the circle of those whom he loved was not large; it was composed chiefly of those of his own family.

But the narrower the circle, the more concentrated and intensified was the affection. Never was there, or could there be, a more generous elder brother, one more anxious to promote the interests of all the younger members of his family. He had seen what a struggle it cost his parents to give him a college education, and denied himself every needless expense. In looking over his letters from College, it is easy to see with what reluctance he writes home for so much as twenty dollars, and he wished that the other children should not require similar sacrifices. On the day that he was twenty-one, although he was but a lawyer's clerk, he wrote to his father that his first desire was to lighten the burden that rested upon him by helping his brothers and sisters to get an education; and the very first money that he saved from his meagre income he sent to his sister Emilia (afterwards Mrs. Brewer), then at a school for young ladies in Hartford.

Three of his brothers went to Williams College, all of whom were indebted to him for assistance to carry them through; Jonathan and Stephen studied law in his office in New York, as did in later years a nephew whom we then knew as "Young David," but who is now Mr. Justice Brewer, sitting beside his uncle on the bench in the well known Court Room in the Capitol in Washington. It was because he could be under the protection of his older brother, that Cyrus was allowed to go to the city at the age of fifteen, when he entered a great mercantile house as an errand boy, and thus put his feet on the first round of the ladder, on which he was to climb so high. Hence in the place of honor in the family, next to the Father and Mother, was this elder brother, to whom we all owed so much.

The Golden Wedding was on the last day of October, 1853. It was a beautiful day in the most beautiful season of the year, when

> "The woods of autumn all around our vale
> Had put their glory on."

As we came together under the old roof-tree, our first thoughts were of the absent and the dead. One child had died in infancy. Another had been lost at sea, though not till he had given promise of a brilliant career. This was the second son, Timothy, who entered the navy as a midshipman, and of whom his comrades spoke as the life of the ship when they went up the Mediterranean, and as foremost in pursuit of the pirates who infested the Greek Archipelago. Stephen was on the Pacific Coast. He had returned from Europe in 1849, when the country was wild with excitement over the discoveries of gold in California, and had gone to the land of promise, where his dreams were fulfilled in his notable career at the bar and in the Convention to form the Constitution of the State; and on the bench, where he was Chief Justice when called by Lincoln to Washington. California was not then so near to the

East as now, and he could not be spared for a voyage of many weeks to go and return. Cyrus too had gone to South America, but arrived home the day before the Golden Wedding. Matthew had been an engineer at the South before the war, and built a number of suspension bridges in Kentucky and Tennessee, one of which spanned the Cumberland at Nashville, but was destroyed in the retreat of the Confederate Army to prevent its being crossed by the army of General Buell. At that time he had returned North and lived in Southwick, his wife's home, and once represented Hampden County in the Senate. Jonathan had settled down in Stockbridge, and was one of the leaders of the bar in Western Massachusetts. So popular was he that, though a Democrat in politics, he was elected by the Republicans to the Senate three times in succession; and each time chosen to be its President—an honor never before conferred on any member of that body. With these brothers we had our two sisters, Emilia and Mary. The latter, as the youngest of the group, was the pet of the family, and yet was the first to be taken from us [only three years later in Paris]; and because of her gentleness and that she died so young, she lives in our memories as the sweetest of us all.

And now the dear old couple stood up side by side, as they had stood fifty years before, to receive the congratulations of their children, in which I know not whether there were more smiles or tears. How happy we all were on that wedding day—a day that could never return! Together we sat round the long table that had been stretched to furnish seats for some forty guests. And then we gathered, as of old, for morning and evening prayers, when the Patriarch, who never looked so beautiful as with that crown of white hair, commended us, with a voice that was still strong, to the God of Abraham, Isaac, and Jacob, praying that we might all be the "children of the Highest," "sons and daughters of the Lord Almighty." Such prayers brought their own answer, and as we went forth from the door of the old home, we felt that we carried a blessing with us that would abide through all the coming years, till we too should be "gathered to our fathers." *

If any apology be needed for the introduction of this domestic episode into a narrative that has to do with grave matters of the law, I answer that my object is to tell the truth, and the whole truth, of a remarkable life

* It was not long before our ranks were broken. Of the group that stood round our Father and Mother on that day, every one of my generation, except myself, has gone to the grave. Mary died in 1856; the dear Mother in '61, and the elder sister, Emilia (Mrs. Brewer), the same year; Father in '67; Jonathan in '68, and Matthew in '70; which left but Four Brothers to represent the family for nearly a quarter of a century; and of these, two—Dudley and Cyrus—are gone. Stephen still lives, but he was not at the Golden Wedding. Soon the generation to which we belong will have passed away, but only, as we hope and believe, that we all may meet on a happier shore.

THE FATHER

THE MOTHER

and character. It is not enough that I hear men speak of him as the honored dead, when to me he is the beloved dead. I wish them to know him as I knew him; to know the sweetness of his nature, as well as the force of his will; and most of all, of the affection that he bore towards those who were of the same father and mother. I could go still farther and tell how intense was his love for his children, and for the grandchildren who were the idols of his heart. But it is enough to speak of the generation to which I belong. As one of the family, I can testify that, next to those who gave us being, we owe what we are to one than whom there was never a more dutiful son, or a more kind and thoughtful brother.

But this family affection is often but a form of family pride or ambition, a clannish feeling, that makes one stand by his own kin against the world. But such an interpretation would do great injustice to one who was not only a lover of his clan, but of his race. I never knew a man who was more quickly touched by sorrow. How often have I heard him, as he came home from the business of the day, tell of some poor woman who had come to him with a pitiful tale of poverty and want, whom he always received with the utmost kindness, and listened patiently to her story, too happy if he could relieve her distress, or put new courage into her sad heart. Or as he walked home in the evening, the gaslight flashed in the face of a poor girl on the street corner, who was trying to earn her bread by selling papers. As he caught sight of the pale wan face, he would stop, making an excuse of buying the evening papers, to say a few words that might cheer her in her loneliness.

This tenderness of nature showed itself even in his Codes, where he always leaned to mercy's side. Rigid as were his ideas of absolute equality before the law, yet he thought it not incompatible with justice that the law should extend its shield most over those who needed it most, and never was it in the more legitimate exercise of its power than when it stretched out its long and mighty arm to protect the poor and the helpless, the widow and the child.

One more picture may close this domestic episode. Among the many charities that have sprung up in our country, none is more beautiful than that of the Children's Aid Society, which takes the little waifs of our cities, and transports them far away from the foul and noisome streets to the green fields and waving prairies of the West, where they can breathe the pure air, and learn the ways of industry and virtue.

Kindred to that, though of more recent date, is the Fresh Air Fund, which takes the same class of children to the country, though for a shorter time, only for a few weeks, that they may romp and play, and fill their little mouths with good things, and get pure air in their lungs and warm blood in their veins. One of these delightful retreats is in Curtisville, a part of Stockbridge, where Mr. John E. Parsons of New York has provided what he calls St. Helen's Home, in memory of a beloved daughter. Here he has laid out some acres, with buildings, clean and sweet, where in the summer hundreds are let loose, and run about the grounds and climb the trees like so many squirrels, and the passer-by may hear their laugh and glee, as a score of little naked legs wade into the clear pebbled stream that rushes under the bridge. They breathe the fresh air all day long, to lie down at night in clean beds and sleep the sleep of innocence and peace. The place had a fascination for Mr. Field, and he often took it in his afternoon drive. Sometimes he would pile a dozen children into a large carriage for a ride. They all knew him so well that they looked for his coming. As he sat on the veranda the tiny little creatures would climb up on his knees two or three at once. I can see him now as he took them in his arms, and tossed them into the air in a grandfatherly way; while the "good gray head" caught the last rays of the sun going down in the West—fit type of the peaceful ending of his own long day. Never was there a more beautiful picture of the two extremes of life than this of sportive childhood in the lap of age, which no stranger could look upon without feeling that, if the "grand old man" had been a man of war from his youth, he had always carried under his martial cloak a warm, tender and loving heart.

CHAPTER VII.

CODIFICATION OF THE COMMON LAW.

The happiest scenes must come to an end ; meetings must be followed by partings ; and so, after we had gathered in the old home under the elms, and paid our tribute to those to whom we owed everything, and received their blessing ; we had to come back to the scenes of common life, and take up again the work that we had to do in the world. And here I resume the thread of my story.

"A prophet is not without honor save in his own country." It was all very well for Mr. Field to be cheered to the echo by English barristers and members of Parliament; but here in America, where the practice of the law was in a process of revolution, there was quite another feeling. There were many lawyers and judges who were not at all disposed to applaud the Reformer; who indeed would have been quite content to have him spend the rest of his days in the mother country, and practise at the English bar, if he would only let his own country, and especially his own profession, alone. They were perhaps in a more critical mood from the fact that a fragmentary Code of Procedure had been adopted in 1848, and made a part of the law of the State of New York, and they were trying to adjust themselves to the new conditions. But there they wished the Reform to end. An Act had indeed been passed by the Legislature appointing a Commission, consisting of Chancellor Walworth and two other eminent lawyers, to codify the whole substantive law. But the slowness of their work was in striking contrast with the celerity of Mr. Field's. After two years' meditation, they reported only a small fragment of law, which they did not recommend for adoption ; and their final report was in substance one of grave doubt as to whether the work assigned to them could or ought to be done at all. Not unnaturally, the Legislature, in April, 1850, repealed the Act itself ! This seemed to be a fatal blow. To resuscitate the Commission would be like raising the dead, and this was not an age of miracles. In fact it was seven years before the miracle was accomplished—years that were to Mr. Field like the seven years that Jacob served for Rachel. But, like the ancient lover, he never lost heart or hope. He pleaded his cause in a series of Law Reform Tracts on "The Administration of the Code"; "Evidence as to its Operation," showing that it had worked well ; "A Short Manual of Pleading under the Code"; and a discussion of "The Competency of Parties as Witnesses for Themselves," in support of which he drew up a memorial to the Legislature for the passage of a law to admit their testimony.

But all this was only preliminary to a still more sweeping Reform, which he proposed in another Tract on "The Codification of the Common Law"—a change that would be almost revolutionary, and which cannot be understood without a brief explanation of this "Common Law" which had not only ruled England for so many generations, but had extended its rule over the greater family of the descendants of Englishmen on this side of the Atlantic.

What was the Common Law? I am but a layman, as unfamiliar with the mysteries of the law as of medicine. But there is sometimes an advantage in looking at a structure from the outside. It gives the spectator a point of view from which he can take in the whole. Looking on therefore, as we laymen do, from a reasonable distance, what are we to understand by the Common Law? The phrase has a certain majesty, as if it were in Law what the Common Faith is in Religion, a symbol of that which, though it be somewhat dim and distant, is still too sacred to be lightly spoken of. Perchance it stands as a synonym for universal justice, and is called common—not because it is in any sense low or commonplace, but because it is for all men. If that were indeed its significance, it would be a noble title for a noble thing. But when we discover that the Common Law is only Common Usage, and is backed by no great legal authority, our reverence begins to abate.

Yet such is the Common Law of England, from which our own is taken. It is not a compilation of the laws of the realm, of acts of Parliament, for with the greater part of them Parliament had nothing to do. It is made up for the most part, not of statutes, but of precedents, of the decisions of judges, of whom some were learned and some unlearned; some wise and great; some weak and wicked. Derived from England as it has been, nobody has spoken of it so contemptuously as Englishmen themselves. "Do you know," said the great Jeremy Bentham, "how judges make the Common Law? Just as a man makes laws for his dog. When your dog does anything you want to break him of, you wait till he does it, and then beat him for it. And this is the way the judges make law for you and me!" To make the best of it, we cannot help seeing that it is a compound of good and bad; that the stream of time, which has brought down to us the wisdom of the past, has also swept along on its mighty bosom other and meaner things, the mere drift of the ages, with which the present generation ought not to be burdened.

"But imperfect as it is, you cannot get rid of it," was the cry; "it is here, and here to stay forever!" And as for Codification, that was impossible! As well might you attempt to imprison the vast and wandering air, or set bounds to the waves of the immeasurable sea.

Even if it were possible, such "narrowing" of the law into a small compass would do more harm than good. Some even thought its vagueness and uncertainty a good feature, as it made it more "elastic," and left more scope to the expansive genius of Young America!

But other objections were less fanciful. When we are told that the great body of lawyers and judges in the State of New York were opposed to it, we are not to infer that it was from merely frivolous considerations. Least of all would we impute to them unworthy motives. A cause quite sufficient to explain it all is found in the simple power of inertia, that weighs upon us all like the power of gravitation. There is in every man a reluctance to change old habits and usages. Nor is this a bad trait. On the contrary, it may be all that saves us from mistakes that might prove our ruin. It may be our only protection from the consequences of our own rashness and folly. Hence it is that we are warned in holy writ to "walk in the old ways." Any departure from this rule must first show that the new way is better than the old. This Mr. Field endeavored to prove by insisting on the absolute necessity of some relief from a burden that had grown to such enormous proportions. The law was so covered up by the deposits of successive generations, that it lay scattered about as if among dead men's bones, so that one might almost as well seek for it in the catacombs. The richer it was in its accumulations, the more unwieldy it became. The greater the number of precedents to be quoted, the greater the perplexity, for in running back to the decisions of the courts for generations, it seemed as if every possible case had been decided in every possible way. So slowly moved the wheels of justice, that in some cases a man could hardly hope for a verdict in his life-time. An appeal to the Court of Chancery, for example, was almost a mockery, as an English judge confessed, when he inquired after a particular case and was told that it had been referred to that Court, at which he asked in a melancholy tone, "Have you the heart to send a fellow-creature there?" This was a paralysis of justice from too much law—a result that is not an infrequent accompaniment of too many refinements in the statutes or in the modes of procedure.

For all this confusion and delay there must be some relief, if there was to be any virtue in the law or the tribunals of England or America. And this could only be by some process of condensation and simplification, both of which were combined in "Codification," whereby the whole of the Common Law could be framed into distinct Codes, which should be so plain and simple that they could be read and "understanded of the people."

Such was the aim of Mr. Field, his one great and overpowering ambition. It was not to be a breaker of the precious traditions of the past. He had no purpose or desire to destroy the Common Law, but to preserve it and exalt it by cutting off its excrescences, and by translating it into the language of the people, so as to make it worthy, not only of the free States of America, but of all English-speaking peoples on the habitable globe.

But the stronger the argument for the Code, the more violent was the opposition. It was a case of an irresistible force striking against an immovable body. And so the battle raged, with constant alternations of advance and repulse. In 1855 a bill was introduced into the Legislature to reorganize the Code Commission, making him one of the Commissioners, but its enemies were alert and fought it at every step and defeated it. The chief opposition came from the older members of the bar, who seemed to have a power in the Legislature to obstruct and defeat any action to which they were opposed. Nor were they always very reserved in boasting of their power, to which the only answer of the Reformer was, "All things come to him who waits!" He did not have to wait much longer before the old conservatism gave way. In 1857, on the 6th of April—a day that was to be forever memorable in the history of Law Reform—an Act which he had himself drawn up with the greatest care, was passed by the Legislature, that a new Commission be appointed "to reduce into a written and systematic Code the whole body of the law of this State, or so much and such parts thereof as shall seem to them practicable and expedient, excepting always such portions of the law as have been already reported upon by the Commissioners of Practice and Pleadings, or are embraced within the scope of their reports."

Very simple words are these to "lay readers," who do not take in all their meaning. But to the legal mind that one sentence, "*to reduce into a written and systematic Code the whole body of the law*," was the foretokening of a Revolution. With this came to Mr. Field the opportunity of his life. From the time that he entered on the practice of law, he had been possessed with the idea of Reform : it had been his one thought by day and his dream by night. A part of his scheme had been realized in the Codes of Procedure, but the greater task of reconstructing and codifying the substance of the Law itself, yet remained. It was the same work of Reform—only in a higher and broader sphere.

The nearer he came to the task, the larger it grew, till the cloud that was like a man's hand expanded till it covered all the horizon. No bounds could be put to its circumference. "Law," says Hooker, "has her seat in the bosom of God, and her voice is the harmony of the world : all things in heaven and earth do her homage, the very least as feeling her care, and the greatest as not exempted from her power." But even this magnificent sentence, one of the most splendid in the English language, does not exhaust the extent of its illimitable reign, for the law of which it speaks is only that of the material universe : but in law that is to rule and govern mankind, there must be more than blind force—more than power, even though it be the power of God ; something that appeals to the moral sense—to reason and to conscience.

Even the law of God himself is not merely the edict of Almighty Power, with no recognition of the wants or weaknesses of men. That would make Him to be like Shiva the Destroyer in the Hindoo theology, whose tremendous power rolled over men like the Car of Juggernaut, crushing all that came in its way. Not so could any one think who had been brought up in a New England home, where from a child he had been taught that the Creator of mankind is the Father of all.

Nor could a Divine authority be claimed for any human decrees. There was no sacredness in law that was simply the creation of arbitrary will—of King, or Kaiser, or Czar—it was only law that was founded in absolute justice that partook of the character of God himself, and had somewhat of His authority.

Approaching the law with such careful steps, it took on a sacred character, as if it were a part of religion, as it well might be, if it were conformed to the highest standard of rectitude. The work of the legislator was not merely to apply the laws of nature to human conduct. Nor was it merely the recognition of a blind force, acting in one fixed and unalterable way, like the law of gravitation. The law for communities and States was for moral beings, and must have in it a moral element—an element of justice so clear and plain as to approve itself to him who was under it, so that obedience should not be a matter of compulsion, but of free choice and will. Justice, in the eye of the Reformer, was the rock, the corner-stone, on which to build the structure of human society. I never knew a man who had a stronger sense of justice. In framing a law it never occurred to him to modify it in the interest of this or that individual, or of this or that class. The first question that he asked—and the only question—was, Is it right? Is it just? Of course, in the work of codification, it was not his business to make the law; but in recasting thousands of statutes, there was boundless scope for improving the language by rejecting all outlandish phrases, and reducing each statute to its simplest form by putting it in plain old Saxon words, which were most familiar to the common ear, and most suited to "the roundabout common sense" of the common people. With these two conditions, the law so plain that every man could understand it, and so obviously just that all should approve it, it would be a moral education of the people, who, in learning at once their rights and their duties, would be better fitted to be citizens of a great and free Commonwealth.

Such was the task. How was it to be done? Though Mr. Field was at the head of the Commission, the work was not left to him alone, for it was too enormous for any one man ; associated with him were two of the most eminent members of the bar, Mr. William Curtis Noyes and Mr. Alexander W. Bradford, and the three were to divide the work between them. They were to report at the next session of the Legislature a general Analysis of the projected Codes, as preliminary to the larger task that remained in the future. To this they gave their first attention, Mr. Noyes undertaking to prepare the Analysis for the Penal Code, and Mr. Field the Analysis for the Political and Civil Codes.

After this they went to work on the Codes themselves, reporting at every session of the Legislature the progress made up to that time. As fast as any part of the Draft was prepared it was to be distributed among the Judges and others for examination, and afterwards to be reexamined, with the suggestions made, and finally submitted to the Legislature. No compensation whatever was to be allowed to the Commissioners.

In this division of labor it will be seen that Mr. Field had the lion's share of the work thrown upon him in having assigned to him both the Civil and the Political Codes. Was it not too much for a man who was no longer young? It was a work for a lifetime, and he was already fifty-two years old. But he was still in the full vigor of his splendid manhood, and the task itself gave him a fresh inspiration. Enthusiasm took the place of young blood, and supplied the vital force to bear the tremendous strain.

Of course an undertaking so vast could not be carried out in detail by any one man, even though he should give to it the undivided labor of the longest life. In his choice of assistants he preferred young men to old men. They might not be so learned in the law, but that was in one view of it a qualification, as they were more free from the paralyzing influence of old traditions; more alert in mind as well as in body; more quick to receive new ideas; and last, but not least, had more power of continued labor. It was no light task to be a co-worker with Mr. Field, for as he never confessed fatigue himself, he made little account of fatigue in others. So long as he was in command, those who followed him must keep up with his tremendous pace. And yet he was not a hard master, for exacting as he was, and imperious in the carrying out of his plans, he appreciated talent in others, and was very proud when one of his adjutants showed uncommon ability. For them it was an admirable training for professional life. In the preparation of the Political Code his assistant was Mr. Austin Abbott, for whom it was a stepping stone to his subsequent distinguished career.*

With a lieutenant so energetic the work did not drag, and on the 10th of March, 1859, Mr. Field was

---

* The recent death of Mr. Abbott was a great loss to the bar of New York. Had he lived, it was hoped that he would furnish important contributions to this biography of one under whom he had served for several years in the preparation of the

able to send out the first Draft of the Political Code to the parties to whom it was to be submitted, by whom it was carefully examined, and returned to him for a final revision, which took another year, so that it was not till thirteen months later, April 10th, 1860, that he was able to offer this Political Code complete. At the same time he suggested the importance of a "Book of Forms," which was provided for by a special statute directing the Commissioners to prepare it. This too was assigned to Mr. Field, under whose supervision it was prepared by Mr. Thomas G. Shearman, in the same manner as the three Codes : first a Draft, or, as in this case, two successive Drafts were circulated, and the revised work was reported to the Legislature on the 30th of March, 1861.

Then came the greatest labor of all in preparing the Civil Code, in which Mr. Field had the invaluable assistance of Mr. Shearman and of Mr. Austin Abbott, by whose combined labors, under his constant oversight, directing, inspiring and pushing on the great work, the first Draft of the Civil Code was sent out on April 5th, 1862. The Draft of the Penal Code, which had been

Codes, and for whom he had the greatest admiration. Of all the tributes to Mr. Field, none was more discriminating, or carried more weight, than that of one who was not only in the front rank of practitioners at the bar, but was also eminent as a Teacher of Law, being the Dean of that Department in the University of the City of New York.

assigned to Mr. Noyes, was not presented till two years later. It had been prepared with the assistance of Mr. B. V. Abbott, and was then read over at meetings of all the Commissioners, and amended by them.

The Political and Civil Codes were left entirely to Mr. Field, except that Mr. Bradford prepared a first Draft of that portion of the latter which relates to the estates of deceased persons. After eight Reports to the Legislature, the Commission submitted their Ninth and last Report on the 13th of February, 1865 (Mr. Field's birthday, on which he completed his sixtieth year), laying the full Penal Code upon the tables of the members. The Civil Code was already in the hands of the printer, but was not issued until the autumn. The revision of the Civil Code involved as much labor as its original draft. In this work, in addition to the gentlemen already mentioned, Mr. Charles F. Stone rendered some valuable assistance on the law of real estate.

These law-reform labors of Mr. Field occupied a large portion of his time for eighteen years, during all of which, except the first two years, he not only received no compensation, but had to pay the expense of his assistants, amounting to many thousands of dollars.

The Codes for New York were written and rewritten several times: every part of the Civil Code at least three times and many parts eighteen times! These Codes, as completed, are contained in five octavo volumes. Three of them—the Civil Code, the Penal Code, and the Political Code—give the substantive law. Two of them—the Code of Civil Procedure and the Code of Criminal Procedure—prescribe the practice of the courts, and define their jurisdiction. In the preparation of the Codes of Procedure, Mr. Field was associated with Mr. Loomis and Mr. Graham; and in the other Codes with Mr. Noyes and Mr. Bradford; all of whom were able and distinguished men in the profession; but they gave to it far less time than he did, and wrought upon it with far less intensity. Of his habits of working, in the early morning hours and late at night, I have spoken elsewhere, a strain that was kept up, not for a few weeks or months, but for eighteen long years. Thus he gave to it more time than all the others combined, indeed all the time which could be spared from the labors of an engrossing profession. With him it was the passion of his life—the work which he was the first to propose, and was the most determined to carry through, and he wrought upon it with all the ardor of personal ambition, so that he is universally recognized, at home and abroad, as the chief author of the Codes.

In a letter to his brother Stephen—Justice of the Supreme Court of the United States—he speaks thus of the opposition he had to encounter :

"Now that my work is finished, as I look back upon it, I am amazed at the difficulties I had to overcome, and the little encouragement and assistance I received.

It seemed as if every step I took was to be impeded by something laid across my path. I was opposed in everything. My life was a continual warfare. Not only was every obstacle thrown in the way of my work, but I was attacked personally as an agitator and a visionary, in seeking to disturb long settled usage, and thinking to reform the law, in which was embodied the wisdom of ages. This was perhaps to be expected when I undertook such radical changes in the face of the most conservative of professions. But he has little reason to complain of the number or violence of his adversaries who finds himself victorious in the end. As to any real service which I may have rendered to American law, and so to the cause of universal justice, of human progress and civilization, in short, as to any claim I may have to the title of lawgiver and reformer, I am willing to be judged by the wise and good after I have passed away.

"One lesson, which I might perhaps have learned by reading, has been taught me by experience, and that is, that he who attempts reform must rely upon himself, and that all such enterprises have received their start and impetus from one, or at most a very few persons."

CHAPTER VIII.

ADOPTION OF THE CODES AT HOME AND ABROAD.

It is one thing to frame an ideal Code, on the strictest lines of justice, and quite another thing to have it enacted into law by the law-making power. I once saw a Revolution, that taught me a good many things, and chief of all, the vanity of human expectations. When I stood in front of the Tuilleries and saw the Royal Palace sacked by a mob, while he who but an hour before was a king, was fleeing in disguise for his life, it seemed as if the bottom was knocked out of everything ; that there was nothing on earth that was secure from being overturned and destroyed. But the next lesson was not less a surprise : it was the marvellous genius of the French people in the creation of a new government. It was not many days before Paris was flooded with constitutions, each of which was believed by its projector to be almost inspired, and that, if adopted, it would cure all the evils of human society. Few of them were ever heard of again. One or two were tried as experiments, but soon broke down for want of some needed balance in the political machine; till, four months after the Revolution, all these wild dreams were exploded in a four days' battle in the streets between the people and the army supporting the government, when the attempt to restore the golden age was finally drowned in blood!

Since then I have not been so sanguine of seeing great reforms carried by *coups d'etat*, whether by rulers or by people. The march of mankind is slow, and it is enough for any generation to help it a little on its way. We in America are not likely to see such a tragic ending of our schemes for the improvement of human society. Happily for us our reforms do not imply revolutions. But for all that, a Reformer is a man who pulls down as well as builds up, and must not be surprised if he meets with criticism, for the mere suggestion of reform is a reflection upon the old state of things as needing to be reformed—an assumption which is resented by those who are satisfied with things as they are. The old ways are good enough for them: and it seems to be almost an impertinence when a man comes along who thinks that he is wiser than his generation; and that he can teach them a better way, whether it be in law, in politics, or in religion. The Codifier therefore had no reason to complain if his new Codes, however skilfully "framed and put together," should not be at once accepted by the public, or by those of his own profession, who were content with the old traditions and usages, which, if not ideally perfect, were practically safe.

On his part he faced the situation squarely, and found no fault with the closest scrutiny. He knew very well that when the Legislature of New York authorized the Commission to prepare the new Codes, it had exhausted its power—that its action could not bind any future Legislature (which might not be chosen until some years later) to *adopt* the Codes so prepared. When they appeared they must stand on their own merits, and thereby be justified or be condemned. As every Legislature was made up largely from the legal profession, he took for granted that, while some might be in favor of law reform, others would be opposed to it; and perhaps the greater number be simply indifferent, looking upon it as merely an experiment. The report bound no one. To the last moment the Legislature held the power in its own hands; and though the country lawyers were quite willing, as a matter of professional curiosity, that Mr. Field and his associates should amuse themselves with their beautiful Codes, it would be quite another thing to ask the whole bar of the State to put their necks under the yoke; and when it came to that point, the "Reformers" might hear from the back districts!

With such natural repugnance to change, it was not surprising that the adoption of the Codes was slow. Even the Codes of Procedure, though they concerned but the outward forms of administration of justice, instead of the substance of the law, met with opposition both within and without the Legislature. Although they had been submitted complete on the first of January, 1850, they had to wait long for recognition, and even as yet are only adopted in part. The Code of Civil Procedure was once passed by the Assembly, but defeated in the Senate ; and a different Code, prepared by M. H. Throop, though mainly founded upon Mr. Field, was adopted between 1876 and 1880. The Code of Criminal Procedure was not adopted until 1882.

Thus the progress of reform was slow : it was only the outer walls of Conservatism that had been carried, the fortress itself was still to be stormed and taken. The revision of the Codes had taken the Commissioners, with all their assistants, eight years of the hardest labor. Not only had they been outlined with the utmost care, but every chapter and article had been revised and re-revised, till some portions were changed no less than eighteen times. But all this was not enough to insure its adoption. There was not a meeting of the Legislature that Mr. Field had not to make a pilgrimage to Albany, to appear before the Committee of the Senate or of the Assembly, where he was always sure to meet the determined opposition of some of the ablest members of the Bar in the State, in which they were supported by a large number of the legislators, who, from professional instinct, were opposed to innovations which would oblige them to re-learn, at least to some extent, both the substance and the practice of the law.

These were heavy odds, against which the Reformer had to stand almost alone, using all his power of argument and of persuasion, with only partial success. The Penal Code was indeed enacted in 1881, and has been the law of the great State of New York for fifteen years ; but the Civil and the Political Codes have not been adopted to this day ! The Civil Code, which he looked upon as the most important of all, has passed one of the houses, the Senate or the Assembly, again and again ; twice it has passed *both* by large majorities ; but failed in either case of receiving the signature of the Governor, who shrank from the responsibility of putting his name to a Reform which reconstructed the very substance of the Law.

These repeated defeats were of course a sore disappointment to the Reformer, but after all they ought not to have surprised him. In any great movement for reform, allowance must be made for the natural conservatism of old institutions, what in mechanics would be called the power of greatest resistance. It could not be an easy thing to move an old Commonwealth, like New York, wedded to old laws, some of which dated from the time when the Dutch held Manhattan Island.

But there was another and broader field in the new States and Territories, where the ground had not been preoccupied, and so "westward the star" of reform, as well as of empire, "took its way." Whenever a government was to be formed, its framers saw the advantage it would be to begin its political life with the very best methods of securing justice. While some of the older States, like Ohio and the Carolinas, adopted only the Code of Civil Procedure, sixteen other States and Territories—Kentucky, Indiana, Missouri, Arkansas, Iowa, Wisconsin, Minnesota, Kansas, Nebraska, Nevada, Arizona, Utah, Idaho, Wyoming, Oregon, and Washington—adopted in substance both the Civil and the Criminal Codes of Procedure; and to outdo them all, California, the Queen of the Pacific, led the way in adopting, not only the Codes of Civil and Criminal Procedure, but also the three Codes, Civil, Penal, and Political; and Dakota, which was the first of the States or Territories to adopt the Civil Code, has in due time taken all the rest, a fitting crown to the great State of the Mid-Continent.

And not Dakota alone! Beyond the Dakotas lies another State three times as large as New York, a Highland region, with valleys between the mountain ranges, rich as the valley of the Nile. But its first occupants were of the lawless character that often hang on the border, so that when the stalwart sons of the West marched across the plains with their rifles on their shoulders, they found that the first thing was to put down lawlessness with a strong hand, after which they proceeded to lay the foundations of a great Commonwealth worthy of its position in the very heart of the Continent. In this no man was more conspicuous than Colonel Sanders, who was the first to represent Montana in the Senate of the United States. But that he owed anything—or that Montana owed anything—to the Reform in New York, was first disclosed in the following letter :

HELENA, Montana, January 24th, 1896.

My dear Dr. Field: I learn that you are to write a biography of your eldest brother, Mr. David Dudley Field, and I am very much pleased to know that so active and useful a life is to be described by so faithful and entertaining an author. The State of Montana will feel a personal interest in this book of yours, as to his labors, more than to those of any other man, is she indebted for the very excellent system of statutory law now in force within her limits.

It was my good fortune to know him for a number of years, and his lively interest in the codification of our laws not only intensified my own interest in it, but gave to it an intelligent direction. For a considerable period we sought to secure legislative action here, and your brother, although he lived remote from Montana, and was always busied with very large affairs, was never so busy but that he took a lively interest in our progress, and by his advice assisted us in the consummation of this great legislation. Although advanced in years, he surprised me by his earnestness and activity in this matter, and comprehended, and seemed to carry in his mind, the smallest details which appertained to the accomplishment of this work. Entertaining a very high opinion of the beneficence of codification, it was my good fortune during the last years of his life to meet him frequently, and to receive from him information and suggestions, which he frequently gave also by letter, not only to myself, but to members of the Commission who had this codification in charge. During these years, while the work progressed, and while we were waiting the passage of the enactment, his lively interest in it and assistance induced me to resolve to furnish him a copy of the statute as it should be finally passed; but the inevitable end came to him before that event.

And so I turn to you with some expression of the thanks which the people of Montana feel, and which I certainly feel, for the labor which he performed, and of which we have been able to avail ourselves in the passage of *a system of law which, for comprehensiveness, coherence and perspicuity, stands without a parallel in the history of legislation.** If our local needs

* To an inquiry whether this included *all* the Codes, the writer replies in a second letter that the legislation came to Montana by the way of California, which had adopted it from New York, and that, though there were some slight changes in the transmission, they do not affect the substantial fact that the laws which rule Montana to-day are the work of Mr. Field, to whom he gives the honor, and to him alone. I quote his very words: "There were thrust into the Codes, as passed in California, certain pre-existing statutes of this State pertaining to the same subject matter, and local as to our conditions and needs; but we have the Political Code of your brother, the Civil Code, the Code of Civil Procedure, the Code of Criminal Procedure, and the Penal Code. These last two, however, are consolidated, and are known in our statutes as the Penal Code, and pertain to crimes, and the methods of their punishment. In a few instances, possibly, our code commission, instead of taking the statutes from California, may have preferred a substantial form of the same statutes taken from Colorado, South Dakota,

and infirmities have thrust into his codification some legislation not projected on the high plane of his code, it is our fault, not his ; and it does not impair the great task which he performed, not only for Montana, but for all other States availing themselves of his noble work. At a period of life when other men would have considered their labors to be over, he was as keenly alive to the adoption of these laws by the various States as any person I have ever known.

He was not acquainted in Montana, nor do I know that he ever visited this State, but he took as lively an interest in improving its legislation as if he had founded it, and was wholly identified with its history. Having edited these statutes and published them, it seemed to me appropriate that some recognition of his services in behalf of improved legislation and codification should be had ; and, in the preface, I took occasion to

---

or some other State ; but these instances are very few, and I *consider the Montana codes substantially the legislation prepared by your brother.* Departures from the form as prepared by him are so insignificant that in generalizing upon the laws they need not be referred to."

To this it should be added that so thorough and complete has been the process of "boiling down" the myriads of enactments and of precedents scattered through libraries in England as well as in America, that the several Codes of Law, Civil, Penal and Political, with the Codes of Procedure, are all compressed into a single volume much smaller than the Revised Statutes of the United States ; so that a citizen of Montana, who has but little money to spend on books, needs to have lying on his table but three : an English Dictionary to teach the knowledge of his own mother tongue ; this Book of the Law, to show him his rights as a member of civilized society ; and the good old Family Bible to teach him his duties to God and to man.

mention his name, regretting only that the opportunity was not afforded me to say more. If the courts whose quandaries he has settled ; the lawyers whose doubts he has resolved ; and the citizens whose legal rights in simple and concise words he has defined ; could speak in your volume, his name and memory would certainly be blessed. His was a great life to look back upon, and I doubt not your volume, which I bespeak, will set it forth in alluring sentences with such detail and generalization as shall make it coveted by all intelligent young men of our country.

The profession to which I belong will appreciate, but cannot exaggerate, the great services rendered by your brother, not merely to it and the courts, but to the humblest citizen of the land, in simplifying the law and bringing it home to their hearthstones. *Indeed codification is peculiarly the boon and benediction of the poor, and it furnishes some facilities whereby the ignorant may become wise.*

His services in endeavoring to secure the settlement of all international differences by arbitration bespoke a noble nature, humane in purpose and enlightened in comprehension ; and in these days, when careless speech seems fraught with so much peril, and the spirit of frivolity pervades so many high places, his words of truth and soberness, born of sanity and prudence, raise him in the esteem of philanthropists throughout the world. It was my fortune to know something of him personally, and these great services which he rendered to mankind in no way oppressed him. He rose superior to the weariness of the daily toil, and was as cheerful and active in social life as any person I ever knew. With my wife I recall a journey with him down the Hudson River one summer day, a stream with which I flattered myself I was somewhat familiar, not merely from personal observation of it, but from the works of Irving and Lossing and Bryant, and others who had exhausted their genius in painting its beauties and describing its history ; but your brother pointed out new places of interest along that historic stream, and related the events which have made it immortal, until from Albany to Manhattan Island it was all aglow with history and romance.

The dullness of appreciation of the legislative improvements with which he was identified, I cannot wholly comprehend, but I am satisfied that the States which have availed themselves of his services count these enactments as among their most precious possessions. To fitly describe such a life as he led is an inspiring task, and I do not doubt but that affection and duty will lift you to the occasion, and give us a biography not only worthy of his own renown, but also worthy of your own pen. Such men never die.

I trust confidently your book will occupy a shelf along with the biographies of Sumner and Garrison and the autobiography of Mr. Sherman, an example and inspiration to the youth of the land, who may learn therefrom the rewards of courageous, intelligent and patient toil. To those of us who knew him and can bear witness to his great service for mankind through so many years, it will seem fitting justice that his name be handed down by dutiful affection to the gratitude and admiration of future ages.

Very truly yours,

W. F. SANDERS.

These are the victories of peace, which are indeed no less renowned than the victories of war. As a messenger of peace Law is next to Religion, and most of all laws adopted by the people themselves from a sense of justice, and for their own protection. No army crossing the Continent could carry in its mailed hand such a pledge of peace to future generations.

Nor was the effect of this legal reform limited to our

own country: the movement was soon felt by our kinsmen across the sea. As we had derived our laws from England, she was equally interested with us in any improvement in that which was our common heritage. This need was felt by her greatest statesmen. In the year 1867 I was in London, and saw a good deal of John Bright, who was full of congratulations on the issue of our civil war, which gave him unbounded hope not only for our country, but for the reaction upon his own. He thought it would be no harm to England to learn a lesson from America. Among other things, he said very earnestly: "I wish we had a man in England to do for us in the way of the reform of the law what your brother has done for America!" But where to find the man was the difficulty. So far as he knew the man did not exist. But there were some of his countrymen who were not above profiting by our example. What America had done England could do. The interest thus excited led to the appointment of a Parliamentary Committee, and a Crown Commission, to consider the whole subject of Law Reform; and twice when in England—in 1851 and in 1867—Mr. Field was invited to meet with them, and explain the methods and extent of codification in New York. On the latter occasion there were present the most eminent legal authorities of the Kingdom, including five Lord Chancellors—Lord Westbury and Lord Cranworth; Sir Page Wood, afterwards Lord Hatherley; Sir Hugh Cairns, afterwards

Lord Cairns; and Sir Roundell Palmer, afterwards Lord Selborne. They sat to a late hour of the night, and when they rose Lord Hatherley took their visitor by the hand and said, "Mr. Field, the State of New York ought to build you a monument of gold!"

It was not long before the American Codes of Procedure were adopted in substance in Great Britain and the Colonies. A few years later (in 1874) Mr. Field went round the world, and found to his surprise his system of practice in use in the courts in India! He could hardly believe his eyes when he was confronted by the rules that he had prescribed, word for word as he had written them in his library in New York; and saw justice administered according to them in those far-off ends of the earth, Singapore and Hong Kong!

This was not "the drum beat, which, following the sun, and keeping company with the hours, encircles the globe with the martial airs of England," but it was something better than the sound of war—the whisper of peace, soft as the murmurs of the sea, yet touching every shore—peace founded upon justice to subject races—the Hindoo, the Malay, and the Chinaman—whose rights are not only guaranteed by England, but may we not add (this, I am sure, will not offend the majesty of England) still further guarded and protected by some wise provisions, that have been adopted from American law.

CHAPTER IX.

"THE COMMANDING FIGURE AT THE BAR."

A man may frame the laws of a country, and never practice in the courts. The two things are distinct, and yet they may be united. Mr. Field was a lawyer before he became a reformer, and one grew out of the other. It was in the daily practice of the law, that he saw its defects, and the need—even the necessity—of its being cleared of all drift wood, and being brought into a compact and orderly form. But who would begin a contest that would continue for a great part of his life; and in which he might sacrifice himself for the public good? As there was no one else who had the boldness—some would call it the rashness—to undertake it, he was forced to the front. Even then his life might have been made easy if he had abandoned the practice of his profession, when he might have shut himself up in his library, and devoted his days and nights to the study of all the Codes from Justinian to Napoleon, from which to construct a more perfect body of law for his country. But to continue at the bar, he would be brought into daily contact and antagonism with those who were bitterly opposed to his reform. Yet, disagreeable as it might be, it had its advantages, as this constant alternation kept him in touch with the practice in the courts, so that he saw at once its excellences and its defects—a knowledge that was indispensable to any system of reform. Here were two lives—the life of the ideal and the life of hard reality—going on at the same time side by side, yet when it came to writing the story, it was necessary to separate them, and treat of each apart in order to keep the unity of the subject, and having struck upon the trail of Reform, it seemed better to follow it to the end, even though it should be anticipating in the order of time, after which we could resume the course of the professional career.

The first part being closed, we now change the scene from the stillness of the library to the excitement of public halls. There is nothing in our American life—not even a popular election, or the meeting of Congress—that stirs the blood more than a trial, on the issue of which may depend men's fortunes, or even their lives. Then the court room becomes an arena of combat, where lawyers are the gladiators, with judges and juries for spectators, and a crowd filling every niche and corner, hanging on the words of the speakers, and waiting, it may be in breathless anxiety, for the issue. In such an arena the subject of our story takes his place. How did he bear himself with the leaders of his day? and what will be his fame with posterity?

No man can speak for posterity, but one who was familiar with all his contemporaries, the late Mr. Austin Abbott, did not hesitate to speak of Mr. Field as "the most commanding figure at the American bar!" This may be taken as the impulsive utterance of a generous friend, whose sense of loss was quickened by the sudden death of the object of his admiration. The bar of New York counts many illustrious names from the days of Alexander Hamilton, whose leadership no man would dispute, unless it were his rival, Aaron Burr. After him came Thomas Addis Emmet, who was living when the young student of law first came to New York. I remember well the picture he gave me of that truly great man, around whom there lingered the sad memories of all that he had done and suffered for "his own loved island of sorrow." Judge Story has described a scene in the Supreme Court of the United States when Emmet was pitted against Pinckney, of Baltimore, a combat of giants, which left on the judges and spectators the highest estimate of the abilities of both. A few years later stood at the bar of that high court Daniel Webster, for whom the admiration of the American people amounted almost to awe. But he too belongs to a former generation.

After these "three mighties," it would be presuming to speak of any one of half a dozen great lawyers of our time as above all others. They are too near us to be rightly judged. There are many stars in our American firmament, and it is only when they have receded into the distance that future astronomers will determine which was the star of greatest magnitude. The writer would think it a very poor tribute to one whom he holds in reverent as well as loving memory, if he were to exalt him by depreciating others. So far is he from this that it is a pleasure to recognize those who upheld the name and fame of the bar of New York. To old citizens whose memories carry them back as far as Thomas Addis Emmet, it may seem as if his greatness were equalled, if not surpassed, by one whose father emigrated from Ireland just before his birth, the late Mr. Charles O'Conor. Mr. William Curtis Noyes also stood in the front rank of his profession. But he died in 1864—thirty years before Mr. Field, who had the mournful duty of pronouncing his eulogy. Had he lived to as great an age, he might have had as great a reputation at home and abroad.

Of this small group of leaders of the bar only one remains, Mr. William M. Evarts, who has had a long life of distinction both in his profession and in the service of his country, as United States Senator and Secretary of State. In legal contests he and Mr. Field were often pitted against each other. One such I remember, in which the famous Thurlow Weed was prosecuted for libel upon Mr. Opdyke, the Mayor of New York, growing out of some transactions in the war.* It was a study to watch the two combatants. No men could be more unlike. Mr. Field, like a powerful athlete, went straight to the mark. No flights of fancy turned him aside from the object he had in view. To this Mr. Evarts was a perfect contrast. Though of slender figure, he had an alertness of mind, a quickness of perception, that made him a very dangerous antagonist. He was famous for his long sentences,† that stretched on and on till sometimes the meaning seemed to be "in wandering mazes lost." And yet it was delightful to hear him, (even though the current of his thoughts was like that of a beautiful river winding hither and thither,) and listeners sat breathless to catch the last word. Such was the great advocate and lawyer who is with us still. Long may he be spared in the city of which he has been a resident for half a century, and in which he is looked up to with universal respect and veneration, for his own great qualities, and as one of a small group of "commanding figures at the bar," of whom he is the last survivor.

It is therefore without raising any question of preeminence, that the biographer gives the outline of another figure that could not but attract attention at any bar or

---

* I saw them again pitted against each other in the arguments before the Electoral Commission in Washington.

† When he was criticized for this, he answered with his pleasant humor that "he did not know that anybody had reason to complain of long sentences except the criminal classes."

in any public assembly, at home or abroad, in Congress or in Parliament, the figure of one whose very presence was "commanding," and served at least as a favorable introduction, when he rose to address any body to which he was a stranger.

As to the standing of a lawyer, how he "ranks," (if we may use a military word,) that probably depends, at least among his professional brethren, quite as much on his knowledge of the law given to his client, it may be in the privacy of his office, or in a brief statement before the court in which there is no attempt at eloquence, as in his most labored efforts at the bar. In this knowledge of the law even those who differed most from Mr. Field would hardly claim that he had any superior. All who call themselves lawyers are supposed to understand its general principles. But few men kept up the study as he did from the very necessity that was upon him in the reconstruction of the law, which compelled him to be familiar, not only with the Common Law of England and America, but with the jurisprudence of other countries, running back to the Roman law, which was the foundation of them all. This vast learning could not but be of service in his professional practice.

Being thus master of the law, it did not take him long to make himself master of a case. No man was quicker to "see through" an involved legal question. But that did not supersede the most careful study to the minutest detail. To those who knew how he was absorbed in his Codes at all hours, early and late; at morning and midnight; the wonder was that he could find time for anything beside. But no trial ever came on and found him unprepared. His power of abstraction was such that he could, if need were, forget everything else, and concentrate his mind upon the special case, analyzing it as a chemist analyzes a compound substance. Under the blaze of this search-light, he took it, as it were, to pieces, separating the immaterial from the material, the essentials, on which the whole question turned, and, like a skilful general, massed his forces on the vital point.

When he had thus made himself master both of the law and the case, he had no difficulty in making others see it. He had a singular precision of language, that came in part from his training in the higher mathematics, so that when he put a proposition in words, it was with a sort of mathematical exactness, until it might be said of him, as was said of Webster, that "when he had stated a case he had argued it."

But an argument, however logical, may fall flat from the coldness of him who presents it. Of this indifference he was never guilty. When he undertook a case, he put his own personality into it, and as he had great confidence in his own judgment, his opinions, when once formed, were very positive. And this was one element of his power—that he believed in himself! It may seem like making a virtue of egotism and self-confidence to say that a man must believe in himself in order to have power over others, but no man ever did much in the world who did not believe in himself.

Of course, as with all lawyers of large practice, the number of his cases in sixty years was beyond counting. At one time his law practice was said to be larger than that of any other member of the New York bar. Some idea of the innumerable litigations in which he was engaged may be formed from a glance at the fifty volumes of "Cases and Points," in which briefs and records are bound together in the order of time. Of course, all such documents were but fragments, huge but unshapen masses of rock that were to be framed into the building of some great argument, but, even as they are strown over the field of legal controversy, they show an almost preternatural activity.*

"But where was the place for Law Reform to come in?" was the question that everybody asked; to which he replied that it was a wonder to himself, but added with his usual philosophy, "In one way this outside work was a benefit to me, for the intensity of my professional life required some relief from the incessant

* These volumes were sent to his brother, Mr. Justice Field, to be kept by him during his life, and at his death to be given to the New York State Law Library in Albany. They are supplemented by a dozen Scrap-books, containing slips from newspapers concerning the same litigations and other points of personal history, that may furnish materials to some future historian.

mental strain, to which the pursuit of an ideal, like that of Law Reform, was a healthful diversion" : ["healthful diversion !"—that is good for a work that occupied him for eighteen years !] "and may thus have kept me from breaking down."

As to the mere "business" of the law, it is for the most part, like any other business, very prosaic, requiring no labored argument or eloquence, but only a clear head, a good intelligence in ascertaining the facts of a case, and what relief or redress may be furnished by the law. This is the every-day round of the profession, in which there is no opportunity for a great advocate to show any superiority to his brethren, all of whom are supposed to be to that extent learned in the law. If anybody were to go to court to hear Mr. Field, and the case were one of some commercial transaction—perchance a question of damages, which might be a matter of figures—he would probably hear only a simple statement of the case, which would be all that it required. But give him a great cause, in which great principles were involved, and he rose to the occasion with a mingling of argument and of eloquence, in which there was a moral as well as intellectual power. When he had such a cause to defend, it was with an earnestness which I always thought he inherited from his father, who, as a preacher of the Gospel, was wont to speak "with authority," because he spoke from the infallible "Word," which no man could question. The same positiveness appeared in his eldest son, whom I have heard laying down the law as founded in eternal justice, in a tone of solemnity that seemed to be an echo of the old Puritan when he read the Ten Commandments with a hushed awe, as if he had been with Moses in the Mount, and had heard the very voice of God!

Then it was, as he drew near to the close of an argument, that the great advocate appeared in his fullest power. It was not that his personal presence, however "commanding," overawed the court, but there was something in his voice which no judicial bench could choose but hear. It was not the soft, persuasive tone of one who pleads for mercy for his client. There was nothing of the abject or even of the humble petitioner; but straightening himself up to his full height, he demanded a just verdict! At that instant there rose before him a sense of the majesty of justice as something greater even than mercy—as the world is "established in righteousness," which is only another name for justice—and that justice he demanded, not only in the name of the law of his country, but in the name of a just as well as an almighty Lawgiver in heaven.

DAVID DUDLEY FIELD

THE FIGURE AT THE BAR

[From the painting by Hardie in the Capitol at Albany]

CHAPTER X.

POSITION IN POLITICS. A DEMOCRAT, BUT OPPOSED TO THE EXTENSION OF SLAVERY. ANNEXATION OF TEXAS. RISE OF THE FREE SOIL PARTY.

Much as Mr. Field loved his profession, he loved his country more. Absorbed as he was in the practice of the law and in his legal reforms, at the same time he kept watch of public affairs, though at first he only looked on from without, as an interested spectator. In his political creed he formed his own opinions from the beginning in a way that was rather surprising in one who was born in Connecticut, a State that when he was a boy was the seat of the rankest "Federalism," and had welcomed in its Capitol the Hartford Convention, which protested against the war of 1812, as threatening to destroy the commerce of New England, and in which there were mutterings of disunion not unlike those that half a century later burst forth in the civil war. That out of an atmosphere thus surcharged with anti-democracy should come one so free from it, would seem to indicate a complete mental evolution. It may have been owing in part to his legal associations in Albany and New York, but most of all was it due to an independence which asserted itself in early manhood. He thought for himself, and studied the questions of political economy, as applied to all governments, and then specially to his own. In general he held that most countries are over-governed, though he would not go quite so far as to adopt the extreme maxim of democracy, "The best government is that which governs least," for that would seem to imply that the ideal state of society was no government at all! But he did believe that the tendency in all governments was toward over-legislation. Sixty years later he wrote an article for the North American Review on the Theory of our Government, in which he says: "There are two theories of government, the liberal and the meddlesome," meaning by the latter that which "dabbles" in all the pursuits and occupations of men, and of necessity grows into a system of favoritism, which leads every kind of industry to hang on the central power, and thus demoralizes the manliness of all who live under it. He would not object to the protection of new industries in time of war, or in the infancy of the Republic, till they were able to stand alone; but the habit of applying to the Government for protection grew to an enormous abuse, that was not at all in harmony with the simplicity of our government. That was what he called a "meddlesome," and he would have added, a "mischief making" government. Instead of this "paternalism," in which the government was to play the part of a "nursing father" to certain interests, whereby the many were taxed for the benefit of a few, he would adopt the wider rule: "Protection to all and favor to none!"

With such principles, between the two parties that divided the country—the Whigs and the Democrats—he sided with the latter, and the first political speech he ever made [in 1842] was in Tammany Hall! a strange beginning for one who was to spend a large part of his life in fighting against it! [The particular occasion, however, was not one of great importance, as it only concerned the nomination of Robert H. Morris for Mayor.] But while thus sincere and outspoken in his convictions, he was not made for a politician. He was too rigid and unbending in his principles, and would not be bound by caucuses or conventions. As the natural consequence, he never held an office in his life, except for two months in Congress, to which he was sent for a special purpose, to prevent what he thought to be a great public wrong. He was once offered the appointment of Judge of the Supreme Court of New York, which he declined, feeling that his place was at the bar rather than on the bench. His only public position was that of Commissioner of the Code, which could hardly be called an office, for, although it involved enormous labor, it was all work and no pay. But if he was hedged about with no official dignity, he had what was far better—absolute independence, freedom to think, and to speak what he thought. The very fact that he asked nothing for himself gave him the more weight, so that few men in public life had a greater influence than he, though he stood apart and alone, determined to follow only what was dictated by his own sense of public justice and public honor.

Here beginneth a chapter of political history that has never been fully written, but which ought to be, as it takes us back half a century, to a period when old issues were gone, and old parties were broken up, and all things became new. In that long conflict, which lasted for a whole generation, there was no bolder or braver combatant for liberty than Mr. Field. Though he was a Democrat, he would not be in bondage to the name, and the moment that he saw that the party was to be used as a means of extending slavery, he spurned its authority, and led the way for others to follow.

The first thing which aroused the alarm of the more independent men in both parties was the movement for the annexation of Texas, then almost a *terra incognita*, so unoccupied as to invite the floating population that always hangs on the border of civilization, who had but to cross the Rio Grande to roam over the land at will, recognizing no authority but their own. When this had gone on for a few years, and the settlers had come to number a few thousand, they declared their independence of Mexico! This was their own affair, with which we had no concern, till it was proposed to annex it to the United States! The motive of this was clear. It was not merely to add to our domain, but to give a preponderance of territory and of representation in Congress to the slave-holding States. The line had been drawn in 1820 by the Missouri Compromise:—that slavery should not extend North of a certain parallel of latitude! But there was no obstacle to its expansion Southward. New territory would bring increased population, that would enable the South to maintain its control of the government.

The proposal to annex a territory large enough for an empire, Mr. Field looked upon as a gigantic robbery, which was all the worse if Mexico was too weak to prevent it. As for title, we had no more right to Texas than to Canada. In April, 1844, there was a great demonstration at the Broadway Tabernacle at which he spoke with the utmost vehemence against what he regarded as a national crime. Thus he began:

"FELLOW CITIZENS: The President has sent to the Senate a treaty to annex to the territories of this Union a tract of country six times as large as the State of New York—a country which till lately was a part of the neighboring and friendly Republic of Mexico, and which even now is engaged in open war for its independent existence. This treaty has been negotiated with a suddenness, a secrecy and haste unparalleled in our annals—a suddenness, secrecy, and haste which have no excuse in the nature of the act itself or in the circumstances of the country.

We are in profound peace with all the world, and tranquil at home. What then can justify the President in entering upon and consummating, so far as depends on him, a treaty of such importance, almost before the country was aware it was contemplated? This annexation was offered to the Administration six or seven years ago, and rejected on grounds in which the whole country seemed to acquiesce. We were, therefore, unprepared for this movement, till it came upon us like thunder in a clear sky. But I trust we have, nevertheless, warning enough to prepare for the storm. The President was not elected with reference to any such question, nor was the Senate, nor the House of Representatives. It is of all questions one in which the people should be consulted, and their will ascertained beforehand. We appeal from the President to the Senate, from the Senate to the States of the Union, from the States to the sovereign people. If they determine that this measure shall be accomplished, let it be; if they do not, let no secret cabal, no set of men in power, effect it. . . .

"Admit that the cause of quarrel between Texas and Mexico was just; yet the struggle was one in which we had no right to interfere; and, if we had followed the advice of the fathers of our country, we should not have interfered.

"How was the revolution accomplished and made successful? By aid from this country; without aid from us, Texan independence could not have been established. It was well known that bands of hunters were organized in the Western States to hunt in Texas, though there was nothing for them to hunt but Mexican soldiers. The aid our people sent them in men, in money, in munitions of war, accomplished the revolution. Mexico complained, and how was she answered by our Government? It said, We mean in good faith to fulfil our treaty stipulations, but it is impossible to prevent our men from going over our immense frontier; we cannot maintain a cordon of troops for a thousand miles, in an uninhabited country; but we will prevent all aid from this country as far as we can.

"That answer absolved the Government; but, if it were not able to prevent the wrong which our citizens perpetrated, let it not profit by it. Let us not proclaim our weakness as our excuse, and then take advantage of the spoliation which our weakness permitted. The state of the case is simply this: Mexico has been despoiled of one of her finest provinces; the spoilers went out from among you, because you could not prevent them. Then take not back to your bosom the spoilers and the spoil. If you receive them, the whole world will pronounce you faithless. . . .

"*The annexation of Texas is war with Mexico!* We have the authority of our venerable President [Tyler] that it is not merely the provocative of war, but war itself. War, moreover, declared by the President and Senate, when the Constitution confided the war-making power to Congress. Consider what must follow such an act. You extend your frontier from the Sabine to the Rio Grande. Your troops must occupy the fortresses of Texas. Your troops instead of Texan troops must defend them against Mexico. *Are you prepared for war?* If you are, in the name of justice, in the name of honor, let it be fairly and manfully waged! I am for war too, when necessary, in defence of the rights and liberties of our country. But I am not for an aggressive war against a weak and unoffending neighbor. The people of this republic are the best judges of that question; let them decide it. If we are to have war, let it be such a war as our forefathers waged, in self-defence, for the maintenance of our rights and honor."

But in spite of all warnings, it seemed that the Democratic party was to be given up to blindness in taking this step. At the Baltimore Convention a few weeks after, Mr. Van Buren was thrown overboard, simply because he had written a letter against the annexation of Texas, and James K. Polk was nominated on a platform committing the party to it. Polk was elected and Texas was brought into the Union. Then came the war that Mr. Field had predicted, which, though we were victorious, was looked upon by the best people of the North with a repugnance that no tidings of victory could remove : as I once heard Rufus Choate say with his inimitable touch of beauty and tenderness : "The wail of the daughters of Mexico is no music to our ears ! "

But when the cruel war was over, it appeared that the South had a larger purpose still, for it ended not only with the annexation of Texas, but of California also, which, however, was obtained, not by conquest, but by purchase ; and with this further acquisition came the demand that it should be admitted as a slave State ! Anticipating this, Mr. Wilmot, a Democrat in Congress from Pennsylvania, had introduced as an amendment to a bill for purchasing Mexican territory, his famous proviso : "That as an express and fundamental condition to the acquisition of any territory from the Republic of Mexico, neither slavery nor involuntary servitude shall ever exist in any part of the said territory," which was adopted in the House, but rejected in the Senate. Soon it became a battle-cry for the

North. At the same time Mr. Field wrote the famous "Secret Circular" and "Joint Letter," designed to rally the anti-slavery portion of the Democratic party. In 1847 he was a delegate to the Syracuse Convention, where the Democratic party was split in two over the question of the extension of slavery, and on that occasion he introduced the famous resolution, long afterward known as "The Corner-Stone," which was for years displayed at the head of the leading column of the Albany Atlas, as the rallying cry of the Free Democracy. It was in these words :

> "Resolved, That while the Democracy of New York, represented in this convention, will faithfully adhere to all the compromises of the Constitution, and maintain all the reserved rights of the States, they declare, since the crisis has arrived when that question must be met, their uncompromising hostility to the extension of slavery into territory now free, or which may be hereafter acquired by any action of the Government of the United States."

Matters came to a head in 1848 with the nomination of General Cass. When the Democrats of New York assembled in mass meeting to hear the report of their delegates to Baltimore, they were very much excited. Mr. Field wrote the address, which declared their strong disapproval. Carrying their feeling into action, a portion of the party refused to support General Cass, and nominated Mr. Van Buren for President, and Charles Francis Adams for Vice-President, on the platform of no more extension of slavery. In support of these principles and candidates, Mr. Field spoke at a large meeting in the city, and wrote the address of the Democratic-Republican Committee to the electors of the State. Nor did he confine himself to New York; he carried the war into New England, into Faneuil Hall, where he was introduced by Charles Sumner, and spoke with a spirit of resistance to the domination of slavery that seemed as if it were an echo of the days of the Revolution.

Here was the beginning of the Free Soil party, which took the field with increased determination when it was proposed to open Kansas and Nebraska to the introduction of slavery! There was a Chinese wall in the way in the Missouri Compromise, which declared that slavery should never cross the line of 36 degrees and 30 minutes! All above that was holy ground, consecrated to liberty. But what spot on earth was ever sacred to an ambitious politician? Stephen A. Douglas, of Illinois, was the most popular man in the Northwest, and if he could make himself equally popular at the South, he would have a triumphal march to the Presidential chair. For this it was only necessary to break down the barrier to the extension of slavery, when Southern statesmen would be able to boast:

> "No pent up Utica contracts our powers,
> But the whole boundless Continent is ours."

But it was a delicate matter to touch the Missouri Compromise. It could not be done openly and avowedly, but it might be made of no effect by giving it a new interpretation, to which Mr. Douglas was competent, preparing a bill in which it was declared to be "the true intent and meaning of the act, not to legislate slavery into any state or territory, nor to exclude it therefrom, but to leave the people thereof perfectly free to form and regulate their domestic institutions in their own way, subject only to the Constitution of the United States." This was not a repeal of the Missouri Compromise! Oh no! Those who voted for it would never lay sacrilegious hands on anything so sacred, which had come down to them from their fathers! That old fortress of liberty was left standing in the wilderness, a picturesque ruin, covered with moss, while the sappers and miners had cut a way through the forest, broad enough for the whole South to march round it.

No sooner had the partition wall been broken down than planters from Kentucky, Tennessee and other States farther South came by boat-loads up the Missouri River, with all the field-hands from their plantations, and swarmed into what was then known as the Platte Country, where the "hot bloods" became the famous, or infamous, "Border Ruffians," that long kept the country in a state of terror. There were also settlers from the East, but "on the side of their oppressors there was power," for they were supported by the national government, which undertook to put down resistance by law, arresting opposers and throwing them into prison, till the blood of the North, that was supposed to be very cold, began to boil as never before. Indignation meetings were held in the Eastern cities, in which collections were taken up to supply the Northern men with rifles. Nor was this confined to New England: the city of New York was the focus of a great popular excitement. Never shall I forget a meeting in the old Broadway Tabernacle, that was crowded by men in a state of irritation that could hardly be controlled. I was in the ante-room with Henry Ward Beecher, who was pacing up and down, like a lion in a cage. As I sat near him on the platform, I saw that he was under the power of a great passion, which culminated in a dramatic scene when he took up in his hands a chain that had been used to bind the limbs of men in Kansas, and raising it above his head, he dashed it to the floor, and trampled upon it in token of his contempt and scorn for a government that could stoop so low. Such was the excitement that, had there been a call for volunteers, many would have been ready to take their muskets on their shoulders, and set their faces towards the West. It was easy to call this fanaticism, but it was the kind of fanaticism that soon after flamed out on the field of battle. Mr. Field was the last man to be called a fanatic, but he was stirred to indignation by the audacity of the South on the one hand, and the cowardice of the North on the other. Of course there was a great outcry that he had deserted his party, and been false to his Democratic principles, to which he replied in a letter to the Albany Atlas, dated May 22, 1856 :

"Though I have not hitherto acted with the Republican party, my sympathies are of course with the friends of freedom, wherever they may be found. I despise equally the fraud which uses the name of Democracy to cheat men of their rights; the cowardice which retracts this year what it professed and advocated the last; and the falsehood which affects to teach the right of the people of the Territories to govern themselves, while it imposes on them Federal governors and judges, and indicts them for treason against the Union because they make a constitution and laws which they prefer, and collects forces from the neighboring States and the Federal army to compel them to submission."

This Kansas business gave a tremendous impulse to the Free Soil Party, which grew to such proportions as to give a strong hope that it might elect its candidate for the Presidency, for which it nominated Fremont, whom Mr. Field supported in speeches in New York and Pennsylvania.

By these successive strokes, the wedge was driven deeper and deeper, by which the old Democratic party, which had so long ruled the country, was cleft asunder, while the Free Soil Party grew stronger and stronger with every battle that it fought, until it united with the Anti-slavery portion of the Whigs, and formed the Republican Party, that was in the fullness of time to gain the control of the government in the election of the man for the hour. Here the curtain rises on a great figure, and on a series of events with whose beginning we enter on the most awful, the most tragical, and yet in the end the most triumphant, period in American history.

CHAPTER XI.

THE NOMINATION OF LINCOLN. A CHAPTER OF UNWRITTEN HISTORY.

Man proposes, but God disposes. Ambition overleaps itself. The political manœuvering which was to make a popular leader President, ended in his defeat, and the election of his rival. It was one thing for Douglas to carry a measure in Congress, and another to settle with his constituents at home. When he returned to Illinois, he found that he had lighted a fire on the prairies that could not be put out. He had to make a campaign through the State, and wherever he went he was confronted by a new antagonist, a tall, lank, ungainly Kentuckian, with not a single grace of manner, but whose long right arm could deal heavy blows. No two men were more unlike even in their personal appearance, for while the new-comer stood six feet four, Douglas was so diminutive in stature that he was nicknamed the Little Giant, a picturesque combination of two such figures on the same stage. But the contrast in the personality of the men was soon forgotten in the earnestness on both sides, which made it one of the most exciting political contests ever seen in this country. The question was one of supreme importance, that of carrying slavery into the new Territories, and roused each to put forth his utmost strength. Douglas had the advantage of a great reputation and the skill acquired in many a hard battle, but with all this he carried the State only by a bare majority, and was reelected to the United States Senate, but the contest for the first time made the name of Abraham Lincoln known to the American people.

There is nothing that rouses popular enthusiasm like the discovery of an unknown great man. The fame of this debate went beyond the bounds of Illinois, till the echo was heard even in the East, and though the scene of contest was so far away that it was like the voice of one crying in the wilderness, yet the voice was so clear and strong that men pricked up their ears to hear, and asked who it was that spoke, and what manner of man he was? The next step was to invite him to come to New York and give a lecture on the political situation. How well I remember his first appearance before an Eastern audience! It was in the Cooper Institute as it was in the old days, when the platform of the great hall was not in the middle, but at the far end, and I can see him now as the door opened, and the tall figure came forward, accompanied by William Cullen Bryant and David Dudley Field. As I sat on the platform close to the speaker, I caught every word, and observed every gesture. He spoke in a high-pitched voice, in which there was not a trace of the smooth-tongued orator; but there was a singular clearness in his style, with a merciless logic which no listener could escape, as he unfolded link after link in the iron chain of his argument.

But there was more in evidence that night than skill in debate: there was a revelation of the man, as one who loved his party, but loved his country more. The fairness to his opponents was quite unusual in political combatants. It was not as if he were fighting an enemy, but reasoning with a friend. The lecture closed with an appeal to the South, that was not at all in a tone of threatening, but of pleading with kindred, with those who were our brothers—if brothers estranged, yet brothers still—partakers with us in the great inheritance of liberty. It was this "sweet reasonableness," this "gentleness of wisdom," and above all, the tone of "sad sincerity" that gave me, who heard him then for the first and the last time, an indelible impression of the character of Abraham Lincoln.

But three months passed and this man of the people was a candidate for the Presidency, a step forward which took the country by surprise, and which to this day is enveloped in some degree of mystery. If we were in France we might say that "it is always the unexpected that happens," but among a people that are not so readily carried away by sudden impulse, events come to pass in a more regular and orderly way.

Since the campaign of Fremont the Republican party had grown in numbers till it was strong enough to make a bold strike for the possession of the government; and when the Democrats split into two factions, and nominated two candidates, while a third party, made up of old Whigs and Know-nothings, nominated a third, the Republicans felt, like Cromwell, that "the Lord had delivered the enemy into their hands."

The custom had long obtained of nominating candidates for the two highest offices of the government—President and Vice-President—by a National Convention made up of representatives from all the States, to double the number of their members of Congress, a fair apportionment, and a good way to get at the will of the people so long as they were left to freedom of choice. The danger came in only when one man undertook to do their choosing for them, in which case the free election became a solemn farce. New York, having two Senators and thirty-three members of the House of Representatives, was entitled to seventy delegates, that were to be designated by a State Convention which met at Syracuse a few weeks before the National Convention. One who was a member of the nominating Committee appointed by this Convention tells me that they came together with all due gravity, as if they were a legislative body to enter into high debate on matters of national importance. "But," he added, "we might have saved ourselves the trouble, for while we were in the room with closed doors, as if deliberating in the profound secrecy of a papal conclave, Thurlow Weed sat just outside the door to tell us whom to nominate!"

Mr. Weed was an old campaigner, who had fought many battles and won many victories. I once heard the late Mr. Edwards Pierrepont, in a case before the courts, speak of him, as he sat at the bar, as "the man who had made Senators, Governors and Presidents!" He was now to try his hand again, and laid his schemes with full assurance of victory. The first thing was to have well in hand the delegation from New York. He knew the men for his purpose. They must be men of good standing in the party, whose names would have weight with the public, but at the same time he wanted supple, pliant men, not too scrupulous about little matters, who held him in awe, and would defer to his political sagacity. Of course, he had no use for men like Horace Greeley or David Dudley Field, who were too independent and self-willed. When they reached Chicago Mr. Greeley (to Mr. Weed's great disgust) was elected a delegate from Oregon! Mr. Field was left standing without, but found that an outsider may sometimes have an influence as great as an insider, of which he was to give signal proof before the contest was over.

The Convention met in Chicago May 16th, 1860, in a huge, barn-like structure that had been erected for the purpose, called "The Wigwam." Here the Republicans, as they answered to the roll-call, mustered 465 strong! All went smoothly for the first two days, and seemed to point to one man who among all the candidates stood foremost, as if appointed by heaven to lead them to victory. This was the distinguished Senator from New York, William H. Seward. Nor did there seem a doubt of his nomination. On the eve of the decisive day Thurlow Weed said that he "was sure of success," and Mr. Evarts, that "the victory was certain, and would be rapid!" Indeed Mr. Greeley, who was strongly opposed to it, gave up the contest, and at midnight telegraphed to the Tribune in New York, that the opposition could not concentrate upon any candidate, and that Governor Seward would be nominated!

But when the morning came, and the divisions of the Republican army marched into the Wigwam and grounded their arms for the more peaceful work of the vote, to the amazement of friends and foes, the natural heir to the crown was defeated, and Abraham Lincoln proved to be the man of destiny. As this was a surprise even to the Convention itself, we cannot help asking by what influences, open or secret, it was brought about, for we cannot exaggerate its importance. It was the turning-point in the life of Lincoln. If he had not been nominated that morning, he would have remained to be, what he was before, a country lawyer in Illinois, making his round with the circuit of the courts. He might still have been a conspicuous figure in Western politics, (for he was not a man to sink into oblivion,) but for the time at least it is probable that he would have returned to his profession and the even tenor of his life would have flowed on as gently as before.

Nor was the result of less moment to the country. With the defeat of Lincoln the hand on the dial of history would have been turned backward. The mighty succession of events that followed—the secession of the Southern States, the call to arms, the four years' war, and the abolition of slavery—all would have been passed over to another generation. Hence it was a critical moment in our national life. In view of the tremendous consequences that followed in peace and war, it is not too much to say that the whole course of American history turned on the decision of that hour !

As we come to the how and the why of this sudden revolution, I turn to a "Life of Lincoln," a massive octavo of nearly eight hundred pages, by a distinguished author, Henry J. Raymond, the founder and editor of the New York Times ; who was thoroughly acquainted with the whole history of American politics ; with the rise and fall of parties and of men. He records briefly that "On Thursday, the 17th of May, the Committee on Resolutions reported the Platform, which was enthusiastically adopted. A motion was made to proceed to the nomination at once, and if that had been done, the result of the Convention might have proved very different, as at that time it was thought that Mr. Seward's chances were the best. But an adjournment was taken till the morning, and during the night the combinations were made which resulted in the nomination of Mr. Lincoln."

So much and no more! This is very calmly stated, as if it were in the natural order of the proceedings. But the reason for this subdued tone is apparent in the Preface, in which the author says that the book was "prepared during the Presidential canvass of 1864," and that "its main object was to afford the American people the materials for forming an intelligent judgment as to the wisdom of continuing Mr. Lincoln for four years more in the Presidential office."

The purpose of the book, then, was to be a campaign document, issued to influence the coming election, a help that was sorely needed at that hour when there was real danger of Lincoln's defeat—a danger that was not removed till after Sherman's capture of Atlanta. While there was any doubt as to the result, it would have been the height of unwisdom to open old wounds, and revive old antagonisms. For the time it was a duty to forget past "unpleasantness," and unite all hearts to save the Republic.

But now that the danger is past, that the war is over, and that we are seeking after the truth of history, we go back to the original documents, and appeal from the Mr. Raymond of 1864 to the Mr. Raymond of 1860, when he was just from the Chicago Convention, and tells a fuller and a plainer story, letting out the real state of things on that memorable night when, as he mildly puts it, "the combinations were made which resulted in the nomination of Mr. Lincoln." Combinations by whom? Was there a movement all along the line? Or was there a secret Gunpowder Plot to make an end of Mr. Seward's political ambition?

Some have found an easy way to explain the result by assuming that there was no plot at all, but only that the delegates, in their calm deliberations in the stillness of the night, had come to the painful conclusion that they must sacrifice their personal preferences to the "political necessity" of having a candidate who could carry the four doubtful States of Illinois, Indiana, Pennsylvania and New Jersey! No doubt that had its weight, but it is one thing to say that it was *a* reason, and another that it was *the* one and overmastering consideration. The latter Mr. Raymond flatly denies, and even goes so far as to say that, on the contrary, "The nomination finally made *was purely an accident*, decided far more by the shouts and applause of the vast concourse which dominated the Convention than by the direct labors of any of the delegates."

Here then we are all at sea. A flippant dismissal of the subject only deepens the mystery. If at midnight it was conceded on both sides that the result was inevitable, that Seward would be nominated the next morning ; and at the appointed hour he was defeated ; then between midnight and morning something happened. What was it? To talk in a general way of "political necessity" is to evade the question : it is an explanation that does not explain. Instead of asking, What did it? it is more to the point to ask, Who did it? for it was not abstract considerations, but a living presence that appeared in the darkness of that memorable night. It was not a miracle, wrought by unseen hands. It was the work of men, who were not only in the flesh, but very much alive. To Mr. Raymond, looking on as a spectator—eager, earnest, and knowing all the actors in the foreground—the contest seemed to be not so much a political as a personal one. There was no difference among the candidates as to the platform of principles on which the battle was to be fought : but there came in another element more powerful than all the logic in the world—the personal antagonism, that no man can tame, and that often carries a public body by storm. Whoever has been present at a political convention—especially if it be to choose a President—knows that it is a cyclone of warring ambitions, of which it is not possible to get any adequate impression except from one who was in the storm-centre, and who can truly say, "All of which I saw, and part of which I was."

If we cannot get such an inside view of the Convention from biographers and historians, perchance we may get it from the newspaper correspondence of the day, where we need no higher authority than Mr. Raymond himself, when the final decision relieved him from all restraint, and he was free to declare the truth, the whole truth, and nothing but the truth. He does not seem to have been in any doubt as to who defeated his candidate. As no one can tell the story so well as himself, it is better to let him tell it in his own words. A few days after the Convention adjourned, there appeared in the New York Times a letter of two columns and a half, whose very date is significant, and prepares us for the melancholy tone in which it begins :

"AUBURN, May 22, 1860.—I have turned aside from my direct route homeward, to pay a visit of respect and friendship to Governor Seward. I found him as busily and happily engaged in directing the improvements in his delightful country residence as if no such incidents as treachery and disappointment ever disturbed the tenor of political life." As to his future, "he regards his public life as definitely closed. You may dismiss all the speculations in which the public journals are just now indulging as to his place in the new Republican administration—if we have one—as idle and useless. Henceforth the only sphere of his labors will be his home, and the society which surrounds it."

From this mournful picture of fallen greatness, Mr. Raymond turns to the author of it, and makes a savage attack upon Horace Greeley, as the creeping, crafty, and malignant destroyer of the great statesman. How a poor young man, coming from a farm in Vermont to be a type-setter in a printing office in New York, could rise to such influence and power, is shown by a reference to his career. As Mr. Raymond would have it, he owed it all to Mr. Seward. "For twenty years Greeley had been sustaining the political principles and vindicating the political conduct of Mr. Seward through the columns of the most influential political newspaper in the country"; during all which "he was proud to have been his personal friend and political supporter," a devotion that continued till he was alienated by the fact that the great Senator did not sufficiently recognize the hard-working Editor, but listened more to the wily influence of Thurlow Weed—a dissatisfaction that grew to such a point that once, in a moment of irritation, he wrote a letter to "the party of the other part," in which he announced that "the firm of Seward, Weed and Greeley was dissolved!" This alienation—though it did not come to an open and public rupture—was never healed. For six years the retired member of the firm was

"Nursing his wrath to keep it warm,"

till the Chicago Convention gave him the opportunity to "wreak upon Mr. Seward the long-hoarded revenge of a disappointed office-seeker"!

This was a heavy charge to throw upon Mr. Greeley.

No matter how much he pleaded innocence—or, to put it more gently, wished to divide the responsibility of the nomination—Raymond retorts bitterly : "He awards to others the credit that belongs transcendently to himself," and to sum it all up he says : "The great point aimed at was Mr. Seward's defeat ; and in that Mr. Greeley labored harder, and did tenfold more, than the whole family of Blairs, together with all the gubernatorial candidates to whom he awards the honors of the effective campaign."

This is sufficiently explicit. But Mr. Raymond has one more indictment to make. The next day he returns to the subject in an editorial in which he brings under the same condemnation "Dudley Field, who labored with equal energy in the common cause," though he does not presume to impute to him the charge of "treachery" to Mr. Seward, to whom he was never under the slightest obligation. He was a Democrat of the old school, who left his party because it had surrendered to the Slavery power ; and had joined the Republicans, but had no part in their family quarrels. But he did not take kindly to the new creation in American politics of a "boss," who, with none of the responsibilities and the restraints of office, assumed absolute control, setting up one and putting down another : and his chief objection to Mr. Seward was, that if "This our Cæsar" were throned in the Capitol, he would have his proconsuls in the provinces, and as the State of

New York was the richest "province" in our American empire, he saw a familiar figure sitting in the place of custom, receiving tribute, and dividing the spoils, in the fine old Roman way.

In coupling together the names of Horace Greeley and David Dudley Field—for he does not mention another man—Mr. Raymond brings the matter down to a fine point, to specific and definite personalities, and singles out the two men who in his opinion were above all others responsible for the defeat of Seward, and the nomination of Lincoln. That the result was not due to Mr. Greeley alone, or chiefly, I have his own declaration, for I once spoke to him about it, giving him credit for the sudden change in what seemed to be the inevitable course of events, which he disclaimed as doing him too much honor.* This at the moment surprised me, until I learned that there was reason for his not assuming too much, since at that dark hour when he sent his despatch to New York, he was thoroughly demoralized as to the event of the coming day, and

* Indeed so far was Mr. Greeley from wishing to pose as the original Lincoln man, that when he went to Chicago he had in view another candidate, Mr. Edward Bates, an eminent lawyer of St. Louis, who, being in a slave State, though only just on the border, would not alarm the timid conservatives, who were frightened by the very name of an abolitionist, and whose nomination might give an impetus to emancipation in Missouri. So fully was he possessed with this idea that, even after

would have "thrown up the sponge" if he had not been literally "held up" by a stronger will than his own, and by more unflinching courage.

To see how critical was the situation, that not a moment was to be lost, we have to introduce another witness, who will take us farther on in unravelling the mystery of Mr. Seward's defeat and the nomination that followed. It was midnight: in a few hours all would be over: whatever was done must be done quickly. It is on the night before a battle that the battle is planned, though it be not till the morning that it is fought and won. It is of the preceding council of war that our new witness has somewhat to relate—not as a reporter of what somebody else said or did not say, but of what he saw with his own eyes and heard with his own ears.

This is the late Mr. James A. Briggs, a man of the best New England stock, a nephew of Governor Briggs of Massachusetts, a lawyer by profession, who had lived for twenty years in Cleveland, during which time he became an intimate personal and political friend of Mr. Chase. In 1857 he removed to New York, having his

---

Mr. Lincoln was nominated, and Mr. Greeley had returned to New York to hear the shouts for "Old Abe," he was not satisfied till he had put himself on record [in The Tribune of May 21st, 1860] thus: "I think that Judge Bates, to whom I never spoke nor wrote, would have been the wiser choice." This at least frees him from the responsibility of having forced Mr. Lincoln upon the Convention.

home in Brooklyn, from which, on November 1st, 1859, he wrote to Mr. Lincoln to come and lecture in Plymouth Church. This was the lecture that was finally given in Cooper Institute. Mr. Briggs was an ardent Republican, and went to the Chicago Convention in hope to promote the nomination of his political chief. Here he was in a position to have a full inside view of the movements of the several divisions of the party that were struggling for the ascendency, and afterwards felt it to be his duty to put on record an account of what passed under his own observation. It is brief, but right to the point. He says:

"I have always thought that Mr. Lincoln was more indebted to Mr. David Dudley Field for his nomination for the Presidency at Chicago in 1860, than to any other one man. I was present at that Convention as the friend of Mr. Chase, but soon found that the nomination was to go either to Mr. Seward or to Mr. Lincoln, and then I was for Mr. Lincoln.

"I was at the Tremont House, with Mr. Field, Mr. Greeley, Mr. George Opdyke, and Mr. Hiram Barney. The night before the nomination, about midnight, Mr. Greeley came into Mr. Field's room, and threw himself down with a feeling of despair, and said 'All is lost; we are beaten!'"

[Mr. Greeley was subject to such sudden depression, and the events of the day, and the anticipations of the morrow, had tried him to the utmost. He had been all the evening in a state of unnatural excitement,* which ended in his sending his message to New York, from which he came back to Mr. Field's room to throw himself down in a state of collapse, till a strong man lifted him up and set him on his feet, and breathed new life into him. Who it was that rendered that kindly office, I leave to Mr. Briggs to tell :] "To Mr. Greeley's cry 'All is lost !' Mr. Field replied 'No, all is *not* lost ! Let us up and go to work !' His energetic voice and manner seemed to inspire Mr. Greeley with new life, and both immediately went out to renew the struggle. Mr. Field particularly worked with a determined will

* When I was looking about for sources of information, Senator Dawes directed me to Mr. Edward R. Tinker, of North Adams, Mass., who was a member of the Convention, and could speak from his personal knowledge. Mr. Tinker went on to Chicago in the train with some of the delegates from New York, and was with them in their quarters in the Tremont House, in what Mr. Weed called "The Conspirators' Room," and was in and out at all hours of day and night. He says that on the night before the vote Mr. Greeley was in a very irritable mood. As the hours drew on, he became more and more excited over the impending defeat, the blame of which he charged upon others, telling them that they were throwing away their votes, at which he raged and stormed, and finally burst away and rushed to the telegraph office to send a message to New York that Mr. Seward would be nominated in the morning, and then, completely exhausted, returned to Mr. Field's room, where he found a man who was not so easily dismayed.

and resolute purpose that seemed to know no such word as fail. He went from delegation to delegation, and as he was from New York, Mr. Seward's own State, and yet was opposed to his nomination, he had great influence in turning the tide of feeling in favor of Mr. Lincoln. Before morning they returned in high spirits, when Mr. Field said: 'The work is done! Mr. Lincoln will be nominated!' Mr. Greeley seemed equally confident—a confidence which was justified by the event. But it was in those midnight hours that the work was done. That was the turning-point in that memorable Convention, and therefore a turning-point in the political history of our country. For the issue then reached, I have always been convinced, from what passed under my own eyes, that more was due to Mr. Field than to any other man."

Here then at last we seem to have come to the Transformation Scene—to the time, the place and the actors. This is the missing link in the history which connects and explains all the rest. We can well understand that the delegations were debating among themselves the means of making some combination without which there was not, and could not be, any hope of success, wavering this way and that, when the sudden inrush of two determined men put an end to the divisions, and led them to form in the ranks that led to victory. I have read many Lives of Lincoln, and have never found any other explanation of what transpired that night that was satisfactory or even plausible.

This testimony of Mr. Briggs is of the direct and positive kind that cannot be controverted except by impeaching a man's intelligence or his veracity; and coming right after that of Mr. Raymond, the one confirms the other, answering to the requirement of the old Mosaic law, that "in the mouth of two witnesses every word shall be established."

But there is other evidence still, for where brave men lead the way, the hesitating and the doubting follow; and it was not long before what was going on was whispered from chamber to chamber, from delegation to delegation, so that when the morning dawned there was a general premonition of what was to come. As the delegates poured out of the hotels on their way to the Convention, the elder Blair, the most sagacious politician in the country, turned to Mr. Field and asked what he thought would be the result? and when he said, "Mr. Lincoln will be nominated," the old man answered in a very positive way, "*Well, if we succeed, it will be owing to you!*". And so spoke New England in the voice of the gallant Anson Burlingame, who, after the decisive vote was taken, came to Mr. Field, as he was sitting on the platform, and said, "You have nominated Mr. Lincoln: now help us to nominate the 'bobbin-boy'" [Governor Banks, of Massachusetts] "for Vice-President!"

Nor was this the observation of but a few individuals: it was common talk among the delegates, and those who had watched the course of events. In the train that brought home many of the members of the Convention, and others who had been spectators, was Mr. Clarkson N. Potter, of New York, afterwards Member of Congress, who told his friends that he saw and heard one and another pointing to Mr. Field, and whispering, "That is the man who nominated Lincoln!" This general rumor is a sort of presumptive evidence, which, when confirmed by divers witnesses, outweighs any number of negatives, which merely tell what this or that man did *not* see or hear, and, in the absence of all opposing testimony, must be considered to decide the question.

If I thus recall a chapter of unwritten history, it is not that I wish to magnify the part of an individual; nor that he ever made any claim to recognition on account of it, (a brave soldier is more concerned to win the battle than to dispute for the honors of victory); but that, since it has fallen to me to write the life of one who had a part in this making of history, I put on record the testimony of others, as but just to the memory of him who has passed beyond the reach of any earthly ambition.

CHAPTER XII.

THE LAST EFFORT FOR PEACE.

It is a brave man who can take the consequences of his own acts. Mr. Field had helped to nominate Lincoln, and to elect him, and he must bear his share of the responsibility. The country was now to face a crisis such as it had never faced before. The clouds began to roll up from the South and gather all round the horizon, till many at the North were frightened at the prospect, and loudly declared that the election of Lincoln was at once a blunder and a crime !

Against all such harsh judgments, or fearful portents, Mr. Field stood firm, prepared to show that it was neither a blunder nor a crime ; that it was the only course that could bring a peace worth having, and re-establish the Republic on everlasting foundations.

It was something to have the issue clearly drawn. Mr. Seward had predicted an "irrepressible conflict," but all good men joined in the prayer, "Give peace in our time, O Lord !" But how could the conflict be kept back much longer ? The country was growing ; the population was increasing by millions, and the South, with its "peculiar institutions," demanded the right of way wherever it would go. Forty years before an effort had been made to divide the country by the line of the Missouri Compromise, but that had been broken down, and now the South claimed the right, not only to march Westward up to a fixed parallel of latitude, but beyond it along the mighty courses of the Mississippi and the Missouri, stopped by no barrier of river, or plain, or mountain, till it reached the Western Sea.

But the election of Lincoln was a danger-signal—a warning not to go too far! Not that he had any design to encroach upon the South. He had no such aversion to slavery as a New Englander might have, for he was born in a slave State, and looked upon slavery as a condition for which the present generation was not responsible, and that was to be tolerated where it existed before. He would observe religiously all the compromises of the Constitution. But beyond that he could not, and would not, go: he would not do violence to his common sense in regarding slavery as belonging to an ideal state of society; nor was he ready to see the Free States of America converted into a great Slave Empire!

But the South was not willing to wait to see the new President installed in office: it looked upon his election as a threat, which it must meet in a tone of defiance. It demanded as the price of its remaining in the Union new concessions, new guarantees, for slavery; that no bounds should be set to its extension now, or in any future time. This was putting the pride of the North to the utmost strain. Yet such was the desire for peace—peace at any price—that it was willing to submit to almost any conditions. Even Mr. Seward, opposed in theory to slavery as he was, was ready that we should bind ourselves hand and foot by such an iron chain as this: "No amendment shall be made to the Constitution which will authorize or give to Congress the power to abolish or interfere within any State with the domestic institutions" [a synonym for slavery] "thereof, including that of persons," [how carefully they avoided the word *slaves!*] "held to labor or service by the laws of said State"!

And this resolution was adopted in the Senate by a two-thirds vote, 24 to 12, and in the House of Representatives by a little more than two-thirds, 133 to 65. Could the spirit of concession farther go?

But the South would not be pacified; it would not listen to anything. Scarcely had the result of the election been declared—to be exact, only six weeks later, December 24th—when South Carolina, which John C. Calhoun had long since familiarized with the idea of separation, took the lead, as if ambitious of the place of honor, in a formal act of its Legislature, by which it seceded from the Union, and the Governor issued his proclamation declaring South Carolina to be a "separate, sovereign, and independent State!"

This was a revolution, but one for which she had been long preparing. Her public men did not hesitate to say that it was but the culmination of events for a long course of years. Mr. Rhett, an old politician, said, "The secession of South Carolina is not the event of a day. It was not caused by Lincoln's election, nor by the non-execution of the fugitive slave law. It is a matter which has been gathering for thirty years. The election of Lincoln was only the last straw that broke the camel's back. But it was not the only one. The back was nearly broken before!"

With such unpleasant memories of the past, it is not surprising that South Carolina felt the step she took to be a happy deliverance. She did not stand upon the order of her going. If she had waited a little longer, with a show of hesitation and reluctance, it would have given a touch of formality and of grace to her good-bye to the sisters with whom she had been so long associated. But she had no farewells to give, and no tears to shed. So far from this, she was in a happy mood, and danced away with that "gayety of heart" with which France ten years later rushed into war with Germany! The parallel might be carried still further!

The business of secession once begun, the work went on briskly. Two weeks later, with the opening of the new year, 1861, Mississippi followed the example of South Carolina. Two days later Alabama and Florida locked arms and went out together; to be followed near the close of the month by Louisiana; and last of all, on the 5th of February, by Texas, the mighty State, for which we had gone to war with Mexico. Georgia, which was kept back by Alexander H. Stephens, came a little later and filled up the procession of States that marched out of the Union before Mr. Lincoln had taken his seat in the Presidential chair!

But the procession was not yet full. Virginia, the mother of Presidents, stood on her dignity, not to be run away with by less important States, and chose to act for herself. With the old memories of the Revolution in her heart, she lingered, and finally decided, before taking the last step, to make one more effort for peace, by way of a friendly Conference in Washington, to see if it were not possible to agree on some method of adjustment. It was a novel proceeding to go outside of Congress, to submit grave questions to a body having no legal authority. But the North did not stand upon formalities, if only it might bring peace, and it responded promptly to the call. As none of the seceded States were parties to it, only twenty-one States were represented, but these sent 133 delegates—a body that was not only respectable in numbers, but one of great dignity in the men that composed it, and that was presided over by one who was himself a Virginian, as well as a former President of the United States, Mr. John Tyler. A committee composed of one from each State, twenty-one in all, was appointed "with authority to report what they might deem right, necessary, and proper to restore harmony and preserve the Union." Of this committee Mr. Field was a member, a position to which he was entitled as the chairman of the New York delegation. Thus he was forced into the place of a leader, though the part of the North was not to propose, but to listen. As it had only exercised its rightful authority in voting for a President, and was satisfied with the result, it had nothing to say except to repeat, with increased emphasis, its readiness and determination to stand by the compromises of the Constitution.

But that was not enough, for the South had been going through an education in its ideas of slavery, until it came to regard it as so far from being an evil that it was a positive good, an institution that was according to the fitness of things; ordained by nature itself, as shown in the natural superiority of the white race. Thus exalted by conscious greatness, the men of the South were not at all abashed at the boldness of the undertaking to make radical changes in the Constitution, that had been framed by Washington, Franklin, Madison, and Hamilton. Slavery must be "unconfined"; it must have full sweep. Into whatever territory a master emigrated, he must have freedom to take his slaves with him; and if, when the population was sufficient for statehood, the majority were for slavery, slavery they should have, no power on earth withstanding!

And there must be a new Fugitive Slave Law, with all the modern improvements! If a master wished to go to Boston, he must be free to take his black man-servant with him, and if the latter, snuffing the air of liberty, were to run away, the city police must find him and deliver him up to his master! He might not be hunted with bloodhounds, but all the minions of the law would be on his track; and if he could not be found, the city or State must pay for his loss!

Even this would not satisfy the South. What most galled the Southern people was not the loss of a slave now and then, but the fact that they could not bring the North to see things as they saw them. They must do violence to our consciences, compelling us to accept as right what we believed to be wrong; to call evil good and good evil. This was asking us to stifle the instincts of humanity. They might as well have demanded that we should stop the beating of our hearts.

Had it been possible to comply with these conditions, even then the seceding States gave no promise of return to the Union, nor had their sister States any authority to make it for them. All that could be said was that they would (if they saw fit) take it into respectful (or not respectful) consideration. They might come back, or they might not even take notice of the invitation. But if they did return, it would not be by any means as prodigal sons, with penitence for the past, or promise for the future. If they came at all, it would be as masters in the old baronial halls. If there was any repenting to be done, it must be by those upon whose tame and cowardly spirits they looked down with just contempt.

These were indeed hard conditions of peace, conditions that we cannot read, even at this distance of time, without being almost ashamed of our country. And yet to this degree of humiliation a large portion of the North—God forgive them !—were ready to submit.

Mr. Field had listened with as much patience as he could to these extraordinary proposals. But while he listened the fire burned, and he could not keep silence. Time was passing. It was the 20th of February, and in less than two weeks there would be a new government in the Capitol. He must give warning of the impending danger. With perfect courtesy to his opponents, but with a firmness that could not but command their respect, he set forth the position of the North in a speech which ought to be preserved in every historical library, as it was an historic scene; the last effort for peace before the breaking out of the most terrible civil war of modern times ! As he rose to speak he felt the gravity of the situation. It was not in his nature to be a prophet of evil ; but lightly as some talked of it, he felt that the government, and the country itself, were in danger of going to pieces, and he spoke with a sad sincerity, which those who heard remembered long after. He did not assume to speak for others, but his own position he would not have misunderstood, and he "cleared the air" in the very first sentence: "For myself, I state at the outset that I am indisposed to the adoption, at the present time, of *any* amendment of the Constitution." This was sufficiently explicit. And now he proceeds to give the Reason Why:

To change the original law of thirty millions of people is a measure of the greatest importance. Such a measure should never be undertaken in any case, or under any circumstances, without great deliberation and the highest moral certainty that the country will be benefited by the change. In this case, as yet, there has been no deliberation; certainly not so far as the delegates from New York are concerned. The resolutions of Virginia were passed on the 19th of January. New York (her Legislature being in session) appointed her delegates on the 5th of February. We came here on the 8th. Our delegation was not full for a week. The amendments proposed were submitted on the 15th. It is now the 20th of the month. We are urged to act at once, without further deliberation or delay.

To found an Empire, or to make a Constitution for a people, on which so much of their happiness depends, requires the sublimest effort of the human intellect, the greatest impartiality in weighing opposing interests, the utmost calmness in judgment, the highest prudence in decision. It is proposed that we shall proceed to amend in essential particulars a Constitution which, since its adoption by the people of this country, has answered all its needs, with a haste which to my mind is unnecessary, not to say indecent.

Have any defects been discovered in this Constitution? I have listened most attentively to hear those defects mentioned, if any such have been found to exist. I have heard none. No change in the judicial department is suggested. The exercise of judicial powers under the Constitution has been satisfactory enough to the South. The judicial department is to be left untouched, as I think it should be. You propose no change in the form of the executive or legislative departments. These you leave as they were before. What you do propose is: to place certain limitations upon the legislative power; to prohibit legislation upon certain important subjects; to give new guarantees to slavery; and this, as you admit, before any person has been injured, before any right has been infringed.

There is high authority, which ought to be satisfactory to you—that of the President of the United States, now in office!—for the statement that Congress never undertook to pass an unconstitutional law affecting the interests of slavery except the Missouri Compromise. Well, you have repealed that! You have also every assurance that can be given, that the Administration about coming into power proposes no interference with your institutions within State limits. Can you not be satisfied with that? No! You propose these amendments in advance. You insist upon them, and you declare that you must and will have them, or certain consequences must follow. But, gentlemen of the South, what reasons do you give for entering upon this hasty, this precipitate action? You say it is the prevailing sense of insecurity, the anxiety, the apprehension you feel lest something awful, something unconstitutional, may be done. Yet the gentleman from Virginia (Mr. Seddon) tells us that Virginia is able to protect all who reside within her limits, and that she will do so at all hazards. Why not tell us the truth outright? It is not action under the Constitution or in Congress that you would prevent. What is it then? You are determined to prevent the agitation of the subject. Let us understand each other. You have called us here to prevent future discussion of the subject of slavery. It is *that* you fear—it is *that* you would avoid—discussion in Congress, in the State Legislatures, in the newspapers, in popular assemblies.

[The reader will observe the peculiar style of the speaker, in which he argues by questions, short and sharp, that he rains upon his opponents as if from a battery or a mitrailleuse, to which they can make no reply—a mode of attack upon dangerous sophistry that has been held in honor from the days of Socrates.]

But will the plan you propose, the course you have marked out, accomplish your purpose? Will it stop discussion? Will it lessen it in the slightest degree? Can you not profit by the experience of the past? Can you prevent an agitation of this subject, or any other, by any constitutional provisions? No! Look at the details of your scheme. You propose through the Constitution to require payment for fugitive slaves—to make the North pay for them. You are thus throwing a lighted firebrand not only into Congress, but into every State Legislature, into every county, city, and village in the land.

This one proposition to pay for fugitive slaves will prove a subject for almost irrepressible agitation. You say to the State Legislatures, "You shall not obstruct the rendition of fugitives from service, but you may legislate in aid of their rendition"—thereby implying that the latter kind of legislation will be their duty. You thus provide a new subject for discussion and agitation for all these Legislatures. In the border States especially, such as Ohio and Pennsylvania, you will find this agitation fiercer than any you have hitherto witnessed, of which you complain so much. You will add to the flame until it becomes a consuming fire.

You propose to stop the discussion of these questions by the press. Do you really believe that in this age of the world you can accomplish that? You know little of history if such is your belief. Free speech is stronger than constitutions and dynasties. You might as well put your hands over the crater of a burning volcano, to extinguish its flames, as to attempt to stop discussion by such an amendment of the Constitution. Stop discussion of great questions affecting the policy, strength, and prosperity of the Government? You cannot do it! You ought not to attempt to do it!

I wish to speak kindly upon this subject. I entertain no unfriendly feelings toward any section. But while you are thus complaining of us in the free States, because we agitate and discuss the question of slavery, are you not, in a great degree, responsible for this agitation yourselves? Do you not discuss it and agitate it? Do you not make slavery the subject of your speeches in the South, and in the presence of your slaves? Do you not make charges against us, which in your cooler moments you know to be unfounded? Do you not charge us in the hearing of your slaves with the design of interfering with slavery in the States, with a design to free them if we succeed?

All this you have done, and if discontent, anxiety, and mistrust exist among your people, such discussion has contributed more to produce them than all the agitation of the slavery question at the North. But your amendments are not pointed at *your* discussions! That kind of agitation may go on as before. It is only the discussion on the other side that you would repress!

If the condition of affairs among you is as you represent it, have *you* no duties to perform? Is there nothing for you to do? Should you not tell your people what we have assured you upon every proper occasion, that the Republican party has always repudiated the intention of interfering with slavery, or any other Southern institution, within the States? This you all know. Have you told your people this? If you would explain it to them now, would they not be quieted? Do not reply that they *believe* we have such a purpose. Who is responsible for that belief? Have you not continually asserted before your people, notwithstanding every assurance we could give you to the contrary, that we are determined to interfere with your rights? It is thus the responsibility rests with you.

Although such is my conviction, supported, as I think, by all the evidence, *I am still for peace.* Show me now any proposition that will secure peace, and I will go for it if I can. We came here to take each other by the hand, to compare views, explain, consult. We meet you in the most reasonable spirit. Anything that honorable men *may* do, we *will* do.

We will go back to 1845 when you admitted Texas; back to the Missouri Compromise of 1820. You certainly can complain of nothing previous to that time. If, since then, there has been any law of Congress passed which is unjust toward you, which infringes upon your rights, which operates unfairly upon your interests, we will join you in securing its repeal. We will go further. If you will point out any act of the Republican party which has given you just cause for apprehension, we will give you all security against it. *We will do anything but amend the fundamental law of the government.* Before we do that we must be convinced of its necessity.

When you propose essential changes in the Constitution you must expect that they will be subjected to a critical examination; if not here, certainly elsewhere. I object to those proposed by the majority of the committee—

1. For what they contain, and
2. For what they do *not* contain.

I do not propose to criticise the language used in your propositions of amendment. That would be trifling. I think the language very infelicitous, and, if I supposed those propositions were to become part of the Constitution, I should think many verbal changes indispensable; But I pass by all that, and come at once to the substance.

I object to the propositions, Sir, because they would put into the Constitution new expressions relating to slavery, which were sedulously kept out of it by the framers of that instrument—left out of it, not accidentally, but because, as Madison said, they did not wish posterity to know from the Constitution that the institution existed.

But I object further, because the propositions contain *guarantees for slavery,* which our fathers did not and would not give. In 1787 the Convention was held at Philadelphia to establish our form of government. Washington was its presiding officer, whose name was in itself a bond of union. It was soon after the close of a long and bloody war. Shoulder to shoulder—through winter snows and beneath summer suns—through such sufferings and sacrifices as the world had scarcely ever witnessed—the people of these States, under Providence, had fought and achieved their independence. Fresh from the field, their hearts full of patriotism, determined to perpetuate the liberties they had achieved, the people sent their delegates into the Convention to frame a Constitution which would preserve to their posterity the blessings they had won.

These delegates, under the presidency of Washington, aided by the counsels of Franklin and Madison, considered the very questions with which we are now dealing, and they refused to put into the Constitution which they were making such guarantees to slavery as you now ask from their descendants. That is my interpretation of their action. Either these guarantees are in the Constitution, or they are not. If they are there, let them remain there. If they are not there, I can conceive of no possible circumstances under which I would consent to admit them.

Mr. MOREHEAD: Not to save the Union?

Mr. FIELD: No, sir—no! That is my comprehensive answer.

Mr. MOREHEAD: Then you would let the Union slide?

Mr. FIELD: No, never! I would let slavery slide, and save the Union. Greater things than this have been done. This year has seen slavery abolished in all the Russias.

Mr. ROMAN: Do you think it better to have the free and slave States separated, and to have the Union dissolved?

Mr. FIELD: I would sacrifice all I have—lay down my life, for the Union. But I will not give these guarantees to slavery. If the Union cannot be preserved without them, it can not long be preserved with them. Let me ask you if you will recommend to the people of the Southern States, in case these guarantees are conceded, to accept them, and abide by their obligations to the Union? You answer, Yes! Do you suppose you can induce the seceded States to return? You answer, We do not know! What will you yourselves do if, after all, they refuse? Your answer is, "*We will go with them!*"

Then we are to understand that this is the language of the slave States, which have not seceded, toward the free States: "If you will support our amendments, we will try to induce the seceded States to return to the Union. We rather think we can induce them to return; but, if we can not, then we will go with them!"

What is to be done by the Government of the United States while you are trying this experiment? The seceded States are organizing a government with all its departments. They are levying taxes, raising military forces, and engaging in commerce with foreign nations, in plain violation of the provisions of the

Constitution. If this condition of affairs lasts six months longer, France and England will recognize theirs as a government *de facto*. Do you suppose we will submit to this, that we can submit to it?

I speak only for myself. I undertake to commit no one but myself; but I here declare that an Administration which fails to assert by force its authority over the whole country will be a disgrace to the nation. *There is no middle ground; we must keep this country unbroken, or we give it up to ruin!*

We are told that one State has a hundred thousand men ready for the field, and if we do not assent to these propositions she will fight us. If I believed this to be true, I would not consent to treat on any terms.

From the ports of these seceded States have sailed all the filibustering expeditions which have heretofore disgraced the land. Their new government will enter upon a career of conquest unless prevented. Even if these propositions of amendment are received and submitted to the people, I see nothing but war in the future, unless those States are quickly brought back to their allegiance.

I do not propose to use harsh language. I will not stigmatize this Convention as a political body, or assert that this is a movement toward a revolution counter to a political revolution just accomplished by the elections. Nor will I speak of personal liberty bills, or of Northern State legislation, about which so much complaint has been made. If I went into those questions, much might be said on both sides. We might ask you whether you had not thrown stones at us!

[Then, turning to the second part of his argument, Mr. Field wished his Southern brethren to understand that, if they were to enter upon amendments of the

Constitution, the North had concessions to ask as well as to give; that it might at least demand protection for its citizens when they visited the South. At present a man from Massachusetts or Vermont could hardly cross the line without danger of insult or of violence, unless he professed entire satisfaction with the patriarchal institution. If he saw slaves sold on the block or flogged on a plantation, he must suppress his indignation, or he would be mobbed! Mr. Hoar, an eminent citizen of Boston, who went to Charleston to attend to a legal case involving the rights of a Northerner, was driven out of the city, and hardly escaped without a personal attack. With the memory of such treatment in mind, Mr. Field proceeds:]

As to what is *left out* in the plan of reconciliation, the majority report altogether omits those guarantees which, if the Constitution is to be amended, ought to be there before any others that have been suggested. *I mean those which will secure protection in the South to the citizens of the free States,* and those which will protect the Union against future attempts at secession; guarantees which are contained in the propositions that I have submitted as proper to be added to the report of the majority.

But, Sir, I must insist that, if amendments to the Constitution are required at all, it is better that they should be proposed and considered in a General Convention. Although I do not regard this Conference as exactly unconstitutional, it is certainly a bad precedent. It is a body nominally composed of representatives of the States, and is called to urge upon Congress propositions of amendment to the Constitution. Its recommendations will have something of force in them; it will undoubtedly be claimed for them in Congress that they possess such force. I do not like to see an irregular body sitting by the side of a legislative body and attempting to influence its action.

Again, all the States are not here. Oregon and California—the great Pacific dominions, with all their wealth and power, present and prospective—have not been consulted at all. Will it be replied that all the States can *vote* upon the amendment? That is a very different thing from *proposing* them. California and Oregon may have interests of their own to protect, propositions of their own to make. Is it right for us to act without consulting them? I will go for a Convention, because I believe it is the best way to avoid civil war.

Mr. WICKLIFFE: If a General Convention is held, what amendments will you propose?

Mr. FIELD: I have already said that I have none to propose. I am satisfied with the Constitution as it is.

Mr. WICKLIFFE: Then, for God's sake, let us have no General Convention!

Mr. FIELD: I think the gentleman's observation is not logical. He wants amendments, I do not. But I say, if we are to have them, let us have them through a General Convention.

And I say, further, that this is the quickest way to secure them. If a General Convention is to be called, let it be held at once, as soon as possible. If gentlemen from eight of the States in this Conference represent truly the sentiment of their people, as I will assume they do, there is no other alternative. *We must have either the arbitrament of reason or the arbitrament of the sword.* The gloomy future alone can tell whether the latter is to be the one adopted. I greatly fear it is. The conviction presses upon me in my waking and my sleeping hours. Only last night I dreamed of marching armies and news from the seat of war! [A laugh from the Kentucky and Virginia benches.]

The gentlemen laugh. I thought they, too, had fears of war. I thought their threats and prophecies were sincere. God grant that I may not hereafter have to say, "I had a dream that was not all a dream!"

For my own State and for the North I have only to say that they are devoted to the Union. The love for the Union is the strongest of our political affections. New York will stand by the flag of the country while there is a star left in its folds. If the Union should be reduced to thirteen States—if it should be reduced to three States—if all should fall away but herself, she will stand alone to bear and uphold that honored flag, and recover the Union of which it is the pledge and symbol. God grant that time may never come, but that New York may stand side by side with Kentucky and Virginia to the end! That we may all stand by the Union, negotiate for it, fight for it, if the necessity comes, is my wish, my hope, my prayer. The Constitution made for us by Washington, Franklin, Madison, and Hamilton, and the wise and patriotic men who labored with them, is good enough for us. We stand for the Country, for the Union, for the Constitution.

Was there ever a more manly appeal to the sense of justice, as well as to the love of country that might linger in the hearts of those whose fathers had fought for American independence? Did it call for any sacrifice of interest or of pride on the part of the South? None whatever. Was there a tone of threatening to inflame the proud Southern spirit? Not the slightest! He who pleaded so earnestly for peace spoke more in sorrow than in anger—not as to enemies, but as to those who were, or ought to be, friends and brothers. Thirty years before Mr. Webster had a vision of a conflict, but only as it appeared far off on the horizon, and in horror he put it out of his sight, only leaving the impression in these sad but immortal words that now seemed prophetic: "When my eyes shall be turned to behold for the last time the sun in heaven, may I not see him shining on the broken and dishonored fragments of a once glorious Union; on States dissevered, discordant, belligerent; on a land rent with civil feuds, or drenched, it may be, in fraternal blood!" His prayer was answered, and the black cloud disappeared, but only to reappear in the next generation. Mr. Field was haunted by the vision of a "gloomy future," that would not let him sleep while his country was going to ruin. He dreamed of "marching armies and news from the seat of war"—the very mention of which in the Convention only provoked the representatives of Virginia and Kentucky to laughter. No wonder that such light-hearted men had nothing to propose, or even to consider soberly, when they could not believe that danger was nigh. The mirthful Virginians who could not repress their merriment at Mr. Field's suggestion of a possible conflict, may have recalled it with an altered feeling when the sound of cannon was heard on the other side of the Potomac, and the fair fields of Virginia were "drenched in fraternal blood."

Alas for the lessons of human experience! In the history of nations, as in the lives of individuals, we are constantly reminded of what "might have been." It was the greatest crisis in American history. The country stood on the brink of civil war. If in that awful hour the South had listened to the warning of one of its truest friends, what might have been! One moment's pause! one step backward! and all might have been saved! And saved, not by any unmanly concession; by any humiliating surrender! It would have been Peace with Honor: with confidence restored and friendship made stronger than ever! True, when the conflict came, the sons of the South fought bravely, for they had the blood of Revolutionary ancestors in their veins. But why should they have fought at all? After four years of battle and of blood they had gained nothing and lost everything!

Here for the present we will let the curtain fall. It will be more pleasant to find, as we shall in a future chapter, that when the cruel war was over, and was followed by the Period of Reconstruction, Mr. Field was the strongest defender of the rights of the Southern States to be restored to their former place, as parts of "a glorious Union," that should be henceforth and forever "One and Inseparable!"

CHAPTER XIII.

THE WAR THAT HAD TO COME.

The war had come! We had shut our eyes to it—we could not and would not believe it till the last. Even the secession of the Southern States was looked upon at first as merely "sulking;" the natural fretfulness of "wayward sisters," whose pride had been wounded by their defeat in the election, but who needed only a little kindly soothing to be reconciled to the inevitable. And so the warlike manifesto did not disturb the equanimity of the North, as it proceeded to the inauguration of the new President, trusting that when the thing was done, and could not be undone, the sober second thought of our Southern brethren would bring them back into the fold. But in twelve months we had been making history very fast. Not quite a year before, on almost the last day of winter, a man of giant frame from the West had made his first appearance in New York. And now reappears the same tall figure, though in another guise, standing erect in a carriage, as he rides down Broadway, bowing to the tens of thousands who crowd doors and windows and housetops—not to see "great Cæsar pass," but to see a man of the people, elected by the people, to rule over the people, of the Great Republic! The joy of the occasion was a little—or not a little—damped a few days later by the fact that as he came nearer to Washington the cheers were not so unanimous, and that at the last moment he had to make his entrance at an unexpected hour, to escape a plot that had been laid for his assassination! But at last he was in the Capital, and had taken the oath of office, and was President of the United States.

For a few weeks there was a lull of excitement—the "silence in heaven" before the thunder-burst—when from far down the Southern coast a dull boom "came rolling on the wind," and instantly the land rose up at the sound of war. That first shot upon Sumter made an end forever of "Peace Conferences." The South had been warned that it "must have either the arbitrament of reason, or the arbitrament of the sword." It chose the latter, and had to take the consequences to the bitter end.

A body of soldiers on parade is always a gay spectacle, and Broadway was crowded more than ever when our gallant Seventh Regiment marched down on its way to the front, soon followed by regiments that came from under the shadow of Bunker Hill, all moving towards the Capital, which was for a time cut off from communication with the North, as if it were in a state of siege.

The unaccustomed and troubled state of things was brought home to me by a little personal experience. One evening a company of gentlemen were gathered round my brother Dudley's table, among whom was Vice-President Hamlin, a very important personage at that moment, when there had been a plot for the assassination of the President. Wishing to send word to Washington by a messenger, I was asked to try to work my way through. I got as far as Perryville, where I found the Seventh Regiment waiting for the means of transport. After some hours the ferryboat from Havre de Grace brought a crowd of refugees, among whom was Rev. Stephen H. Tyng, Jr., then a student at the Episcopal Theological Seminary in Virginia, where the political atmosphere had become too warm for him, and he started North, but found it not easy to get through Baltimore, as every stranger was an object of suspicion. Seeing the danger, he put on a bold face, as if he were a Southerner to the manner born, and drove to Barnum's Hotel, entered his name and took a room, by which the watchers were thrown off the scent, and then sauntered down the street till he could turn a corner, when he jumped into a cab and drove to the boat, which was just pushing off from the wharf. It was a narrow escape, and he warned me against running into the same danger, telling me that I could not possibly get through Baltimore, where I might be subjected to very rough treatment. Yielding to his earnest representations, we came back together to New York. To what dangers we might have been exposed we saw a few days after, when the Sixth Massachusetts Regiment, which was the first to respond to the call of the President, was stoned and fired upon in the streets of Baltimore, and had to force its way to the Capital.

While such clouds were gathering Mr. Field could hardly restrain his impatience at the pettiness of politics that was sometimes forced upon him by the importunity of others. At the outset of a new administration there are always rivalries among the seekers for office. Mr. Lincoln knew how his nomination had been opposed by the supporters of Mr. Seward. But he was the most forgiving of men, and with his native generosity he had put Mr. Seward at the head of his Cabinet, which led some of his followers to push themselves to the front with a haste that, to say the least, was not quite dignified. For this Mr. Field personally cared nothing; but he was not willing that his brave companions in arms, the old Free Soilers, who had fought the battle against slavery, and formed the most radical and determined wing of the Republican party, should come in as the rear-guard to a crowd of office-seekers. In justice to them he had a long interview with the President, in the presence of Mr. Seward, Mr. Chase, Mr. Welles, and Mr. Preston King, in which the matter was fully explained, and both parties were relieved of any further responsibility. Mr. Lincoln took in the situation at once, and with his usual tact settled these family differences, so as to unite all in the one purpose of saving the country—an issue that now extinguished the thought of anything else. As soon as the people of the United States found themselves plunged in a tremendous conflict, all personal interests gave way to the one thought of the common safety, and those who had been divided in their political relations stood side by side in the ranks of war.

Then events came thick and fast. An army recruited from the North was soon massed in Washington for its defence, while an opposing army mustered on the other side of the Potomac, where on the 21st of July, 1861, was fought the battle of Bull Run, which, though not a great battle as compared with those of a later time, has a place in history as the first conflict of four terrible years.

When it was thus made evident that we were to have war in earnest, Mr. Field offered his services to Mr. Lincoln, who, recalling perhaps the saying, "Old men for counsel and young men for war," might well think that a man fifty-six years of age could be more useful to his country in sustaining the spirit of the people, than at the head of a regiment or a division.

This is no place to enter into a history of the mighty events that followed. As I look back upon it, it seems like a horrible dream. Why then should we recall it?

It is more than thirty years since the last shot was fired, and a new generation has come upon the stage, to which it is all ancient history. Why should we revive such painful memories? Not to reopen old wounds, but to heal them. Great historical events are seen best at a distance, when the passions they aroused are gone. That time has come. When the leaders of armies on both sides can meet on their fields of battle and rear monuments alike to friend and foe, we may well say that the old bitterness between the North and the South is past, and that we can now look upon the great struggle in the calm light of history.

But at the time there was no "calm light of history." Events were all in the future. Was there a hope of success sufficient to justify a conflict so awful? Some of our best friends abroad thought not. John Bright saw from the first that it was a death-struggle between Freedom and Slavery, and stood firm for the North. But Mr. Gladstone was so shocked by the horrors of the war that he looked upon it as one of the most awful tragedies in history. That a nation like ours—of one race and blood, all speaking the same language, and having the same religion—should go to war among ourselves, and engage in the work of mutual destruction, seemed too horrible for belief, and he would fain shut his eyes from the sight! Near the close of the second year of the war he wrote a letter to the late Mr. Cyrus W. Field, which is one long and passionate outcry, that shows his utter despair. The historical value of such a letter from such a source will justify its quotation here :

11 CARLTON HOUSE TERRACE, November 27, 1862.

My dear Sir: I thank you very much for giving me the "Thirteen Months."* Will you think that I belie the expression I have used if I tell you candidly the effect this book has produced upon my mind ? I think you will not ; I do not believe that you or your countrymen are among those who desire that any one should purchase your favor by speaking what is false, or by forbearing to speak what is true. The book, then, impresses me even more deeply than I was before impressed, with the heavy responsibility you incur in persevering with this destructive and hopeless war at the cost of such dangers and evils to yourselves, to say nothing of your adversaries, or of an amount of misery inflicted upon Europe such as no other civil war in the history of man has ever brought upon those beyond its immediate range. Your frightful conflict may be regarded from many points of view. The competency of the Southern States to secede ; the rightfulness of their conduct in seceding, (two matters wholly distinct and a great deal too much confounded) ; the natural reluctance of Northern Americans to acquiesce in the severance of the Union, and the apparent loss of strength and glory to their country ; the bearing of the separation on the real interests and on the moral character of the North ; again, for an Englishman, its bearing with respect to British interests—all these are texts of which any one affords ample matter for reflection. But I will only state, as regards

---

* "Thirteen Months in the Rebel Army. By an impressed New Yorker." The letter is taken from the Life of Mr. Field by his daughter, published by the Harpers.

the last of them, that I, for one, have never hesitated to maintain that, in my opinion, the separate and special interests of England were all on the side of the maintenance of the old Union; and if I were to look at those interests alone, and had the power of choosing in what way the war should end, I would choose for by the restoration of the old Union this very day.

But there is an aspect of the war which transcends every other: the possibility of success. The prospect of success will not justify a war in itself unjust, but the impossibility of success in a war of conquest of itself suffices to make it unjust; when that impossibility is reasonably proved, all the horror, all the bloodshed, all the evil passions. all the dangers to liberty and order with which such a war abounds, come to lie at the door of the party which refuses to hold its hand and let its neighbor be.

You know that in the opinion of Europe this impossibility has been proved. It is proved by every page of this book, and every copy of this book which circulates will carry the proof wider and stamp it more clearly. Depend upon it, to place the matter upon a single issue, you cannot conquer and keep down a country where the women behave like the women of New Orleans, where, as this author says, they would be ready to form regiments, if such regiments could be of use. And how idle it is to talk, as some of your people do, and some of ours, of the slackness with which the war has been carried on, and of its accounting for the want of success! You have no cause to be ashamed of your military character and efforts. You have proved what wanted no proof—your spirit, hardihood, immense powers, and rapidity and variety of resources. You have spent as much money, and have armed and perhaps have destroyed as many men, taking the two sides together, as all Europe spent in the first years of the Revolutionary war. Is not this enough?

Why have you not more faith in the future of a nation which should lead for ages to come the American continent; which in five or ten years will make up its apparent loss or first loss of strength and numbers; and which, with a career unencumbered by the terrible calamity and curse of slavery, will even from the first be liberated from a position morally and incurably false; and will from the first enjoy a permanent gain in credit and character such as will much more than compensate for its temporary material losses? I am, in short, a follower of General Scott. With him I say, "Wayward sisters, go in peace." Immortal fame be to him for his wise and courageous advice, amounting to a prophecy.

Finally, you have done what men could do; you have failed because you resolved to do what men could not do. Laws stronger than human will are on the side of earnest self-defence; and the aim at the impossible, which in other things may be folly only, when the path of search is dark with misery and red with blood, is not folly only, but guilt to boot. I should not have used so largely in this letter the privileges of free utterance had I not been conscious that I vie with yourselves in my admiration of the founders of your republic, and I have no lurking sentiment either of hostility or of indifference to America; nor, I may add, even then had I not believed that you are lovers of sincerity, and that you can bear even the rudenesss of its tongue.

I remain, dear sir, very faithfully yours,

W. E. GLADSTONE.

CYRUS FIELD, ESQ.

This was a terrible indictment of our country, the more so as the words were those of a friend. But one assumption, which the writer took for granted—that it was impossible to subdue the Rebellion—has been answered by the event. Our country, with the help of God, *did* achieve the impossible!

But the moral question still remains, Was it a just war, or a wicked war? the answer to which we rest on two points: that the conflict was, sooner or later, *inevitable*, (as we have shown by the estrangement between the North and the South, that grew year by year, till it culminated in the secession of eight States;) and that, at the same time, *a separation into two countries was impossible.*

If Mr. Gladstone would divide the United States into two nations, where would he draw the line? There is no natural boundary between us—no dividing seas, nor chain of mountains. Switzerland is throned upon the Alps, whose snow-clad heights are a barrier against invasion from her more powerful neighbors. India is protected by the Himalayas from the descent of any modern Alexander the Great. But we have no such ramparts to defend us one from the other. Nor are the North and the South divided by great rivers, as Canada is separated from us by the St. Lawrence and the Lakes. We have indeed one mighty river that drains the Continent; that is to North America what the Amazon is to South America; but it does not, like the Amazon, run Eastward to empty into the Atlantic, but Southward to empty into the Gulf of Mexico. Wherefore the line of division that is drawn between our two Republics must be purely an artificial one. Nor could it be even a straight line, on one parallel of latitude, but, following the borders of the States, it would zigzag across the Continent. These irregular boundaries would not matter so long as the States were all one Country, for this very interlocking of territory would not be driving so many wedges into one another's sides, to split them apart, but so many bolts of iron to hold them together.

But the situation would be changed utterly if the great expanse of territory were divided into two countries, peopled by two powerful nations. The closer the contact the worse for both when there was one ever-present source of irritation, since on one side would be a Republic built on Freedom; and on the other a Republic (?) built on Slavery! The States of Kentucky and Ohio are divided only by the Ohio River. What power on earth could keep the slaves on one side from stealing across the water in dark nights to the land of liberty? There would be no Fugitive Slave Law to bring them back. The movement Northward would be as constant as if it were led by the Polar Star. With such provocation, how long would the fiery Kentuckians restrain their anger? The only protection for the South would be a standing army, a demonstration on one side that would provoke the same on the other, till the zigzag line across the continent would be like chain lightning, flashing incessantly, and keeping two great nations forever on the verge of war! Seeing all this, the men of the North, who were not "fire-eaters," and had no love of war for its own sake, said, Since the issue is inevitable, we may as well meet it in our day as leave it to our children. If the war must come, let it come now! Better—a thousand times better—to have a war of four years, than a war, like that of the Spaniard and the Moor, to be handed down from generation to generation!

Of all public men in the country, no one saw more clearly the inevitable issue than Mr. Lincoln. Long before he was President he said to himself and to others: "A house divided against itself cannot stand. I believe this government cannot endure permanently half slave and half free. I do not expect the Union to be dissolved—I do not expect the house to fall—but I do expect it will cease to be divided. It will become all one thing, or all the other. Either the opponents of slavery will arrest the further spread of it, and place it where the public mind shall rest in the belief that it is in the course of ultimate extinction; or its advocates will push it forward till it shall become alike lawful in all the States—old as well as new, North as well as South."

What Mr. Lincoln saw from his point of view in the West, Mr. Field had seen even at an earlier date in the East. For years he had been fighting against the slave power, which was steadily advancing to the complete control of the government. At last the issue had come, to be settled, not by political conventions, but on the field of battle; and if he could not march with the regiments, he could at least support them by keeping up the patriotic spirit at home. Again and again he went on to Washington, where he had frequent interviews with Mr. Lincoln and the members of his Cabinet, of whom he was most attracted to Mr. Chase and Mr. Stanton, as they were old Democrats, and as on them fell the chief burdens of the war.* They in turn found support in his unconquerable spirit,

---

* Several years after—when the war was over—in an argument before the Supreme Court of the United States on "Military Tribunals for Civilians," Mr. Field thus referred to Mr. Stanton: "It has been my fortune to be with him in some of the darkest hours of the tempest, and I can bear personal witness to his indomitable energy; to the erect front which he maintained against all disaster; to his industry, which knew no weariness; and to his absolute devotion to the public service. Next to the President himself, and to the illustrious man who organized that gigantic system of finance which carried us through without a shock to the public service, to the amazement of the Old World and the admiration of the New; next, I say, to the President and his Minister of Finance, the country owes more to him than to any other civilian. His services may be for the time lost in the blaze of military glory. His laborious days, and the plain building where he passed them, are now eclipsed by the clouds that rolled from the fields of Vicksburg and Shiloh, from Gettysburg and Antietam, from Atlanta and Petersburg, but when history writes the record of this war, we shall find there, in light, the name of Edwin M. Stanton."

that never gave up even in the darkest hour. After the great defeat of the Second Bull Run, Mr. Stanton telegraphed to him to come to Washington. He went on the same night, and going to his house early the next morning, he found the great War Secretary at breakfast, as calm as a man could be at that terrible moment, when despatches were pouring in with one continued tale of disaster ; that our army was falling back, as if it might be compelled to seek for safety behind the defences of Washington ! Together they went over to the War Department, where they found the President, with Mr. Chase and General Halleck. It was no time to exchange compliments, and Mr. Field felt that he must speak plainly as to the anxiety that pervaded the North at the result of the campaign, in which McClellan, after leading a mighty host almost to the gates of Richmond, had been driven from the Peninsula, and Pope had been defeated in the very sight of the Capitol. At this freedom of speech Mr. Lincoln took no offence, but turning to Mr. Chase, said, "Mr. Field has a right to express himself freely : let us explain the situation to him," and sitting down before a large map that hung upon the wall, he gave a general outline of the plan of the campaign, which showed how perfectly he understood it, and how competent he was to give, not only suggestions, but, if need be, commands, as to the conduct of the war.

The same lesson he had at another time when he was invited to accompany the President, with Mr. Chase, Mr. Stanton, and Admiral Dahlgren, in a government steamer down the Potomac to Acquia Creek, where General McDowell was then in command, who was sent for to come off to the steamer, and came with one or two of his aides, all bespattered with mud, from riding over the horrible roads. But neither Mr. Lincoln, nor anybody else, cared for the outward appearance of these rough riders, but only for what they knew and could report. To hear this all gathered round the cabin table, where was spread out a map of the country, on which they studied the whole field of the contending armies as if in a council of war.

These interviews and conversations raised Mr. Field's estimate of Mr. Lincoln's ability, as he saw under that plain exterior a man, not only devoted to his country, but of such quickness of observation and excellent judgment, even in a subject so foreign to him as that of war, that he had a better idea of the way to conduct a campaign than many an officer, with his glittering sword and epaulets. This combination of intelligence with frankness won, not only the heart of Mr. Field, but his fullest confidence, as he saw that the government was not, like a great ship of war in a tempest, drifting to destruction for want of a capable commander. However threatening the storm might be, there was a master on the deck, of cool head and brave heart, whom it was the duty of all on board to support till the storm blew itself out, and the ship, though with broken masts and torn sails, floated into the haven where she would be.

Thus strengthened in heart and hope, Mr. Field came back to impart to others the same confidence, of which at times there was a pressing need. There was no want of courage in the soldiers. The army was always ready to do its part. Nor were the most trying moments those of battle, for then all were strung up to the highest pitch of daring. But for the country at large, for those far away among the Northern hills, the great trial was the long suspense, the slow movement of armies, the horrors of the battle-field, from which thousands were borne to the hospitals, where were mingled the dying and the dead. All this made the hearts sick of those whose sons and brothers were in the field, to a degree that at times almost paralyzed the nation. Then the great demand of the country was not so much for more soldiers at the front, as for more supporters in the rear, a mighty reserve of invincibles, who never despaired of the Republic.

And now, standing off at the distance of thirty years—the lifetime of a generation—we may venture on one or two general reflections upon the Civil War. Leaving aside the purely moral considerations, it may not be going beyond the mark to say that, next to the Revolution, it was not only the most stupendous, but the most beneficent event in American history. War is not always a curse : it may be the necessary means of the greatest good. Our country has passed through three wars, each one of which has had a part in the making of the nation. It was by an eight-years' war that the Colonies gained their independence ; the War of 1812 raised the United States, if not to a position among the great military powers of the world, yet to one that promised to make it next to Great Britain on the sea ; while this last array of a nation in arms forced upon the world the question : If the States were so terrible when divided and warring against each other, what would they be when united ?

We may even go a step farther, and say that the war for Disunion was indispensable to the Union itself, since it eliminated the only cause of separation between the North and the South, to the happy issue that they should be One Country thenceforth and forever !

At the same time it inspired both with a mutual respect, which is the first step to any closer relations. In this primary discipline war is the greatest of all teachers. Nothing subdues the loftiness of an opponent like an unexpected show of power. Up to this time the people of the two great Divisions did not know each other. Separated, not only by distance, but by different social systems, they grew up with a traditional dislike and aversion. The Southern planters formed an aristocratic class, made up of landed proprietors, who, living by the labor of others, were apt to despise those who worked with their own hands. They looked upon the people of the North as a race of canting hypocrites, who worshipped the almighty dollar, and who were so lacking in manly spirit that they could be treated with a want of respect bordering on rudeness, and yet not be provoked into resistance ! From this impression they had a rude awakening, like that of the French when they rushed into war with the slow, plodding Germans, but soon found themselves engaged in what, to use a modern phrase, might be called "a campaign of education." The North and the South were never really acquainted, till they were introduced to one another on the field of battle. From that time they came to regard one another with profound respect, for both sides displayed the qualities that compel honor and admiration. "Braver men never to battle rode." And the bravery seems to have been equally divided. If our imagination be taken by what the German poet pictures to the eye as "the battle's splendor," we have it here, for never in the history of war was greater courage shown on both sides, if it be measured by the number of the wounded and the dead. In the Franco-Prussian War the greatest carnage was in the cavalry charges at Mars-le-Tour, when nearly one-half fell killed or wounded, a proportion that was surpassed in many of the regiments on both sides at Chickamauga. The battle of Waterloo began at noon, and continued to the going down of the sun : that of Gettysburg was fought on and on for three days, and ended at last by the repulse of a charge that was more desperate than that of the Old Guard.

And is all this glory of the battle-field to be put away and forgotten ? On the contrary, we cherish the memory of it as that of which we are justly proud. Our country has passed through the greatest civil war in history —a war that raged over half a continent—and it still lives, and is stronger than ever. And what is more, we of the North are proud of those who fought against us, of their courage and endurance, in the strength of which we both share, as we are no more twain, but one.

If there was nothing so terrible as Disunion, there has been nothing more glorious than Reunion. Foreigners do not know what to make of it, when they see Northern and Southern Generals meeting at Gettysburg and Chickamauga, raising monuments to those who fought and fell on both sides. But these heroic memories are the proud possession of us all. Nothing in our country reflects more honor upon the generosity of the American people than the vast cemeteries, North and South, in which are gathered the forms of those fallen in battle, with this inscription :

> " On Fame's eternal camping ground
> Their silent tents are spread,
> While glory guards with ceaseless round
> The bivouac of the dead."

But this is anticipating the times of reconciliation, while in the order of our chronicle we are but at the close of the war, which, if it had its burst of sunshine, had also its dark cloud that covered the whole heaven. In the midst of our rejoicing at the return of peace, came the assassination of our beloved President, and for the time all our pride was turned into mourning for him who had carried us through the great ordeal of our national existence. Overwhelmed at the country's loss, Mr. Field went to Washington to attend the funeral, and rode from the Capitol in the carriage with Mr. Stanton, who told him of the President's dream on the night before the fatal event. As the members of the Cabinet were coming in, Mr. Lincoln said that he had a presentiment that something was going to happen, for he had had a dream like one that he had before the battle of Chickamauga. He was standing by a river where the current was swift, rushing by like a torrent, which seemed to prefigure a course of events that could not be checked or controlled. What could be more significant of an event that was coming very near, that was to sweep him away from all part in human affairs? That very night the flood came and bore this emancipator of a race out of human sight, leaving behind him as his only memorial a country saved and an immortal name.

CHAPTER XIV.

RE-ESTABLISHMENT OF THE REIGN OF LAW.

The war was over; but it left wreck and ruin behind. North and South had both suffered immeasurably; but the North the less, as its population was double, and its resources were ten times greater, while the South was left almost a desert. Towns and cities had been bombarded, and the cotton fields, for the product of which the looms of England and the Continent were standing still, presented a scene of blackened desolation.

But even this was less appalling than the sacrifice in tens of thousands of Southern homes, from which sometimes father and sons had gone out together, of all whom but one or two returned. The angel of death had been abroad in the land, till it might almost be said, as in the plague of the first-born in Egypt, that there was not an house in which there was not one dead!

The North too had the joy of victory dampened by what was harder to bear than the loss of a battle. Our country never witnessed a military pageant so imposing as the return of the army through Washington, where from morning to night was heard the tramp, tramp of the legions that had been through the fire, carrying proudly the flags that had been torn by shot and shell. But in all the triumph of that day there was one bitter sorrow : that their beloved President was not there to answer to the roll of the drums and the waving of banners.

The assassination of Lincoln was a national calamity. Great as was the blow to the North, it was still greater to the South, which lost in him its best friend. But for that, the sufferings of both, instead of being a source of mutual irritation, might have brought them into a sympathy of sorrow, that would in time have softened into a feeling of tenderness even among those who had fought against one another. But that fearful tragedy tore open the old wounds, so that it was years before they could be healed.

One of the legacies of the war was martial law, which is the law of barbarism, that must be endured so long as the savagery of war continues, but which quickly demoralizes those who have been accustomed to the gentler ways of peace. To soldiers in command it very soon becomes the natural course of justice, with the advantage that judgment is quick, and may be followed by speedy execution. It certainly affords great facilities in judicial proceedings. There is none of the "law's delay," which is so tedious to a man of high spirit, who is invested, not with "a little, brief authority," for if it be "brief," it is not "little," as it involves the power of life and death. A captain, put at the head of a command in the backwoods, in his small dominion is as absolute as the Czar of Russia. Let him but fix his "glittering eye" on some backwoodsman who does not do him reverence, and he has but to send a troop of horse, and take the man out of his cabin, and bring him before a "drum-head court martial," and he can be tried, sentenced, and shot and buried in an hour! He need not fear the consequences, for dead men tell no tales, and can make no appeals. But with all its facilities, this "happy despatch" may have unexpected issues. In his haste to do justice he may shoot the wrong man! Such accidents will happen now and then to a soldier who "does not stand on ceremony," and, under the form of military law, he may be guilty of a cold-blooded assassination!

This was one of the abuses of power on both sides that are almost inevitable in a civil war. But I speak here only of our own sins, not of the sins of others. In the Northern States, and especially in the Border States, there was many a man who was suspected of want of loyalty to the government, of sympathizing with the enemy; and who for such suspicion was branded as a "copperhead"—which meant a rebel in disguise, and very thin disguise at that—and was liable to be arrested and tried before a court martial, and executed, before there was an opportunity to appeal to a court that could stay the hand of the executioner. How near one might come to the scaffold, even though he escaped it, appears in a case which is the more notable as it occurred near the end of the war, after the capture of Atlanta, and when Sherman was preparing for his March to the Sea.

In October, 1864, a man in Indiana was arrested at his home, and thrown into prison at Indianapolis, and two weeks after was brought to trial by a "military commission" upon "charges of conspiracy against the authority of the United States, inciting insurrection, disloyal practices, and violation of the laws of war!" This was a vague, general charge, that would seem to be barred by the fact that, even if it were true, a military commission had no business to try it, since Indiana was not the theatre of war, and no more under martial law than Massachusetts. If a man had been disloyal to his government, the courts were open, and he was entitled to be tried, not by soldiers, who were not the best men to weigh evidence, but by a judge and jury. There was clearly a "want of jurisdiction." But this objection was overruled—the man was brought before a court martial and convicted, and sentenced to be hanged! The sentence was approved by the President, and he was to be executed on the 19th of May, 1865—more than a month after the surrender of Lee—a grim tragedy to be enacted at the close of the war, in the first joy of peace, to send to the gallows a man who had never taken up arms against his country ! But his time was getting short. It was but little more than a week to the day appointed for his execution, that a petition was filed in the Circuit Court of the United States for Indiana, showing that a grand jury of that Court had convened after his arrest, but that no indictment had been found against him ; and that he had at no time been in the military, naval, or militia service ; nor within any State engaged in rebellion against the United States at any time during the war. The petition demanded that he be delivered to the proper civil tribunal to be tried, or discharged from custody.

The defence was that Congress had authorized the President to suspend the writ of *habeas corpus* during the rebellion ! Yes : but that authority was not unlimited either as to time or place : it was not to be continued after the war was over, nor was it to be exercised in every part of the United States. Indeed the act expressly excepted "States in which the administration of law had not been disturbed, where any who were arrested as prisoners should be brought before the Judges of the United States Circuit and District Courts, and if the grand jury did not bring in an indictment against them, they were to be discharged !"

Here then was the question—whether martial law could be assumed and enforced in a State that had not been touched by war ; and a private citizen could be seized by military order; tried by a court martial, and sent to the scaffold!

The case was one that appealed very strongly to Mr. Field, and he entered into it, not as a matter of professional business, but from a sense of justice. While the war lasted, no one was more earnest that it should be carried through to the end. But when the war was over, it was time that the Temple of Janus was shut; and that the people should return to the ways of peace. True, some ardent partisans thought the advocate was deserting his principles; "going back" on his party. But he knew no party in the Courts of Law. If that was treachery to his party, he had at least good company, for there stood by his side, not only that sturdy old Democrat, Judge Black, of Pennsylvania, but a distinguished Republican who had fought in the war, and was afterwards President of the United States, General Garfield. But the burden of the argument fell on Mr. Field, who rose to the height of the occasion, in exposing the injustice of carrying martial law into a State where there had been no war. The court listened in fixed attention to the very last word, as he closed in a tone of the deepest solemnity:

"Thus, may it please the Court, have I performed the part assigned me in the argument of this case. The materials were abundant. I only fear that I may have wearied you with the recital or erred in the selection. I could not look into the pages of English law;

I could not turn over the leaves of English literature; I could not listen to the orators and statesmen of England; without remarking the uniform protest against martial usurpation, and the assertion of the undoubted right of every man, high or low, to be judged according to the known and general law, by a jury of his peers, before the judges of the land. And when I turned to the history, legal, political, and literary, of my own country—my own undivided and forever indivisible country—I found the language of freedom intensified. Our fathers brought with them the liberties of Englishmen. Throughout the colonial history we find the colonists clinging, with immovable tenacity, to trial by jury, Magna Charta, the principle of representation, and the Petition of Right. They had won them in the fatherland in many a high debate and on many a bloody field; and they defended them here against the mercenaries of the crown of England. We, their children, thought we had superadded to the liberties of Englishmen the greater and better guarded liberties of Americans.

"These great questions, than which greater never yet came before this most august of human tribunals, are now to receive their authoritative and last solution. Your judgment will live when all of us are dead. The robes which you wear will be worn by others, who will occupy your seats in long succession, through, I trust, innumerable ages; but it will never fall to the lot of any to pronounce a judgment of greater consequence than this. It will stand when the statue which with returning peace we have raised above the dome of the Capitol shall have fallen from its pedestal, its sword broken and its shield scattered in pieces ; nay, when the dome itself, which, though uplifted into the air, seems immovable as the mountains, shall have crumbled ; it will stand as long as that most imperishable thing of all, our mother-tongue, shall be spoken or read among men.

"That judgment, I hope and I believe, will establish the liberty of the citizen on foundations never more to be shaken, and will cause the future historian of our greatest struggle to write that, great as were the victories of our war, they were equalled in renown by the victories of our peace."

This was the language, not only of conviction, but of a courage which cannot be fully appreciated at this distance of time. *Now* the case seems so plain that we wonder that any judge on the bench could hesitate a moment as to his decision. But thirty years ago the people of the North were thinking of their dead lying on a hundred Southern battle fields. To say a word for those who fought against us, seemed to be false to our country. This feeling was in the air, and could not but invade the bar and the bench. Though it seems now that there could be but one side, then there were two ; and the other side was argued by a lawyer of the very highest rank, Mr. Stansbery of Cincinnati, then Attorney-General, supported by the ability (which no one could dispute), as well as the bull-dog pugnacity, of General Butler. That their arguments had weight was proved by the fact that the court was divided; of the nine judges four voted to sustain the decision of the court martial, which would have sent the prisoner to an ignominious execution.* It was a narrow escape, but one of immense significance. When the prison doors were opened for a man who had been standing for weeks and months in the shadow of the scaffold, it was a signal to the nation that martial law was ended; that the reign of terror was over; and that the reign of peace and justice was begun!

So far, so good! But that was not the last echo of the Civil War. If disaffection to the government was

---

* The opinion in the case was written by Mr. Justice Davis of Illinois, of whom Mr. Lincoln was wont to speak as "the best friend he had in the world." No man knew better the natural sympathy, even to tenderness, of the late President, and how, if he had lived, instead of taking the airs of a conqueror, who would triumph over the vanquished, he would have been the first to pour oil into their wounds; to soothe their pride; and to turn away their thoughts from the sad legacies of war to the brighter hopes of peace. In reading the opinion of the Justice, one cannot help thinking that, both in its preparation and delivery, he must have been conscious that he gave expression, not only to his own sense of justice, but to what would have been the first prompting of a great heart that had ceased to beat.

not a capital crime, it could be punished in other ways. If the law could not take a man's life, it could deprive him of the means of subsistence by imposing conditions that would shut him out from the practice of his profession. This was effected by the cunning device of a "Test Oath," a form of torture worthy of the Inquisition, as it was expressed in the new Constitution that was framed for the State of Missouri, in which a man who would hold an office, or be a lawyer or a minister of the Gospel, must swear that he had never had any part in the Rebellion, *or sympathy with it*, without which oath he could not "hold any office of honor, trust, or profit, or be permitted to practice as an attorney, or counsellor at law ; nor be competent as a bishop, priest, deacon, minister, elder, or other clergyman of any religious persuasion, sect, or denomination !" The penalty for neglect to take this oath was, not only immediate stopping of the practice of his profession, but a fine of five hundred dollars, and imprisonment from six months to two years !

The provision of the Constitution which lays down these requirements is very long and minute, pointing out the offence with such manifold specifications as to show that it was a net carefully woven to catch the smallest offender. Or, to take another illustration, it was like the scythe of Father Time,

> "Which cuts down all,
> Both great and small."

Monstrous as all this was, it could not be said that it was a new thing under the sun. The passion for vengeance after war is as old as history. Rome made her captives pass under the yoke. Nor was it the first time that it had appeared in American history. At the beginning of the Revolution there were in the colonies many who still longed for peace, and who could not see that there was any sufficient reason for rushing into war with the mother country because of some petty impost such as a tax on tea! But they were branded as Tories. Some moved across the border into Canada; others emigrated to Nova Scotia. Those who remained kept very quiet. But no sooner was the war over than they were required, as the condition of citizenship, to swear, not only to be loyal to the government, but that they had always been so! This was putting a premium upon falsehood and perjury, against which Alexander Hamilton protested, as a direct violation of our Treaty with Great Britain, as well as of the Constitution of the United States, so that Mr. Field, in his argument against Test Oaths, was not fighting a new battle, but only against the same injustice that roused the indignation of Alexander Hamilton nearly a hundred years ago.

But he had no occasion to refer to a treaty with England: it was enough to appeal to our own Constitution, as against that of the State of Missouri, which contained such sweeping disqualifications that it must be itself put to the test to see whether it did not violate a higher law. To this end it was first brought before the Supreme Court of the State of Missouri, which upheld it, from which it was appealed to the Supreme Court of the United States, where we are now to follow it. As if to show in full relief the "tall heads" that it was to strike down, the test case was that of a priest of the Roman Catholic Church, who had been convicted by the State courts of Missouri of the "crime" of teaching and preaching without having taken the oath prescribed by the Constitution! Here again Mr. Field appeared before the Court, and in the very opening of his argument, thus analyzed the new form of Inquisitorial justice:

"Dividing this oath into all its separable parts, it will be found to contain eighty-six distinct affirmations or tests! It is both prospective and retrospective; that is to say, it speaks from the time when it is actually taken by each person, and relates to all that has gone before; so that, if taken by Mr. Cummings (the priest*) now, it will embrace all his past life, and, if taken five years hence, it will embrace not only all his life that is now passed, but the five years from this time forward.

"Altogether, it is a novelty in this country, and I

---

* There was also the case of a lawyer the issue of which would depend upon the decision in this, which explains the allusion on the next page to more than one client.

believe it is a novelty in the world. I have searched in vain for anything in history so sweeping and severe.

"The State of Missouri steps between the Christian flock and its pastor. He cannot ascend the pulpit and preach to a devout congregation the resurrection of the dead and the life of the world to come; he cannot teach the forgiveness of sins at the bedside of a dying penitent; he cannot bless the bride at the altar; without calling God to witness that he is superior to all these tests.

"The Supreme Court of Missouri, the highest tribunal known to the laws of that great Commonwealth, has affirmed the judgment of the Circuit Court, and thereby declared that there is nothing in the political system of *that state* to forbid the imposition of such a test. It is for you, Supreme Judges of all the land, to declare whether there is anything in the political system of the *nation* to forbid it."

The legal argument which follows, though not so long as that in the preceding case, which made an end of martial law, had the same cumulative force, as one proof was piled upon another, till the advocate dismissed the question in these words:

"Here I leave the cases of my clients—cases important not to them only, but to the whole people of Missouri. That State was born in conflict. The dispute about her admission into the Union seemed likely to divide the Union. Slavery, which she then warmed in her bosom, stung her, viper that it was. The poison entered her vitals, and she has been purified from it only by blood and fire. An avenging Nemesis decreed that her deliverance should be effected through suffering proportionate to her error.

"She is now free. This oath, so vindictive and repulsive, is her last deformity. Let her be rid of that, and she will stand erect as well as free.

"My clients, defeated at their own firesides, seek protection here. They know that to this chamber they can come for shelter, as fugitives of old sought refuge beside the altar. You stand the ultimate arbiters of constitutional rights; immovable, however tumultuous passions may surge and beat around you, the one stable and permanent element in the government of the country. Presidents appear and disappear like shadows. Senators and Representatives enter the doors of their chambers, and go out again, no one knows whither. You remain the ornament and defence of the Constitution—*decus et tutamen.*"

The decision of the Court soon sent the Test Oaths in the way of Martial Law, and it was a special pleasure to Mr. Field that the opinion was delivered by his brother, who had been appointed to the Bench by President Lincoln in circumstances somewhat peculiar.*

* After the war with Mexico the discovery of gold had caused such an emigration to the Pacific Coast that California soon had a population that justified its admission as a State.

These two decisions of the Supreme Court of the United States settled two great questions, and settled them forever. There was no more danger to life or liberty by martial law, or that a man should be deprived of the right to practise his profession, because he could not, or would not, swear that he had taken no part in the Rebellion, or had any sympathy with it. The law-

---

But the settlement of titles to land was made very difficult by the fact that large tracts were overlaid by Spanish grants and Mexican grants, and later by the "squatter sovereignty" that seized whatever was unoccupied. This conflict of claims made endless perplexity. Whichever way a case was decided, it was sure to be appealed, till it drifted on to the Supreme Court of the United States, where the Judges themselves were confused by the contradictory opinions. To get some light on these vexed questions, a law was passed by Congress creating another seat on the Supreme Court, to be filled by a Judge from the Pacific Coast, whereupon the Senators and Representatives from California and Oregon went in a body to President Lincoln, to ask for the appointment of Mr. Stephen J. Field, then Chief Justice of California, whose name they presented, not as their first choice, but as their only choice. While the nomination was pending, Mr. John A. C. Gray, a well known citizen of New York, and an old friend of Mr. Lincoln, went to speak to him about it. He found the President agreed entirely in the fitness of Judge Field, and had but one question to ask: "Does David want his brother to have it?" "Yes," said Mr. Gray. "Then he shall have it," was the instant reply, and the nomination was sent in that afternoon, and confirmed by the Senate unanimously. This was the Justice to whom it fell four years later to write the opinion in the Test Oath cases.

Stephen J. Field

yer was free to practise in the courts, and the priest to appear in the pulpit or the confessional, or kneel at the bedside of the dying. So far every man in the South had recovered his freedom, and had all the rights of a citizen of the United States. But where were the States themselves that had taken part in the Rebellion? Were they once more equal members of the Union, or were they conquered provinces to be held in a state of vassalage to await the pleasure of the conqueror? If they were restored at once without conditions, and with their old institutions—slavery and all—they would be left just where they were before, and would need but a few years to recover their strength, when the battle might be renewed. The old State governments, that had been fighting the Union for four years, could not be left in possession. But when they were deposed, who or what should take their place? There must be some sort of government, or the whole South would relapse into anarchy. The natural suggestion was that a commander who was at the head of a Department should take possession of the State Capital, as a nucleus round which the loyal elements might gather until the time of full reconstruction should come. Meanwhile the first necessity was to get rid of Slavery. Mr. Lincoln had issued his Proclamation as a war measure, but it was all-important that it should be confirmed by an amendment imbedded in the Constitution of the United States, which was accomplished in the Constitutional way, by being proposed by a vote of Congress, and confirmed by the votes of three-fourths of the States.

When this was done so that it could not be undone —that the spectre of Slavery and Disunion would never come back to plague us—it would seem as if the Provisional Governments in the South had accomplished their mission, and might be allowed to depart, to return no more. But what authority established by force of arms ever willingly resigned its power? An officer placed in absolute control of a State, felt the dignity of his position, and would make the most of it; and if a Legislature was refractory, would turn it out of doors, as Cromwell dismissed the Long Parliament. Even four years after the war, when General Grant was President, General Sheridan, who was in command in New Orleans, asked permission to arrest the whole Legislature of Louisiana, but fortunately the cooler head of his chief restrained the impetuosity of his lieutenant.

Meanwhile the reign of the carpet-baggers had begun, and men who had hung round the camps during the war, but never showed their faces in the front of battle, were made Governors, and, supported by a Legislature of negroes just off the plantations, went in for a general spoliation. There was not much left in the South to steal—the freebooters might as well have undertaken to rob the dead—but they could at least issue bonds, which, though sold at a low rate, would yet accomplish the purpose to gather in the spoils.

How long this would have continued, and how far it would have gone, it is hard to say if the inrolling tide of corruption had not struck against the breakwater of the Supreme Court of the United States, which in the memorable "McCardle Case" took in review the whole question of the Constitutionality of the Reconstruction Acts of Congress, which, its opponents claimed, was a flagrant invasion of the liberty and rights, not only of a single individual, but of millions of our countrymen.

In this case, as in all the great cases that he undertook, Mr. Field threw his whole soul into it. He was indignant at the continuance of military rule after the war was over: that regiments should be kept in Charleston and New Orleans as if they were in a state of siege. When was the reign of peace and of law to begin?

This argument has a special interest to me as I happened to be in Washington at the time and heard it in part, when it was interrupted by a singular circumstance. While Mr. Field was speaking a messenger came to summon the Chief Justice from his place on the bench to a duty to which no Judge had ever been called before—to preside over the Senate sitting as a Court to try an impeachment of the President of the United States! This postponed the case in the Supreme Court for several weeks, when Mr. Field resumed and concluded his argument. Without undertaking to follow it in detail, it is enough to quote a single passage to show the vehemence with which he spoke, and how he carried his position by the continued thrust of questions to which there could be but one answer :

"A point very much urged in the argument, and constantly referred to in public speeches, is *Necessity!* These military governments of the South, they say, are legal because they are necessary. The usual phrase is : 'This government has a right to live, and no other government has a right to contest it ; and whatever Congress determines as necessary to this national life is right.' What necessity do they speak of ? There is no Federal necessity. The Federal courts are open ; the Federal laws are executed ; the mails are run ; the customs are collected. There is no interference with any commissioner or officer of the United States anywhere in the country. There is no necessity, therefore, of a Federal kind for an assumption of the government of Mississippi. What, then, is the necessity ? Is that the reason why the military government is there ? If you are to wait until you get repentant rebels—or I should perhaps rather say, if you wait until you make rebels repentant by fire and sword—you will have to wait many generations. Of all the arguments, that of necessity has the least force. 'We will not allow the Southern States to govern themselves, because, if we do, the government will fall into the hands of unrepentant rebels !' Well, what is that to you, if they obey the laws—if they submit to your government ? Do you wish to force them to love you ? Is that what you are aiming at ? Of course, it should be the desire and the aim of all governments to make the people love as well as obey ; but as an argument for a military government, it is an extraordinary one. 'Well then,' they say, 'we must protect the loyal men at the South, and therefore the military government, which is the only one adequate to the end, must be kept up.' To that I answer, first, that the General of your armies, the person upon whom this extraordinary power has been thrown, himself certified that there was order throughout the South, so far as he could observe. But are there no other means than military coercion? The Union men of the South, we have been told, were in the majority, and have ever been in the majority, and it was the minority by which the people were driven into secession. Is government by the United States necessary to sustain the majority—a majority, we are told, of the white people? They say that secession was carried by a minority of the whites against the majority, and that the majority have always been loyal. That is a perfect answer, then, to the objection. 'Necessity' is the reason given by tyranny for misgovernment all the world over. It was the reason given by Philip II. for oppressing the Netherlands by the Duke of Alva; it was the reason given for the misgovernment of Italy by Austria; it was the reason given for the misgovernment of Ireland by England.

"'This Nation has a right to live!' Certainly it has, and so have the States, and so have the people. Every one of us has the right, and the life of each is bound up with the life of all. For who compose my nation, and what constitutes my country? It is not so much land and water. They would remain ever the same though an alien race occupied the soil; there would be the same green hills, and the same sweet valleys, the same ranges of mountains, and the same lakes and rivers; but all these combined do not make up my country. They are the body without the soul. That word, country, comprehends within itself place and people, and all that history, tradition, language, manners, social culture, and civil polity, have associated with them. This wonderful combination of State and nation, which binds me to both by indissoluble ties, enters into the idea of my country. Its name is the United States of America. The States are an essential part of the name and of the thing. They are represented by the starry flag, which their children have borne on so many fields of glory, the ever-shining symbol of one Nation and many States. They are not provinces or countries; they are not principalities or dukedoms; but they are free republican States, sovereign in their sphere, as the United States are sovereign in theirs; and all essential elements of that one, undivided and indissoluble Country, which is dearer than life, and for which so many have died. As the State of New York would not be to me what it is, if, instead of the free, active Commonwealth, it were to subside into a principality or a province, so neither would the United States be to me what they are, if, instead of a union of free States, they were to subside into a consolidated Empire. For such an Empire we have not borne the defeats and won the victories of civil war.

The case had this further remarkable issue: that it was never decided by the Supreme Court, though previous decisions indicated clearly what the result would be. Having been interrupted while the impeachment of Andrew Johnson was going on, the decision was postponed, perhaps that Congress might be spared the humiliation of having its own act declared null and void. The Court therefore deferred judgment, and the act was speedily repealed, a victory in another form, which emphasized still further the wantonness and wickedness of this cruel legislation.

After such heavy bombardments the iron gates of military rule seemed to be giving way. If the military occupation continued, it was not quite so arrogant. The South no longer felt the pressure of the iron hand. The arguments against Military Tribunals for Civilians, and against Test Oaths, had done their work ; and that in the McArdle case required no judicial decision, inasmuch as Congress itself hastened to repeal the act in which it had assumed an authority which it did not possess. But there is nothing that men or governments are so reluctant to abdicate as power, and if it be restrained in one form, it will appear in another. There was still an opportunity for Congress to accomplish by indirection what it did not dare to claim openly. The right of suffrage had been given to the colored people of the South. But how to enforce it was the problem. To that end Congress passed an Enforcement Act, which provided that "if two or more persons should band or conspire together . . . to injure, oppress, threaten, or intimidate any citizen with intent to prevent or hinder his free exercise and enjoyment of any right or privilege, granted or reserved to him by the Constitution or laws of the United States, said persons should be held guilty of felony !" Nearly a hundred persons were indicted in Louisiana, eight of whom appeared before the Circuit Court, and three of them were convicted, from which they appealed to the Supreme Court of the United States. This was the famous Cruikshank case, in which Mr. Field appeared for the defendants.

The act had been skilfully framed. One word in it was enough to rouse the suspicions of the North—the word "conspire," which suggested that there was a dark and deep-laid conspiracy to defeat the result of the war by secret combinations to spread terror among the colored people, and so to drive them away from the polls, and deprive them of the fruits of their new-born liberty. To this Mr. Field replied :

"An accusation of conspiracy is of all accusations the most dangerous to meet, and the easiest to make men believe, in an excited community. It is the harshest engine of tyranny ever used under the form of law ; and its frequent use is the strongest evidence of misgovernment. From the bloody days when the compassing or imagining the death of a king was the miserable pretence upon which tyrants took the lives and confiscated the estates of their victims, to the present hour, no surer proof of good or evil government can be found than the chapter on conspiracies in the statute-book of a country. One has but to compare the statutes of well-governed Connecticut with the statutes of misgoverned Ireland, to learn what an odious engine of oppression is the law of conspiracy."

But his main argument turned on the relation of the States to the general government. Overstrained as had been the doctrine of State rights by the South to justify secession, yet it would be going too far the other way, if the result of the war should be to destroy the States, uniting them all in one consolidated government. The States still existed, not to be overrun and trampled down by armies or by undue assumptions of the central authority. If Congress could by its action destroy the rights of the States, so that they would be but weak and helpless members of one central power, the Republic would have passed into a Kingdom. And when it undertook to lay down stringent prohibitions as to interference with the ballot in the States, it must go one step farther and consider how it could enforce its prohibitions without running against the buckler of State sovereignty. As Mr. Field put it :

"Congress cannot destroy a State. If to-morrow the Legislature of Massachusetts should pass a law denying the right of suffrage to every colored man in the Commonwealth, Congress could not authorize the President to march the garrison of Fort Warren into the State House, and turn the members out of doors. Why could not Congress do this ? The answer is that Massachusetts is a self-existing and indestructible member of the American Union, and neither Congress, nor any other department of the Federal Government, has power to destroy any essential attribute of the sovereignty of that Commonwealth. In saying this I am justified by recent decisions of this Court. No longer ago than 1868 this Court, speaking by its late Chief Justice (Mr. Chase), uttered these memorable words, which will live in constitutional history as long as the Constitution lives in its vigor : 'Not only can there be no loss of separate and independent autonomy of the States, but it may be not unreasonably said that the preservation of the States and the maintenance of their governments are as much within the design and care of the Constitution as the preservation of the Union and the maintenance of the National Government. *The Constitution in all its provisions looks to an indestructible Union composed of indestructible States.*'" The language of an older Judge, the venerable Justice Nelson, was not less emphatic. Five years before he had said from that bench: "The General Government and the States, although both exist within the same territorial limits, are separate and distinct sovereignties, acting independently of each other within their respective spheres. The former in its appropriate sphere is supreme, but the States within the limits of their powers not granted (or reserved) are as independent of the General Government as that government within its sphere is independent of the States. . . . The two governments are upon an equality. In respect to the reserved powers the State is as sovereign and independent as the General Government."

Here the differences of opinion were distinctly outlined. The two positions involved two theories of government. If the General Government were to take to itself all that came within the range of life, liberty and protection, what was there left for the State Governments to do? Their occupation was gone. "For what is there in the world," said Mr. Field, "for State legislation, but life, liberty, and the protection of the law?" If the General Government assumed this, it assumed everything, and the States were but the executors of its imperial will. That was a perfectly intelligible form of government, but it was not the government that was established by the fathers of the Republic in the Constitution of the United States. This was the Ark of the Covenant, that must be kept sacred from the touch of any destroying hand. In the previous generation the Constitution had the greatest of American statesmen as its Defender and Expounder. But Mr. Webster never saw the nation under such a strain as that of the Civil War—a convulsion so awful that it seemed to turn back the course of nature, and we had to look round to see if it had not destroyed both Liberty and Law in one tremendous ruin. Then the work had to be done all over again by men of the *post-bellum* period, like Mr. Field, who, seeing how vital was the Constitution to the National existence, "compassed it about on every side," buttressing the ancient walls, till now the Citadel is stronger than ever, standing

"Four square to all the winds that blow."

CHAPTER XV.

WORK AND PLAY. HOW HE "WARMED BOTH HANDS AT THE FIRE OF LIFE."

The greatest service that Mr. Field ever rendered to his country (always excepting his Codes) was the long, stout and stubborn fight for the rights of the South —a contest, not in battle, nor on the floor of Congress, but in the highest Court of the land, where it went on year after year, till justice triumphed at last, but only at the sacrifice to him who led the fight of many old ties and friendships. This was the painful thing about it, that he had to part company from many of his dearest friends, to whom it seemed a kind of treachery to the "grand old party" that had carried the country through the war, to unloose its iron grasp on the "conquered" States. But Mr. Field's party ties had been long weakening. He was too independent to be a politician. Though he was one of the founders of the Free Soil party, and took all the hard knocks in the days of conflict, he left to others the spoils of victory; while his connection with the Republican party may be said to have ended with the death of Lincoln. The day after the funeral he had an interview with Andrew Johnson, in which they discussed the political future. As both had been old Democrats, they were agreed as to the general principles of republican government. In the immediate crisis Mr. Field's most earnest hope was that the new President would carry out the conciliating policy of his predecessor. But Johnson was so wanting in tact, that he was soon at loggerheads with Congress, which threatened him with impeachment. Yet headstrong as he was, Mr. Field always thought that he was right and Congress wrong. But so eager was the latter to crush out whatever stood in its way, that it did not always stop to consider its own constitutional powers. Its assumptions of authority were checked only by the decisions of the Supreme Court, and even then the policy of the Government was to rule the South by force. Seeing this tendency in the Republican party towards what he looked upon as a great political heresy, the centralizing of all power in the general government; (a power that had become still more odious by giving the vote to millions of negroes, who could neither read nor write ;) this old Free Soiler gradually withdrew from the party which he had done so much to create, hoping for some better leadership from the lesson of sore experience.

But the administration of Grant was a disappointment almost equal to that of Johnson. He was a great soldier, but he carried too much of military authority into civil life, and thought he could govern the country as he commanded the army. So apparent was this that many of those who had supported him for the first term hoped that his own good sense would lead him to retire with dignity, and that the country would choose some wise statesman to preside over it. But could there be anything more grotesque than the nomination of Horace Greeley, who, with all his talents as an editor, was a man of great weaknesses, of a childish vanity, which those about him would use for their own selfish purposes? So absurd did the nomination appear, that Mr. Field could not bring himself to take any part in the canvass, nor even to cast his vote.

Thus relieved from all political ties, he was free to give himself up wholly to his legal practice, which had grown to immense proportions. In looking over his papers, I find huge folios filled with reports of the great cases in which he was the leading counsel, and I am amazed at the multiplicity and variety of the questions raised. The principles of law may be few and simple, but their applications are infinite. And here comes into exercise a penetration which is a sort of genius, as it belongs only to a very high order of mind, a quality which, when united with eloquence of speech, makes the great advocate like Rufus Choate, a combination of talents that is inherited by one who bears that illustrious name. *

* Mr. Joseph H. Choate, of New York.

A practice so large was of course a constant strain upon Mr. Field's intellectual and even physical strength. But did he count it a hardship ? On the contrary, it gave him the keenest enjoyment. No profession is a drudgery to him who is a master of it. An artist loves to paint, if he can paint *well*, and a great advocate is not unwilling to show the "hidings of his power." The harder the case the better ! The more it tasks his strength, the greater its fascination ! He is attracted by its very difficulties, as the man of science is attracted by a problem that taxes all his powers. The greater the issue, the greater the courage it demands, and the strategy in laying out the field and marshalling the evidence. But in all this there is a mental excitement, not unmixed with pleasure, especially by one who is conscious of his strength, and is of that combative temperament, which I must confess was fully developed in Mr. Field. As he was very positive in his opinions, so he was in his likes and dislikes. He was a man after Dr. Johnson's own heart, who "loved a good hater." He did not merely have a mild disapprobation of wrong : he hated it, and hated the man that did the wrong. And hence he looked upon fighting as in many cases not only the natural thing, but the right thing. If this wicked world was ever to be reformed, so he reasoned, it must be turned upside down ; and in order to this there must be fighting and a great deal of it. It was one of his maxims that the only men who made any lasting impression on the world were the fighters! Where would have been the Reformation if Luther had not been a man of war? And so he reasoned that, in his own profession of the law, "the combat" must "deepen" for years, and perhaps for generations, if there was to be any progress.

With this instinct of the warrior, he never counted the odds, though he should be warned that there were many adversaries, nor even though it were added that there were giants among them! He always preferred "a foeman worthy of his steel." Nothing irritated him more than to have a weak opponent, whose mind was so flabby that there was nothing to take hold of, or to make an impression upon. But give him a powerful antagonist, and he was more than willing to take the heaviest blows, as it was with him a point of honor to return them with interest.

This was one side of the man. But were it all I had to say of him, it would do him great injustice, as it would give the impression that he was a man of iron (as he *was*), but that he was nothing more; that he was a cold, hard man, with few friends and many enemies; and withal that he was so preoccupied with the duties of his profession, that he had little time for the courtesies, the amenities, and the enjoyments of life.

Nothing could be more unjust or untrue. He was indeed a many-sided man, engaged in manifold activities, and enjoyed them all; and was inflamed with the *gaudium certaminis*—"the rapture of the strife" —when he entered into the contests of the bar.

But the bravest soldier sometimes longs for the quiet of his tent, and no one ever welcomed it more than Mr. Field. Though his professional life was in the city, he loved the country. He was a country boy, born on the banks of the Connecticut, where he loved to sail on the broad river, or to ramble among the hills—a passion that remained with him till the last hour of his life. When he was fourteen years old, his father removed to Stockbridge, one of the most beautiful villages of New England, where his son, even when grown to manhood, and occupied with large affairs, always spent his vacations, and the happiest day in all the year was that on which he turned his back on the city, and started for his summer home. He was particular as to the very day of going, and would take his flight, if possible, on the 20th of May, partly because it was his father's birthday, but also because it was the time of the apple blossoms. The valley of the Housatonic is full of orchards, which are then all aglow with their delicate white blossoms, and the air is laden with their perfume.

His first home was at Laurel Cottage, near the foot of Laurel Hill, which Miss Sedgwick has made the scene of a very thrilling passage in "Hope Leslie"; but a few years later he bought a large farmhouse, perhaps a hundred years old, with two or three hundred acres of ground, on the top of a hill, that is a background for the village which it looks down upon, taking in the valley of the Housatonic, and having a wide sweep of mountains all round the horizon.*

About the same time I bought a more modest farmhouse, with a few acres, a little farther to the West, so that we saw each other every day, and almost every hour of the day. He was very regular in his habits, rising early for his morning ride, in which I was often his companion. Nothing could be more exquisite than those rides over the hills, drinking in the dewy freshness of the morning air, with the song of birds, and all the sights and sounds that mark the wakening of nature to a new day's life. If I was detained from going, I kept a lookout for him, and saw him at a distance, as that tall figure came up the road under the willows, and if he caught sight of me, he was sure to turn into our grounds and ride up to the door to give me his morning salutation. He had been accustomed in his boyhood to hear the old divines of New England speak of this world as "a wilderness," which was fit only for a state of probation, and would call out to me, "Well, Henry! for this 'wilderness world' this is pretty good!" and then turn with a hearty laugh, and ride away, repeating some fragment of poetry, of which

* Dean Stanley, who spent several days with Mr. Field, said the view was the most beautiful he had seen in America.

his head was always full. If it was after the summer was past, I could hear faintly the murmur of the familiar lines :

> " Ere, in the Northern gale,
> The Summer tresses of the trees are gone,
> The woods of Autumn, all around our vale,
> Have put their glory on." *

Nor was he limited to his morning rides. Such was the exhilaration of being in the country, and living in the open air, that he was always getting up excursions to Monument Mountain, or Mount Everett at one end of the county, or Greylock at the other, from which he now and then rode over the mountains, and came down into the valley of the Connecticut.

But the climate of New England is variable, and sometimes even in midsummer there was a day that was dark and dreary. But the sudden change did not trouble him. He was but too glad to have the excuse for a blazing fire, where, stretched in an easy chair, his "creature comforts" were complete, and if he had a few friends around him, he asked for nothing more. Then was the time to see him at his best, as he was free from care, and running over with reminiscences of past years and distant lands.

---

* Written by Bryant when he was a young lawyer in Great Barrington, and published in the United States Literary Gazette, October 15th, 1824.

From this animated conversation he would turn to reading. He had but little taste for music or painting. He was not a connoisseur of pictures, and he hardly knew one tune from another. But he devoured books. He was fond of poetry, and had innumerable pieces at his tongue's end. Even the dullest listener could not but be roused by his ringing voice, as he read "The Ride of Paul Revere" and "How they brought the good news to Ghent." Then turning to Milton, he would quicken his pace to the dancing gait of L'Allegro, and after a pause reduce it to the slow and measured steps of Il Penseroso.

But for sublimity of style there was nothing to him like the Bible. As he had been brought up to read it at morning prayers, he was familiar with it from Genesis to Revelation, and turned to it for its poetry and its eloquence. In this he was like Mr. Webster, of whom the late Chief Justice Chapman, of Massachusetts, once told me that the greatest intellectual treat of his life was in hearing him, not in a public lecture, but in private conversation, discourse of the Book of Job, of which he would talk by the hour, and on which he had sometimes wished to write a commentary! Mr. Field had the same enthusiasm for his favorite psalms, such as "The Lord is my shepherd, I shall not want"; and Luther's psalm, "God is our refuge and strength, a very present help in trouble." In certain passages, such as "They that go down to the sea in ships; that do business in great waters; these see the works of the Lord and his wonders in the deep"; there was a majestic roll like the roll of the sea, to which there came back a response like the sound of many waters, "Oh that men would praise the Lord for his goodness and for his wonderful works to the children of men!" But his enthusiasm did not stop with the poetry of the Bible: he found poetry in its prose: in the stately rhythm of the old Hebrew, as in Solomon's dedication of the Temple, or Jacob's farewell to his sons. I can hear him now reading: "Reuben, thou art my first-born; my might and the beginning of my strength," and "The sceptre shall not depart from Judah, nor a law-giver from between his feet, till Shiloh come, and unto him shall the gathering of the people be."

These are sweet memories of a brother's life, but there was something nearer and sweeter still. While he had good will toward all men, his affection was reserved for an inner circle, into which no stranger could intrude. What he was to his daughter and her children will appear in the next chapter, when we follow him in pursuit of them round the globe. But what he was to his brothers I can tell. Our father's family was a large one—ten children in all—eight sons and two daughters. But one by one they dropped away, till, a full quarter of a century ago, the two sisters and four of the eight brothers were gone, leaving behind

Dudley, Stephen, Cyrus, and myself, as the only survivors. As three of us lived in New York, it needed only a visit from the Judge in Washington to bring us all together. Those were our happiest moments, when we could sit round one small table—"we four and no more!"—and all be boys again. We talked of all things past, present and to come; of school days and College days; of our modest ambitions as we looked out from the Berkshire Hills upon the great world at a distance, and began to dream dreams and to see visions; of our early struggles and disappointments; and of the varied life of the after years. Into all this no one of us entered with more of abandon to the spirit of the hour. As he talked of his youth, his youth came back again; the old light was in his eyes; and an inexpressible sweetness (of which no man had more for those he loved) flushed in the noble countenance. And now—as I think of the immense vitality that carried him into his ninetieth year; of the great part that he acted in the world; and of all that he was to us who knew him best; whereby he drew to himself love at home and honor abroad—it seems as if he touched life at every point, and got out of it as much as it had to give, or that was worth living for. If it were all to be put in a single line, I know of none more fitting than that which was written of Walter Savage Landor, "He warmed both hands at the fire of life!"

CHAPTER XVI.

AN INTERNATIONAL CODE. ARBITRATION INSTEAD OF WAR.

The year 1866 will be memorable in history as that in which two hemispheres were united, so that it could be said, in a real and true sense, that there was no more sea! The honor of that great achievement belongs to an American, as was fully recognized by the best authorities, who knew its whole history from the beginning to the end, such as Lord Kelvin and the late Sir James Anderson and Sir John Pender. There was nothing in which the Great Commoner of England, John Bright, delighted more than to refer, as he did in his speeches again and again, to "his friend Cyrus Field," as "the Columbus of our time, who, after no less than forty voyages across the Atlantic in pursuit of the great aim of his life, had at length by his cable moored the New World close alongside the Old!" That magnificent tribute was simple justice. But there was an inside history to the great undertaking. No one outside of his own family will ever know the terrible strain of those twelve long years, and how the spirit of the projector, when cast down by defeat, was rallied and reanimated by the undaunted courage of his eldest brother, who saw in this iron link between the two countries, not only a commercial benefit to both, but a new tie drawing nearer together those who were of the same blood. Now that the work was done, and that the two countries were no more divided by the sea, but were literally within speaking distance, why could they not be brought into the closest relations of mutual confidence?

This was a dream that Mr. Field had long cherished. Every summer he spent a few days or weeks in England, where he had a large acquaintance with public men—lawyers and judges, and members of Parliament—among whom he found a great liberality of thought on all political questions. Indeed he often said that, while America was more democratic in her institutions, there was more individual independence in England. We were too much in bondage to parties, or to public opinion, the most despicable tyrant that ever reigned over a high-spirited people. A democracy might be the most galling tyranny in the world. Better have one tyrant than a thousand! Hence he felt that, in the great lesson of good government, we had much to learn as well as much to give. So he exchanged experiences with his English friends with the utmost frankness, both assured that, no matter how many defeats the cause of liberty might suffer, right and justice would prevail at the last: that

> "Freedom's battle once begun,
> Though often lost, is ever won."

The first thing was to have a perfect understanding between the two countries. To this end he spoke in England as he spoke in America, with the utmost frankness; aiming to exorcise distrust wherever he found it on either side, and to allay the sensitiveness that made it a matter of pride that each should stand in armed defiance of the other. Such an attitude of jealousy and suspicion was unworthy of either. Instead of this he would that there should be a union in the two peoples of all true-hearted men—the good, the wise, and the brave—in a brotherhood that might in time take a legal form by act of Congress and of Parliament. Nor need it stop there, but extend from country to country, till all nations should be bound together in a Holy Alliance, not of despots and tyrants, but of the kindred races of mankind.

That very year (1866) Mr. Field was present at a meeting of the British Association for the Promotion of Social Science at Manchester, and, perhaps inspired by the great event that had sent an electric thrill through two continents, he proposed the appointment of a committee to prepare the Outlines of an International Code,*

---

* Happily this scene is not left entirely to the imagination. At the time an enterprising searcher after situations that promised to be turning points of history, took a photograph of "Mr. Field proposing the preparation of an International Code," in which appear the well-known faces of some of England's most illustrious men.

which it should report for correction and amendment, and that, when thus completed, should be presented to the different countries represented for their adoption. The suggestion was welcomed with enthusiasm, and a committee of eminent jurists appointed on the spot. But when it came to carrying it out, they found an embarrassment from their wide separation, so that each one would have to work as it were "at arm's length," when they needed to be in constant consultation. Mr. Field, however, did not lose heart or hope, but returned to the charge the next year at the meeting of the Association in Belfast, in an address on the Community of Nations; all of which were one in that their interests were one; while England and America were so bound together by ties of blood that war between them would be nothing less than fratricide. No matter which was victorious, it would be an unspeakable calamity to both. He said:

"We may look upon England and America frowning at each other across the Atlantic; mutually jealous, slow to redress injuries, and ready to offer or receive affronts. Stimulated by bad men, in the passionate madness of the hour, they rush into war for what is foolishly called the supremacy of the seas. Let it become an internecine war. We should fight each other by sea and land. There would be battles in the Atlantic, the Pacific, and the Indian Oceans. Wherever we could strike each other, we should strike. You would batter down some of our towns, and we some of yours. Timid merchantmen flying from pursuing cruisers, burning houses along the coasts, and ships sunk upon the sea, would bear witness to the madness and fury of the great contending nations. At the end of all, after each had burned and killed enough, one might be driven from the sea, leaving the other in undisputed supremacy. But would either be better off than when the war began? Would the beaten and humiliated combatant be as useful to the victor as before? Would the victor be wiser, better, or happier; to say nothing of that store of hate which would be accumulated and laid aside for the renewed strife of a later generation? Would the merchants of London and New York, or of Belfast and Boston, have gained by turning rich and useful customers into exasperated and impoverished enemies? Would the institutions of England or America be improved by the conflict? Would not the wealth and culture of both—all, indeed, which makes man better and happier in each—be lessened in the waste and desolation of the struggle?"

This was not the language of fear, deprecating a contest for which one side was unprepared—it was the manly utterance of reason and justice, spoken in the name of humanity, and in the name of Almighty God, who is the Father of all the nations of the earth, and would have His children dwell together in unity.

That this might be our inheritance forever, it should not be left to rest only on sentiment, but be assured by a recognition of the Community of Nations, which were indeed but separate members of one great family. This was a part of modern civilization, of which the ancients knew nothing. Two thousand years ago every state that was conscious of its power stood apart, sovereign and alone, in proud isolation and defiance:

"Old empires sat in sullenness and gloom,"

hardly recognizing a common humanity. In the Latin language the very word *hostis* meant at once stranger and enemy. There was no right but that of the strongest. As Rome and Carthage looked across the Mediterranean, the highest ambition of each was to destroy the other. The Carthaginians claimed the supremacy of the sea, and if any strange sail rose above the horizon, they pursued it as if it were a pirate, and seized its crew and threw them overboard. Nor did a Roman feel that he violated any law, human or divine, if he killed a Carthaginian. That two great powers, looking out upon the same blue sea, could live as friendly neighbors, never occurred to them. The idea of the brotherhood of the whole human race was born with Christianity.

But century after century had to come and go before this brotherhood was recognized among communities and states. It was not till what are comparatively modern times, less than three hundred years ago, that Grotius gave form to international law in his great work on the Rights of War and Peace [De Jure Belli et Pacis], which was followed by Pufendorf some fifty years after. But what they wrote then may not serve the purpose now, for this is not the same world as that of Grotius and Pufendorf. The nations do not stand apart as they did three hundred, or one hundred, or even fifty years ago. The ends of the earth are coming together till it may almost be said that there are no more "foreign countries." With our ease of communication it is as if we were of one language and of one speech, and international communication leads almost of necessity to international law. But it may be more easy to understand one another's language than their ideas of justice. If those who are brought in contact were homogeneous, their relations would easily adjust themselves. But in many cases their ways and ours are not only different, but antagonistic, as we are of different races and religions. There are in the world a hundred and twenty millions of Moslems, to whom the only law is that of the Koran, so that between Egyptians and Englishmen justice has to be administered by mixed tribunals composed of representatives of both. With such confusion of ideas, it is not always possible, even with the best intentions, to be just to others, and just to ourselves.

Who then shall make the law for nations? Is it not almost inevitable that it will be made by force; that the will of the stronger will be imposed upon the weaker?

And where should a reformer begin? Was it necessary to turn upside down the whole fabric of existing law, crude as it might be? By no means. Mr. Field was no iconoclast to break in pieces the idols of the past. His idea was not to destroy, but to improve. The world would move slowly at best, but it might be kept moving in the right direction. With no visionary dreams of a millennium, or of an ideal state of society, he believed that it was possible for nations to adjust their relations to one another on such a broad plane of fairness and mutual benefit, that they should no longer dream of the glory of conquest as the height of their ambition.

But the preservation of peace was only one part of International Law, though it might be the most important part. Yet in its full extent it included all the relations of one country to another. As Mr. Field puts it:

> "International law is that body of rules recognized among nations, defining their rights and duties toward each other, and the rights and duties of their people respectively, as growing out of international relations. The law is vast in extent and infinite in detail. It encircles the earth, holds or assumes to hold the strongest nations in its grasp, and affects to a greater or less extent the relation of every human being. You may intrench yourself in camps and fortresses, yet its voice will reach you; you may take the wings of morning, but you cannot escape its presence. Its office is to regulate the conduct of your own nation toward all other nations and all strangers; and to govern and protect you into whatever part of the world you go. No sovereign is so haughty, no subject so poor, as to be beyond its authority. It knows neither latitude nor longitude, wears the same face under northern and southern skies, and utters one voice to the Caucasian, the African, and the Mongolian."

So vast was the realm over which International Law had sway. It was a power like gravitation that held the world together. But to some it seemed to be an indefinite and almost intangible thing, which it was quite impossible to reduce to any fixed form. It was like one of the forces of nature, which, however powerful, could not be confined, and, as it were, imprisoned within the iron bars of a Code. So thought Lord Russell, the Lord Chief Justice of England, who is certainly one of the first authorities in the world. In a recent Address before the American Bar Association, he refers to the work of Mr. Field, but thinks he attempted the impossible. He says:

"The rules of international law are not to be traced with the comparative distinctness with which municipal law may be ascertained. I would not advocate the codification of international law. The attempt has been made, as you know, by Field in this country, and by Professor Bluntschli of Heidelberg, and by some Italian jurists, but has made little way towards success. Indeed, codification has a tendency to arrest progress. It has been so found, even where branches or heads of municipal law have been codified, and it will at once be seen how much less favorable a field for such an enterprise international law presents, where so many questions are still indeterminate. After all it is to be remembered that jural law in its widest sense is as old as society itself; *ubi societas ibi jus est;* but international law, as we know it, is a modern invention. It is in a state of growth and transition. To codify it would be to crystalize it; uncodified it is more flexible and more easily assimilates new rules. While agreeing, therefore, that indeterminate points should be determined and that we should aim at raising the ethical standard, I do not think we have yet reached the point at which codification is practicable, or if practicable would be a public good." *

But Mr. Field, with American audacity, saw no such impassable barriers in the way. He had read the prophecy of the last days, that the valleys should be exalted and the hills made low to prepare an highway for the coming of the Prince of Peace, and every strong-armed toiler could help to clear obstructions out of the way. As to the impossibility of framing a 'Code,' he had said long before :

"There is no more difficulty in framing a Code of International Law than of national, or (as it is sometimes, though inaccurately, called,) municipal law. The established rules of International Law have already a written record ; they are contained in the treaties entered into between nations, in acts of legislation, in the decision of courts of law, and in treatises of publicists. All that is thus contained can be gathered from its various repositories, condensed, analyzed, and arranged, and stated in distinct propositions."

* Lord Russell adds in the very next paragraph, "Among the most successful experiments in codification in English communities have been those in Anglo-India, particularly the Penal Code, and the Codes of Civil and Criminal Procedure." He was probably not aware that this was, in part at least, a contribution from Mr. Field, who, in his journey round the world, spent a few days at Singapore, and inquiring of the Attorney-General, who called to see him, what was the Code of the Straits Settlements, was answered, "The Code of New York" ! and indeed, turning to the printed page, he read the very words that he had written in his library on the other side of the globe.

Between two such authorities, it would be presuming to give an opinion, but for Mr. Field it must be said that he claimed nothing more than to be a pioneer of reform, leading the way where others would follow. Though for convenience he used the word "Code" * as part of a title, he took good care to define the limits of what he undertook. In the preface he says: "This work should be taken for what its name imports: Draft Outlines of an International Code. It is not put forth as a completed Code, nor yet as the completed Outlines of a Code, but as a Draft of the Outlines." Surely it would not be possible to take a more unpretentious title. It was an experiment rather than a finality. He said: "It is intended for suggestion, and is to undergo careful and thorough revision." He was content to labor, and that other men should enter into his labors. In the second edition he makes full acknowledgment of what he has received from others: "I have had the advantage of many suggestions, and have given the work a careful revision." Nor was he disturbed if others should claim all the honor, quite willing to leave it to those who should come after him to do him justice.

---

* Even the word "Law" itself has to be used in a peculiar sense, for strictly speaking there can be no such thing as law which does not emanate from a lawgiver, who has the authority to make the law, and power to enforce it, both of which are wanting in the case of International Law.

The first step was a study of the existing state of International Law as laid down by writers of authority on the multitudinous subjects which it embraces, and as recognized in treaties between different countries. The treaties made by Great Britain, if not a law to the world, were a law to herself, so far as concerned the countries with which they were made. If other countries were to adopt the same rules, there might grow up a general consensus of opinion and practice, which would have the force, if not the form, of an enactment of law. Another authority was found in the diplomatic correspondence between different governments; and another still in the judicial decisions of the higher courts in cases involving contested points. These investigations, spread over a field so vast, were reduced to a general result by drafting into separate articles what were accepted as rules of law, with comments and arguments in their support. The burden of this original examination and analysis of authorities, throughout the greater part of the work, was borne by Mr. Austin Abbott and his partner, Mr. Howard Payson Wilds, and, on certain special subjects, by Mr. Charles Francis Stone, all members of the New York bar. Mr. Wilds was engaged in these researches for nearly five years.*

* President Barnard, of Columbia College, prepared the titles on "Money," "Weights and Measures," "Longitude and Time," and "Sea Signals."

With such experts ransacking libraries and exploring every source of information, there was accumulated a mass of material that would have dismayed a man of less courage than Mr. Field. But with his temperament, the greatness of the undertaking only stimulated his indomitable energy, and all the hours that he could snatch from his professional engagements—his mornings and his midnights—were given to the work of International Law.

And what came out of all these busy years? A brand new Code, evolved out of his own brain? Not at all! It was the same old law with modern improvements. Was the law the only branch of human knowledge in which there was no such thing as progress? The world was changing and the law must change with it. If this was taking liberties with the past, it was a liberty that must be taken by any generation with the work of its predecessors.

But modest as were its pretensions, the "Outlines of a Code" grew and grew into a volume that quite appalls the ordinary reader. If I do not attempt a critical analysis of such a work, it is because that is too high for me; it belongs to one whose life has been given to legal studies, who only can appreciate the vast range of subjects (the table of contents alone covers forty pages!), and is competent to analyze each separate part, so as to judge how far it is a real contribution to International Law.

Without attempting anything so ambitious, it may be permitted to one who is not a lawyer to dwell briefly on the last third of the book, which is given up to War, in which it is apparent that the author has put into it, not only his legal knowledge, but his whole heart, hoping that long after he had passed away it might remain as a plea for peace and good will among men.

To begin with, he did not deny that a war might be sometimes inevitable—coming like a convulsion of nature, a storm or an earthquake, which man was powerless to resist. Nor would he deny that wars had sometimes subserved the cause of liberty and of civilization. The gallant fleets of England destroyed the Spanish Armada. By a seven years' war our country won her independence. By a civil war of four years slavery was destroyed. By war Italy was made united and free. No appeal to justice could have persuaded Austria to give up Lombardy and Venice: they had to be wrenched from her on the field of battle. The tyrant Bomba ruled Naples and Sicily till he was driven out by the invasion of Garibaldi. In such cases war was the only relief from a situation that was too terrible to be borne.

But for the most part wars were precipitated by pride, hatred or ambition. For such a war Mr. Field had a double abhorrence: not only because it was wicked, but because it was insane, in that it did not settle anything but the question of brute force! It did not prove that the victorious power was right; that its cause was just; and that the conquered state, which shrank back defeated and almost destroyed, was a sinner above other nations, or indeed above its victorious enemy. Nor did it even settle the question of peace. On the contrary, one war sowed the seed of other wars, that might be continued from generation to generation, till one power or the other was destroyed; or if permitted to exist, it was only as a subject or a slave!

Looking then at the question from before and after, Mr. Field reasoned that the proper moment to stop a war was before it was begun; before any rash act had put either power where it could not retreat with honor, or at least without a sacrifice of national pride. Therefore he reasoned that in case of differences between two countries, the mode of procedure should be settled *beforehand*, so that neither should be thrown off its balance by some sudden irritation, but could look at any question in the clear light and tranquil atmosphere of peace and friendship. To this end he suggested three simple provisions, which, if followed, would make war almost impossible:

"First: that there should be a simultaneous reduction of the enormous armaments which now weigh upon Europe!" That alone would save millions of dollars a day, and thus lift a burden that presses sorely upon every power on the continent; while the mere pause would cool the hot blood of the belligerents.

"Second: that if any disagreement or cause of complaint should arise between nations, the one aggrieved should give formal notice to the other, specifying in detail the causes of complaint and the redress sought, and that this complaint should be formally answered within a certain period." This would prevent hasty action, and give time for both parties to think it over, and to ask themselves if there were really anything in dispute that was worth fighting about. If such a course had been pursued by France and Germany before the fatal declaration of July, 1870, we should probably have been spared the last Franco-German war; although it must in truth be said that the French were so mad for war, to show that France, and not Germany, was the great military power of the continent, that it is doubtful whether anything could take the conceit out of them but a few tremendous defeats. Then, indeed, they began to open their eyes, and would have gladly retreated. But it was too late, and they had to drink the cup of humiliation to the very dregs. We on this side of the Atlantic have taken care to avoid any possibility of misunderstanding with our neighbors by inserting a provision in our treaties with Bolivia, Guatemala, Peru, San Salvador and New Granada, that a blow should never be struck without full notice of any grievance that might be peaceably composed.

"Third and last: If the parties did not agree, they were to appoint a Joint High Commission";

[representing the two countries] "and if that failed, a Tribunal of Arbitration" [made up of representatives from other nations friendly to both].

Could there be anything more simple than this? Would it involve any sacrifice of dignity on the side of either party? Was there any humiliation in arguing a question in a tone and temper of mutual respect, as if each had the fullest confidence in the sincerity and fairness of the other? Such frankness would be a lesson in national manhood.

We need not theorize about it when we have a case in point, that is the best of all arguments. At the close of our civil war there was a very bitter feeling against England, from whose ports had gone out the ships that had preyed upon our commerce till they had nearly driven it from the ocean. The case lingered for six years till Mr. Gladstone, seeing that the fires were still smouldering, with a frankness that did him infinite honor, made advances towards having the question settled forever; and, as if to show that England was ready to meet us more than half way, instead of inviting the American representatives to come to London, he sent the English representatives to Washington, to deliberate with us under the shadow of the Capitol, where both sides went to work with such earnest purpose, that in a few weeks they had agreed to submit the whole question to a Tribunal of Arbitration, to be composed of five members; one to be designated by the Queen, and another by the President; with a request to the King of Italy, the President of the Swiss Confederation, and the Emperor of Brazil, each to name an arbitrator, and in case of the failure of either to act, the request was to be transferred to the King of Sweden and Norway.

When the treaty was duly signed and sealed, the English representatives came on to New York to embark for home, and the night before they sailed, they were entertained by Mr. Cyrus Field at Delmonico's, where they had the opportunity of meeting several hundreds of our most eminent citizens. The feeling on both sides was one of unbounded relief and satisfaction. I can hear now the ringing voice of the Marquis of Ripon saying proudly, "The treaty between the two countries is an honest treaty, of which neither has reason to be ashamed!" Ashamed indeed? There is nothing in all our history of which we have more reason to be proud.

A few months later the Tribunal met in Geneva, and after listening to the arguments of great advocates on both sides, gave their decision that England should pay an indemnity of fifteen millions of dollars! Was it a humiliation of England that the case went against her? Then was it a humiliation for us that another arbitration a year or two later about the fisheries on the coast of Newfoundland went against us! The only difference was that we had to pay but five millions, while England had to pay fifteen! Does that seem a great deal of money? Both together would not have paid the cost of war for a week! But really the question of money is too paltry to be so much as named when two governments have to decide the policy of two great countries that profess to be civilized and Christian.

In closing the address with which he presented the International Code, Mr. Field took good care to guard himself from misrepresentation:

> "I do not mean to say that every claim which one nation may make upon another should be submitted to arbitration. There may be claims which no self-respecting nation would submit to any arbiter, such as those which touch its equality or independence. To put an extreme case: suppose Spain were to claim the sovereignty of Holland, pretending that it had not been lost by Philip II, or by any of his successors, I would not have Holland submit such a claim to the decision of any arbiter or of any human power. It is not difficult to draw the line between questions which *can*, and those which *cannot*, be submitted to arbitration."

But if war is inevitable, or has already come, then how shall it be conducted? There is such a thing as civilized war. War does not destroy all rights on either side, for even enemies have rights. First of all, war cannot be waged upon women and children, or peaceable citizens going about their lawful occupations. If a city is to be attacked, notice should be given to non-combatants, that they may get out of the way. To bombard a city with a hundred thousand inhabitants in their houses, or going about the streets, would be an act of barbarism, as atrocious as to set it on fire. The people of Moscow indeed put the torch to their own city as a means of self-defence. But if Napoleon had set fire to it, his name would live in history as that of another Attila, the scourge of God !

The first principle of civilized warfare is that it shall be waged only between armed forces on land or sea. This is imperative if we are to preserve the character of civilized nations, and not wage war as savages and barbarians. Against this savagery the proposed revision of International Law sets up every barrier of civilization. If nations are seized with such madness that they *must* have it out on the field of battle, let them fight like men, and not like demons, whose only thought is that of destruction, of the innocent as well as the guilty, of the helpless as well as the strong. There is at least a certain decency to be observed in the way that nations begin and conduct a war. Here are a few of the barriers that must not be broken down. There shall be no wanton destruction of private property. Armies may fight with swords and guns and cannons, but not with poisoned weapons, nor explosive bullets that not only kill, but tear the body in pieces. And the Sisters of Charity and other good angels that hover over the battlefield or watch in the hospitals to relieve the agony of the wounded and the dying, shall be sacred from all rude hands. Nor shall any fierce invader bombard towns and cities that have no defence.

All these ways of making war are relics of an age of barbarism. Then follow chapters with such suggestive titles as these:

"*Of those who may wage hostilities; against whom hostilities may be waged; the instruments and modes of hostilities; truce and armistice; medical and religious service; prisoners; hostilities against property; contraband of war; visitation, search, and capture; blockade; prize; and the effect of war upon the obligations of nations and their members, upon intercourse and the administration of justice. In respect of neutrals, the absolute right of a nation to remain neutral while others are at war is asserted in the strongest terms.*"

Here is an array of topics, each of which is enough for a treatise or a volume. But the end to be secured was worthy of all the labor of the greatest and the best of all countries, for it is a combined effort to put an end forever to one of the greatest calamities that can afflict mankind.

"I do not say," said Mr. Field, "that war is the greatest of all calamities, for I think that national degradation and slavery, or general corruption and the reign of fraud, are evils still greater. An oppressed people may and must rise against its oppressors. A nation attacked may and must defend itself. He who would not fight to the death in defense of his family or his country is not fit for this world. But, in proportion as the defense is just, the attack is unjust. There would be no occasion for the rising of an oppressed people if there were no oppression, and no need of defensive war if there were not first an aggressive war. And, of course, in proportion as you diminish the aggression you diminish the defense. In other words, if there were no aggressive and unjust war, there would be no war of defense—that is to say, no war at all.

"Nor would I detract in the least from the merits of those great captains who, fighting for the rights of their countrymen, have earned renown; nor would I dispute that there is in war frequent occasion for, as there has often been a display of, high heroic virtues. But the great men who displayed these virtues have themselves deplored the occasion and the evils of the war which they had been obliged to wage. Our own Washington was not only first in war but first in peace, as he was first in the hearts of his countrymen; and it was the Duke of Wellington, if I remember right, who said that there was nothing worse than a battle gained except a battle lost.

"I would not, indeed, discourage the cultivation of the heroic virtues or take away the opportunities of their exercise; but, assuredly, war is not the only school where they can be cultivated or exhibited. There will always be suffering enough in the world for the exercise of all the virtues. Does not the shipmaster who puts his ship about in a stormy sea at the signal of a shipwrecked brother, and stays by him through the dark and perilous night till the daylight comes, that he may save him at the risk of his own life, exhibit as much heroism as any of those who fought at Waterloo? Did not the captain of the Northfleet, who the other day calmly accepted death that he might save women and children, exhibit as much heroic virtue as any of the brave six hundred who charged at Balaklava? Was Howard less a hero than Marlborough? Would you not as soon deserve the eulogy which Burke pronounced upon the former, as the poem with which Addison celebrated the victory of the latter? Let him who would win renown through labor, endurance, and self-sacrifice, go abroad into the world and make war upon the wrong with which it is filled."

With such devotion to the welfare of our race, the "good time" for which we have been waiting through all the centuries would soon come. Indeed in the vision of the speaker, it was coming *now*, and with this glimpse of the dawn he brought his words to a close:

"I am not sanguine enough to suppose that war is in our time to be put an end to altogether, but I do suppose that increased intercourse and the general progress of civilization have more and more inclined men to the ways of peace. The armor that now hangs useless in our baronial halls; the battlements that now serve for ornament in place of defense; the walls of cities once formidable but now converted into promenades; are so many witnesses of successive steps in the progress from continual war to frequent and long-enduring peace. I do suppose, further, that, by judicious international arrangements, the chances of war occurring may be lessened, and that when, unfortunately, it does occur, its evils may be mitigated. Such has been the object of the imperfect work which I now place, with all its defects, in the library of this Association, the closing act of a task undertaken seven years ago, and now fulfilled."

With this Mr. Field laid down the burden that he had taken upon him seven years before. It was a work in which it was impossible to make rapid progress. He had to advance slowly, revising and re-revising every page and line—only to feel at last that it was still very "imperfect," and to submit it "with all its defects!" From this self-depreciation we may appeal to the judgment of eminent jurists in Europe, and to the fact that it has been translated into French and Italian. Yet to a work on which he spent years of labor, he gave only the title of "Outlines," as if it were but the dim foreshadowing of what he would have it to be. Such indeed it was. This was not an affectation of modesty, but an expression of his sense of how little he, or any one man, could do. He would have been the last to ask others to be satisfied with what did not satisfy himself, for he looked upon International Law as a progressive science, which must advance with the progress of mankind. The utmost he hoped to do was to make his contribution to the "common weal" of the world. Those who came after him would have far greater opportunities, as they would have the wisdom of all the ages. He was but one of the pioneers that went before the grand army of progress to point the way. To the future it belongs to fill up the "Outlines" that have here been sketched on a broad canvas by a master's hand.

CHAPTER XVII.

THE LONG VACATION : GOING ROUND THE WORLD.

In the army of the United States officers of high rank are retired at the age of sixty-four ! Their days of battle are over ; their names are placed on the roll of honor, and they can take their seats, like Roman emperors, in the Coliseum, and look down serenely upon those who are still engaged in the combats of the arena. But in the professions there is no limit of age. There may be veterans, but there are no pensioners, who are provided for by a grateful country. Nor would a man like Mr. Field accept any price, or any honor, that retired him to the rear, which he would have looked upon as a gilded exile from the stormy activities of life. To live he must keep in the ranks of war. That inaction would have cut short his days seems probable, when we recall the fact that, after he passed the age of military retirement, he not only survived, but was an actor in the stirring events of his time, for another quarter of a century !

But he must have now and then a change of scene, which he found by frequent visits to England and the Continent, where he had so many friends that he was as much at home as in his own country. He had also travelled in the East. But now there was an attraction which drew him farther still. He was nearing the line of seventy when he set out on the longest journey of his life—to go round the world; and not by the shortest line, straight east along a Northern latitude, but by the longest, that crossed the Equator, and reached far down into the Southern Hemisphere. The distance was great, but the attraction was greater, for there at the Antipodes was the idol of his heart, his only daughter, who was predestined to a life in "lands remote" when she became the wife of a Governor of a British Colony. Sir Anthony Musgrave was the Governor of Newfoundland at the time of the laying of the Atlantic Telegraph in 1866, and gave a hearty English welcome to Mr. Cyrus Field. This was the beginning of an acquaintance, not only with his family, but with that of his brother Dudley, whose only daughter he married in 1870, when Sir Anthony was Governor of British Columbia. From this distant post he was sent half way round the world to Africa, to be Governor of Natal; and next was promoted to the Governorship of South Australia, where Mr. Field set out to seek his child, literally at the world's end.

But he could not go anywhere, to any part of the habitable globe, without keeping in mind the great mission of his life, the Reform of the Law. He had finished his New York Codes, and they were fighting their way across the Continent. When he went abroad, he found a similar movement in other countries, which, if not inspired from America was along the same lines, and working to the same end, so that their reformers and ours could exchange ideas in the most friendly way, as fellow-workers in the same good cause. We could reach out our hands across the sea, not only to the great nation from which we are sprung, but to all the races to which we were more distantly allied. Mr. Field's ideas always had a logical relation one to another ; and in his mind the natural order of progress was that justice should go before, and liberty would follow after ; and that "the fruit of righteousness would be peace," not only in the spiritual life, but in all the relations that are formed among men.

This would be better than all the Peace Societies, which had attempted much, but accomplished little. There was a Peace Society in this country, which held an anniversary once a year in Tremont Temple, in Boston ; as another society met in Exeter Hall, in London ; at which good men and good women deplored the great armies and great battles, and prayed for universal peace. But so far as stopping war, they did not so much as stir a ripple on the mighty waters of public opinion in Europe or in America. This was brought home to us very clearly one evening in May, 1873, when Mr. Field invited a few friends to his house in Gramercy Park, to hear the report of Dr. James B. Miles, who had been abroad as the agent of the American Peace Society. It was the same old story. Everybody in England was in theory as much for peace as John Bright, and yet that did not prevent constant warlike preparations. Was there not a better way to cultivate the amenities out of which grow friendly relations by looking into kindly faces, and listening to kindly voices? This was a large question to be discussed before a small company in a private parlor. But tall oaks from little acorns grow, and that very evening these gentlemen resolved themselves into a modest "Committee"—out of which grew a body more imposing in name, as well as in numbers and in power, as it brought together a few months later at Brussels some of the most distinguished publicists of England and the Continent, to form "An Association for the Reform and Codification of the Law of Nations," of which Mr. Field was chosen the first President.

The movement was a success from the very beginning. The peculiar charm of the new organization was its unpretentiousness, its simplicity and its absolute freedom. It claimed no authority. It was in no sense a political body, composed of delegates from different countries, to advocate some policy that might be more favorable to one than another. It was more like the scientific associations that meet from year to year, now in London or Edinburgh, and now in Paris or Vienna, to record new discoveries in science, and lead the way to still greater achievements. Nor was it limited to jurists, but included statesmen and political economists, with perhaps here and there a dreamy philosopher, who had in his brain some social reorganization, that would be a cure for all the ills of the human race. But this only enlivened the discussions, as it showed the wide range of opinion that was allowed, and the contact, or even collision, of such theorists with men who were nothing if not "practical," might enlarge the ideas of both. Naturally an intercourse so free and unrestrained led to the formation of many friendships, as all national prejudices dissolved in the warm atmosphere of a generous enthusiasm for a great cause, that of universal justice and peace.

At the close of this first meeting Mr. Field gave a dinner to the members, at which the burgomaster of Brussels and the English Consul at Antwerp were guests. As might be supposed, the occasion was one of mutual congratulation between the representatives of different countries, who felt that it was indeed one step forward in the progress of the world.

This was sowing the seed that was to bear fruit in many directions. The report of that first Conference in Brussels (which was in its purpose and spirit, if not in name, a Peace Congress,) attracted immediate attention beyond the border of Belgium, so that when Mr. Field arrived in Paris, he was fêted by the French as well as by Americans. In passing through Turin, he paid a visit to Count Sclopis, who had been President of the International Tribunal at Geneva, (when they celebrated the event that was uppermost in both their minds in a cup of tea, that was served for the first time from the silver service presented to him by the United States Government;) and in Rome he formed a very warm friendship with the Prime Minister, Signor Mancini, and other Italian statesmen.

But now he was to leave Europe behind, and the long journey began when he embarked with his wife from Brindisi for Alexandria. He had been in Egypt nearly a quarter of a century before, in 1850, but had only gone as far as Cairo, to get a sight of the Pyramids; but now he went up the Nile in a steamer to the First Cataract, nearly six hundred miles.

But it was not till they returned to Cairo, and crossed to Suez and took the steamer for Bombay, that they felt that they were indeed bound to the Far East. The voyage down the Red Sea, with Asia on one side and Africa on the other, is full of historic interest. Walking on the deck, when the sun is setting over the Dark Continent, one can see on the other side his last rays fall on the cliffs of Mount Sinai. Had my brother been landed on that barren Arabian coast, as I was nine years later (in 1882), he too might have been mounted on his camel, measuring off the long stretches of the Desert, "the great and terrible wilderness," on his way to the Holy Land. But he kept down the Red Sea, and at Aden sailed out into the Indian Ocean ; and in another week came in sight of the great wall of mountains that are known as the Ghauts of Western India.

To the traveller there is no country in the world more fascinating than India, which Mr. Field took in to the full, as he went up the country to Allahabad, where the two sacred rivers, the Jumna and the Ganges, mingle their waters, and millions of pilgrims come to wash away their sins ; and thence to Agra, with its wondrous Taj, the most exquisite tomb in the world in architectural beauty and grace ; to Delhi, the capital of the great Mogul Empire ; to Cawnpore, where the blood of the great massacre still cries from the ground ; to Lucknow, that will always have a place in history for its heroic defence in the terrible siege ; to Benares, the holy city ; and last of all came down to Calcutta, the capital of British India.

From Calcutta they sailed for Ceylon. While waiting at Point de Galle for the steamer that was to take them to Australia, Mr. Field went up to Colombo and thence to Kandy, which is to Buddhists what Jerusalem is to Christians, or Mecca to Mohammedans ; where is a shrine which they visit with the utmost veneration, as it contains a sacred relic in a tooth of Buddha ! Here are the two High Priests of that faith, to whom he was introduced by the English official, who said, to give him an idea of their exalted dignity, "This is the Buddhist Archbishop of Canterbury, and this the Archbishop of York!" He asked them about their doctrine of Nirvana, which they said "was not that the souls of the departed sank into annihilation, but found rest in a place of eternal and conscious repose."

Returning to Point de Galle, they embarked in a Peninsular and Oriental steamer and bore away into the vast Southern Ocean, to which all other oceans are but seas. Never before had Mr. Field such an impression of the waters that girdle the earth. Day after day, and week after week, they sailed on, and saw nothing but the heavens above and the waters below, till, as with the Ancient Mariner,

> "So lonely 'twas that even God
> Seemed not there to be."

But there was a fascination in this very silence and immensity. The sea was calm, and as he sat on deck at night, above him shone the Southern Cross and all the constellations that revolve round the Antarctic pole. But of land there was not a sign, not even an island thrown up by an earthquake, like the Peak of Teneriffe. Nor was there a sign of human life, not even a sail on the horizon, save once, when an Italian barque rose up like a phantom ship, as it came out of the East and sailed into the West, "looking," said Mr. Field, "as it passed over the water, like a great white flying eagle."

But all voyages must have an end, and after three weeks they had their first sight of Australia in the port of New Albany, where they hailed their country's flag, flying from the peak of two American whalers, which had gone thus far from home in search of a cargo. One of the captains was from New Bedford, Massachusetts. His wife had accompanied him in his long voyage, and made a little flower garden out of a box on the deck, where were growing her native flowers to remind her of her New England home.

Passing along to South Australia, they reached Kangaroo Island, off Adelaide, on a bright moonlight night. Never was a scene more striking. The ship was moving on without a sail, every rope of her cordage distinctly traced on the background of the clear sky, the shore visible along the island and up the bay, while the revolving lights told them that they had reentered the regions of civilized life.

The next morning the Governor's secretary came on board to greet them and tell them the glad news that Lady Musgrave had that morning, March 10th, 1874, borne another son, for whom the bells were ringing out a welcome as they drove into Adelaide from the port of Glenelg. The little fellow for whom the bells rang, is now Lieutenant Arthur Musgrave in the English army.

Although Mr. Field had been led to undertake this long voyage to the Antipodes by the yearning of his heart to see one who was inexpressibly dear to him, yet he never visited any foreign country without making a careful study of its natural features and resources; of its towns and cities; and above all, of its population. In every place to which he came he had his eyes open, observing and reflecting as to the future of the new world which was rising in the Southern Hemisphere. Though Australia was no longer to be drawn on the map, and spoken of in geographies, as an island, but as a Continent, it had many disadvantages in the vast wastes of the interior, that were as desolate as the steppes of Siberia, or the Desert of Sahara. Yet it had many compensating advantages in its coast line of thousands of miles, indented with bays and ports for commerce, and above all in being settled by the mighty English race, who have been the colonizers and civilizers of so large a part of the world.

Thus delightfully occupied in observations of everything round him, and above all in the charming domestic scene in the Government House, the weeks in Adelaide flew quickly. But at last he had to tear himself away, and they took a coast steamer for Melbourne, where he was surprised to find a city not forty years old, (it was first settled in 1835,) with over two hundred thousand inhabitants; with streets as wide as our New York avenues; with stately Parliament Houses; an University and a Cathedral; libraries and museums; a Royal Park and other public gardens; with courts of law and banking houses, representing the great firms of London; and clubs and theatres and all the signs of European civilization. Best of all, were the private residences, whose architecture and tasteful surroundings showed that they were the abodes, not only of wealth, but of English culture and refinement.

Another sail along the coast brought them to Sydney, the old Botany Bay, to which at the beginning of the century England transported its criminals, but that had proved itself worthy of another population, which gave it a character befitting the capital of New South Wales, whose schools and colleges and churches showed that it too, like Melbourne, was modelled after dear old England.

Continuing northward, the steamer stopped for a day at Brisbane, the capital of Queensland, where Mr. Field went up to the city and dined with the Governor, Lord Normanby, little dreaming that his son-in-law, Sir Anthony Musgrave (after being five years Governor of Jamaica), would be Governor of Queensland, and there die and be buried far from his native England !

And now they were no longer on the open sea, as they passed inside of the Great Barrier Reef, the most extensive range of coral reefs in the world, which forms a mighty breakwater within which they had as complete inland navigation as if they were on the coast of Norway or the voyage to Alaska.

The last persons they saw in Australia were two American missionaries, husband and wife, standing on the high bank of Cape Torrens, and waving them a farewell, a benediction which they heartily returned, for one result of Mr. Field's journey round the world was to exalt his opinion of the character of the missionaries, and of the work they were doing, and he was often heard to say that, if he had to choose between them and our consuls, or even many of our ministers, he would take the former as the best representatives of his country.

As they approached the Equator, the sun was more directly over their head, and the heat was so oppressive, though relieved somewhat by the trade-winds, that they were more than willing to take a long siesta in the midday hours, and keep watch by night. It is commonly supposed that the constellations of the Northern Hemisphere are more brilliant than those of the Southern, but in those midnights it seemed as if the stars came nearer to the earth, and the heavens glowed with immeasurable splendor.

The culmination of their long voyage was in the Arafura Sea, where, between the islands of Bali and Lombok, they were so near the shore that they saw the natives about their cabins, while above them rose the Peak of Bali, twelve thousand feet high—just the height of the Peak of Teneriffe—which was girdled with three zones : one from the sea upwards to the clouds ; the second a robe of clouds, where a storm with lightning was playing ; and the third the clear top, shining in the sky.

And now they were sweeping along the shores of Java, one of the richest islands in the world, with its background of lofty mountains, and its foreground of rich tropical vegetation, over which towered its majestic palms; an island that supports a population of thirty millions, ten times that of the whole continent of Australia! It was night before they anchored off Batavia, but so eager was Mr. Field to go on shore, that he went at once, and at daybreak was exploring a city which, by its innumerable canals, showed that it was in many features a reproduction of its ancestral Holland.

Turning Northward from Java, they had in view for two days the island of Sumatra, a thousand miles long, and larger than all Great Britain. In this last stretch they crossed the Equator, and were once more in the Northern Hemisphere, as they landed at Singapore, the Southern point of Asia!

Here they were still under English dominion. The Governor was Sir Andrew Clarke, who invited Mr. Field to dinner, at which he met the Maharajah of Johore, who came in Oriental dress, and brought his cook with him, that he might not eat forbidden meats. The Attorney-General also called on Mr. Field, and when asked what was the judicial procedure of the Straits Settlements, answered that they had the New York Code, which, of course, was very gratifying to one who had the chief part in framing that Code on the other side of the world. It seemed to say that justice is of no country; that it is the same in all latitudes and longitudes; the rightful inheritance of all climes and of all the races of men.

From Singapore it is a week's sail to Hong Kong, but here too he did not come as a stranger, for his Codes had gone before him, and the Governor, Sir Arthur Kennedy and Chief Justice Smale joined to do him honor; while Messrs. Burroughs and Russell, American merchants, received them with that generous hospitality which the great mercantile houses in the East are always so ready to show to distinguished visitors.

From Hong Kong it is but a few hours' sail across the strait and up the Canton River to the great city of that name, where Mr. and Mrs. Field were received by Mr. Cunningham, agent of the firm of Russell and Company, whose ample establishment was put at their disposal, and partly fitted up to receive them. Here they were treated with great hospitality; every day English or American residents were invited to meet them at dinner. Archdeacon Gray of the English Church accompanied them in their excursions; the most remarkable of which were a visit to the place of beheading, a real Potter's Field, (where they were shown the cleaver with which heads were struck off, and a bag containing heads that were waiting to be sent to the homes of those who had suffered death;) and a visit to the Courts, where the accused were brought in with chains about their necks; one end of which was passed through a hole in a heavy stone, that the poor wretch had to carry when he moved. As he came before the Judge, he laid the stone on the floor and prostrated himself, when the charge of crime was read to him, and he was sternly interrogated about it, and his answers written down. One of the accused denied his guilt and stoutly protested his innocence, at which the Judge ordered him to be put to the torture, not by the rack, or by the touch of red-hot iron, but by hanging him up by the thumbs and toes, which was agony enough. The man stood it for about ten minutes, when he confessed and was let down—a short way to extort a confession, not always from the guilty, for it might be from the most innocent, who would confess any crime rather than suffer an agony that was worse than death itself. This Chinese justice showed that China had hardly emerged from barbarism. Instead of being a sign of civilization, it was but a ghastly token of man's inhumanity to man.

They returned by Macao, which is a little peninsula long ago granted to the Portuguese, and once a place of some commercial importance. It is now as quiet as a country village, but the beauty of nature still remains, enhanced by an interesting historical association, as the visitor is taken into a pretty garden in which Camoens, the Portuguese poet, wrote the Lusiad.

From Hong Kong the travellers took passage by the French steamer to Shanghai, where they had a hearty welcome from our Consul, Mr. Seward, and Mr. William H. Fogg, a merchant from New York. As Mr. Seward had an official visit to make to the Tao-tai, the head man of Shanghai, answering to a French Prefect, he asked Mr. Field to accompany him. So one morning they set out in their sedan chairs, winding through the narrow streets till, as they approached the official residence, they were saluted with fireworks like Roman candles. The Tao-tai came forward to meet them, and took them into a room with benches on three sides, where he waved them to the right and left, and took his seat between them. Tea was then brought in, which is always preliminary to any official discussion, and when the latter was ended, they retired with the same courteous formality.

But still more interesting to Mr. Field was it to see the administration of justice, which had also its peculiar features. As Shanghai had quite a large foreign population, there were mixed tribunals, in which foreign Consuls sat with the Chinese authorities to watch the proceedings. Mr. Field was present one morning when Mr. Seward sat with a Chinese judge who despatched business without much ceremony, as in a case where there was a contest over a pile of silver dollars, which were laid on the table. He made short work of it by reaching out his hand, and taking a part and passing it over to one man, and the remainder to the other.

The next case was a criminal one. The culprit was found guilty and sentenced to be flogged, which was done at once. He was laid upon his face on the ground, while the executioner took a bundle of rods and began to whip his bared legs. The man cried lustily, and when he got up was further punished by the *cagne*, which is made of two pieces of board, each with a half circle cut in it, to be put together round the neck, so that the man could not lay his head on a pillow or on the ground, nor reach his face with his hands. A more cruel punishment it would be difficult to imagine. Is it that the enormous population of China makes them indifferent to human life or human suffering ?

Leaving Shanghai in one of the Pacific Company's steamers for Japan, they passed through the Inland Sea, which, with its thousands of islands, is the most beautiful Archipelago in the world. The American passengers were reminded that they were nearing home as one evening they heard voices on the upper deck singing "Marching through Georgia !"

From Yokohama Mr. Field made a visit to Tokio, and an excursion to Inoshima and to the great statue of Buddha at Dai-Butz. The evening before he left he dined with Iwakura, the Prime Minister of Japan, at his palace, in company with Mr. Bingham, the American Minister. Except for the swarthy figures and Oriental costumes, the dinner might have been given in Paris, as the service was in the French style, even to the champagne.

In Yokohama he met Sir Harry Parkes, the British

Minister, who had been long in the East, and had a life of incident, not unmixed with danger. One evening, as they were talking of the old times, he told of an attack made upon him and his party by fanatics in Osaka some years before. They were passing through the streets escorted by English soldiers, when some Japanese fanatics rushed upon them with sharp drawn swords and began cutting at the soldiers. They did bloody work, and one was bleeding freely, when Sir Harry rushed up to him and bade him stand his ground, saying, "Remember that you are an English soldier!"

He had come as near losing his head in China as in Japan. Dean Stanley told Mr. Field that Sir Harry once described his conversation with a fellow-prisoner, who with him was condemned by the Chinese authorities to be executed the next morning! They passed a part of the night in comparing the sensations they expected to feel when led out to execution! A gruesome subject indeed for their midnight hours! But by some happy intervention the morning brought light into the prison cell, and the execution was indefinitely postponed.

When our travellers left Japan, they said good bye to the Old World. As they steamed out of the harbor of Yokohama the crews of the American ships of war gave them three cheers. That was their last recognition, for once on the Pacific they saw not a sign of life for seventeen days as they bore away to the East, over a sea as calm as that of the Southern Ocean, and which gave them the same sense of the infinite. Day after day they saw nothing but the blue sky above and the blue waters below, with the long swell, that never broke into a ripple, over which the great ship moved as if conscious of her strength. On the last day, as they approached the coast, they ran into a heavy fog, which compelled them to slow up for two or three hours, when all at once it lifted and disclosed the bright top of a mountain ten miles below San Francisco. At this the good ship seemed to lift up her head, and dashing on with the speed of a race-horse, passed the Golden Gate into the great harbor of the West, and stood still.

Their arrival was not unexpected, as Mr. Field's brother, the Justice, who was here from Washington, was waiting for him, and with other kinsfolk, the Ashburners, made the wanderers feel that they were once more at home, and in a few days they were rested from their voyage. A special car was put at their disposal as far as Salt Lake, where they halted and visited the Mormon City, and had an interview with Brigham Young, who generously offered to introduce Mrs. Field to his seventeen wives—an honor which she politely declined ! The next day they continued their journey, and reached their Stockbridge home in July, 1874, where, looking down from the hill top, they felt that in all the world there was no spot quite so restful as this "Happy Valley" nestled in the Berkshire Hills.

CHAPTER XVIII.

A NEW CHAPTER IN POLITICS. A DISPUTED PRESIDENTIAL ELECTION. TWO MONTHS IN CONGRESS.

When a man has just returned from a voyage to the Antipodes, he might be excused if he should take at least a breathing spell before he starts off on a new expedition. But Mr. Field was not as other men are. He was still in his prime, in his seventieth year, and it was not in him to rest while there were new worlds to conquer. The year before, when he helped to form the Association in Brussels, he promised to be present at the next meeting, though meanwhile he had to make the circuit of the globe, and the very next month after he reached home, he was again on the sea.

This time the meeting was at Geneva in Switzerland, where he found that the good seed had taken root, and was bearing fruit in the Old World as well as the New. It received a new impulse from the very place of its meeting, in the "Salle d'Alabama," so called from the fact that in it had met the representatives of different nations to arbitrate between England and America as to the claims of the latter for the ships destroyed by the Alabama in our civil war, for which the arbitrators awarded to our country an indemnity of fifteen millions of dollars. This had made the hall historic, in memory of which it was ornamented with agricultural implements, which had been moulded out of cannon, to signify that the reign of peace was approaching, when the nations should learn war no more.

During the year past the Association had become known even in the Far East. When Mr. Field was in Japan he dined with the Prime Minister Iwakura, and in the course of conversation mentioned that on his return to America he was again to cross the sea to attend the meeting of the Association for the Reform and Codification of the Law of Nations, which was to be held in October at Geneva, and suggested that Japan should send a delegate! The Minister was at once interested, but did not know whether the Council, or some official body mentioned by him, would approve of it in the time required. But when the time came and Mr. Field was on his way to his destination, he saw in the papers that the Japanese envoy to Rome was also *en route* to Geneva to attend the meeting. There he was indeed, with his wife, and two very intelligent and interesting persons they were, and added much to the pleasure of the European delegates.

These annual meetings were getting to be great events in the life of Mr. Field. As he was a good sailor, he thought nothing of the week's voyage. The change from life on shore was grateful to him, and he could sit on deck in any weather, and drink in the salt sea air with a feeling of exhilaration.

The next year the Association met at The Hague, where it was received with great distinction, not only by the notables of the bench and the bar, but by the court. As the King of the Netherlands was absent, the Queen and the Ministers, and the two Chambers, honored them with all manner of attentions, ending with a reception by the Queen at the "Palace in the Wood." In two weeks he was again on the ocean on his return.

At home he took life more easily, going up to Albany now and then to argue a case before the Court of Appeals, where he was a little—or not a little—shocked at the free and easy way of conducting the proceedings, and finally persuaded both judges and advocates to adopt a little more of ceremony: the judges to wear gowns, like the judges of the Supreme Court of the United States, which seemed to be the fitting "robes of justice"; and the bar to rise as the judges entered, and stand till they had taken their seats. A little of this observance of the stately forms of the past, he thought, by adding to the outward dignity, added also to the respect due to the highest courts of justice.

From Albany it was an easy change to Washington, where he was still more at home, not only in the Supreme Court, but among the old habitués of the National Capital, some of whom seemed to belong to another generation. Thus he writes March 1, 1875:

"Being in Washington, I paid a visit to the elder Mr. and Mrs. Blair, both of whom are more than eighty years old, and yet vigorous in mind, and (except that he is a little weak in the legs) strong enough in body to ride on horseback ! What a picture from the days of our fathers it must be to see this aged couple riding together over the hills, as we may suppose that Martha Washington rode beside her husband a hundred years ago !"

The greatest satisfaction to him was to find that "the war was over," not only on the battle-field, but in personal relations, as well as in political life. After four years of war, it had taken ten years of peace before the angry waves were lulled to rest. But that happy time had come at last. On the same date he wrote :

"I think the revolution in our politics is over, and that hereafter we shall see things moving in their usual channels. A Democratic House of Representatives comes into power on Friday, the 4th of March, and we shall have no more Enforcement Acts, Force Bills, Civil Rights Bills or suspension of the Habeas Corpus."

This blissful state of mind continued through the year, and on the next first of January (1876) he wrote :

"At midnight the bells rung out their chimes to salute both the parting and the incoming year. I listened till they died away at half-past twelve. This morning the flags are flying on every flag-staff in the city, to greet the centennial year. This patriotic fervor is a beautiful thing. With it no nation can fall ;

without it no nation can stand long. We have many faults, but there is at bottom a fund of good sense, energy, love of right and love of country, that will, I believe, carry us through all perils. Every man, hewever, must do his duty to the public. The trouble with us has been that each has been too much absorbed in seeking his own prosperity. As if in sympathy with the time, the weather has become perfect. The air is like May and the sun warm."

Little did he think that a new storm was impending, that would try the strength of our institutions almost as much as the war itself, and bring him quite unexpectedly into public life. The crisis was one unknown in our history, and which the fathers of the Republic never dreamed of, even as a possibility—a disputed Presidential election! Through the ordeal of an election the country had to pass in every four years, and the time came round in the Centennial year of 1876, as that completed a hundred years from the date of the Declaration of Independence. But of the course of events that year I knew little, as I had been for more than a year following my brother round the globe, and I remember well that, as we entered the harbor of San Francisco, and the custom house officers came on board, in my eagerness for news, my first question was, "Who has been nominated for President at the Convention in Cincinnati?", fully expecting to hear the name of James G. Blaine, when to my surprise the answer was "Rutherford B. Hayes," then Governor of Ohio, a name that, however honorable in peace and in war, (for he had been in the army, and borne a brave and a manly part in fighting for his country,) I had never happened to hear before ; while on the other side had been nominated Mr. Samuel J. Tilden, the Governor of New York, whom I had known for twenty years, as he was not only a resident of the city, but lived on Gramercy Park, a few doors from my brothers, so that I knew all his goings out and comings in. Between these two candidates, I thought we were sure to have a good man, who, if not a great President, like Washington or Jefferson or Lincoln, would be at least a figure-head of the Great Republic, of whom we should have no reason to be ashamed.

The election took place on the 6th day of November, and the next morning it was announced all over the country, without a dissenting voice, that Mr. Tilden had received 203 votes in the Electoral College, while Mr. Hayes had received but 166. It was a very simple sum in arithmetic for any school-boy to subtract the one from the other, which gave Mr. Tilden the handsome majority of 37 electoral votes, so that he was duly elected President of the United States ! The Republicans gave it up. The New York Tribune admitted it without a question, explaining it in the only simple and natural way, that it was all because "Mr. Tilden had too many votes !"

But those were the days of the "carpet-baggers," when the Southern States were still in the hands of Northern men, many of them worthless adventurers, who had gone South after the war to spoil the Egyptians, and who had the votes in their hands, and the battle was not lost until they had made out the official returns, and if perchance the majority happened to be on the wrong side, what more easy than to throw out a sufficient number, on the plea of fraud, to turn the scales the other way? The Democrats might do the voting, but as long as the Republican "returning boards" did the counting, they could laugh at any Democratic majorities.

This was a line of operation of infinite possibilities, and a certain "managing editor" figured it out that if the returns from Louisiana, which had eight electoral votes, and from South Carolina, which had seven, and from Florida, which had four, making nineteen in all, could be taken from the column of Tilden, and put to the credit of Hayes, it would give the latter a majority of one! This was a scheme fitly hatched in the dark hours of night, which had been no sooner conceived than the plotter, eager to set it in motion, hastened up town, to the Fifth Avenue Hotel, and waked a Western Senator, who was one of the war horses of the Republican party, and who believed that in politics, as in war, anything was lawful to beat the enemy! To him was communicated the Gunpowder Plot to blow the Democrats sky high! "But the election was over!" "Oh yes, but it was not too late to change the result, for the whole business was not settled till the official returns were made!" The policy was to keep these back till it should be seen just what change of votes would be necessary to make a majority on the other side! To help them in their plot, the conspirators had a private code by which they could communicate with the boards at the South, telling them not to make their returns to Washington till they had received the fullest information and instruction from the North!

Never was a plot more skilfully laid, nor one in which the engineers were more completely masters of the situation. The wicked partners at the South were ready to swear to anything! If the Democrats had carried Louisiana by a few hundred, or a few thousand majority, the Republican managers would take their solemn oath that there had been *much more* than that number of fraudulent votes, for it was always wise to have a liberal margin!

But was it possible that such a made-up majority reversing the actual vote would be accepted by Congress? That was the question. As if to complicate the case still more, the two houses were divided—for while the House of Representatives, which had been more recently elected by the people, was largely Democratic (so that if there were no election by the Electoral College, and the choice were thrown into the House, it would immediately elect Mr. Tilden), yet the Senate, which held over, was still strongly Republican. Between the two there was a strife that agitated the whole country to such a degree that there were fears that it might culminate in another civil war. Some bold hunters of Kentucky threatened to march on Washington with a hundred thousand men! "And they will soon see what we shall do with them!" was Grant's quick reply. But the uneasiness was universal. Congress met on the 4th of December, but business was paralyzed by this all-engrossing question.

Mr. Tilden had the good fortune to be represented in the House by his most intimate personal friend, Mr. Abram S. Hewitt, afterwards Mayor of New York; but it was important to have also a legal representative to meet the constitutional questions that might arise, and as there was a vacancy in the delegation from the city by the resignation of Smith Ely, who had been chosen Mayor, Mr. Tilden wished Mr. Field to take the vacant place, and he was accordingly nominated and elected, and served to the end of the term.*

No sooner had he entered the House of Representatives than he became a very conspicuous figure by his attacks upon what he regarded as the brazen infamy of the false returns. One of the side scenes was the examination of the Boards of Louisiana and Florida, for which the House had appointed a special committee.

---

* Strange to say, Mr. Field had voted for Hayes, but so convinced was he that Tilden was elected, that his sense of justice revolted from an intrigue to rob him of the high office to which he had been chosen by the American people.

At one or two of these examinations I was present, and it was truly pitiful to see how the perjurers writhed under the questions of their merciless interrogator. It was only necessary to look in their hang-dog faces to see that they were well aware that they did not, and could not, deceive their inquisitors ! And yet one could only look at them with a sort of contemptuous pity for the poor creatures who were throwing away their honor, if they had any to lose, for the benefit of outsiders who took good care not to expose themselves to the just punishment of the law.

But the work to be done was not confined to the exposure of false witnesses. There were legal questions to be settled by the highest authorities. As a superiority to the House was assumed by the Senate, as the body that was to receive the returns, to open the certificates, and declare the result, it became necessary that the House should assert itself, and Mr. Field drew five resolutions on the power of the House in respect to the electoral count, which were reported from the special committee by Proctor Knott and Randolph Tucker. He drew also the objections to counting the votes of Louisiana and Florida ; and further, as some timid folk were afraid that the country would go to pieces if it should be without a President for twenty-four hours, he drew a bill, which passed the House, to provide for the administration of the Presidency in case of a failure to elect ! One step farther was the drawing of a bill for the legal procedure called *quo warranto*, which the Democratic caucus voted to have brought in, and which Mr. Field *did* bring in, but which did not pass the House. Here he thought his own party flinched from their guns, for he was very confident that if he could once get the case before the courts, Mr. Tilden would have established his title within six months, unless indeed all law was trampled down by the violence of party spirit.

But now all these dreams and warlike preparations were laid aside by a new proposal. As there was a dead-lock between the two Houses, wisdom finally prevailed to this extent, that their difference of opinion should be submitted to an impartial tribunal composed of five Senators, five Representatives, and five members of the Supreme Court, fifteen in all, which sat for several days in the court room, where Mr. Field and Mr. Charles O'Conor were on one side, and Mr. Evarts on the other. The argument of the latter it was my privilege to hear, and it was a great forensic display, although his opponents might say that it showed more ability than fairness. His whole argument revolved round one point: that the Commission had no *power*—as Congress had no *power*—to go behind the returns. Even though they believed them, or even *knew* them, to be false, there was no remedy! The constitutional provision was simply that "The President of the Senate shall, in presence of the Senate and House of Representatives, open all the certificates, and the votes shall then be counted." But *what* votes ? The real votes deposited by lawful voters, or the result of stuffed ballot boxes, or a false count ? No matter for that ! Right or wrong, just or unjust, it must stand ! I can hear him now saying, and repeating, that there was no power that could go behind the Returning Boards ; that the work was put into their hands "to be *done*, and so done that it could not be *undone !*"

This was the argument used in the Electoral Commission, when they sat by themselves to render their decision. In vain did Mr. Justice Field put an imaginary case :

"Suppose the canvassers had *made a mistake* in footing up the returns, that changed the result of the election—a mistake that they discovered before the vote was counted : was there no remedy ?" "No !" was the answer. "Then," said the Justice, "a mistake in arithmetic, in the adding up of figures, may elect a President of the United States, and Congress is powerless to prevent it !" Again he asked :

"Suppose the canvassers were *bribed ;* or had entered into a *conspiracy* to commit a fraud ; and in pursuance of the bribery or conspiracy, *altered the returns*, declaring elected persons not chosen by the voters, and had transmitted their vote to the President of the Senate, but that before the vote was counted *the fraud was detected and exposed :* was there no remedy ?"

Again the same answer, "No ! whatever fraud there

may have been must be discovered and protested against before the Boards made their returns" [an impossibility when the Boards were themselves the conspirators to defraud !] ; to which the Judge answered :

"If this be sound doctrine, it is the only instance in the world where fraud becomes enshrined and sanctified behind a certificate of its authors. It is elementary knowledge that fraud vitiates all proceedings, even the most solemn ; that no form of words, no amount of ceremony, and no solemnity of procedure, can shield it from exposure or punishment."

Once more he put the question in this form :

"Suppose the canvassers were *coerced by force ;* by men putting pistols at their heads, and threatening to blow out their brains if they did not perjure themselves, and swear to a lie : was there no remedy ?"

Again "No ! No !" an answer which not only condoned clerical errors and mistakes, but in giving the highest reward to perjury, held out a bribe to every degree of villainy and crime !

"But," said one of the leaders of the Republicans, "if you had the trump card, wouldn't you play it ?" "the trump card" being the perjured returns ! This was a taunt worthy of the gamblers of Monte Carlo, but hardly to be thrown in the face of the august Electoral Commission ! But weak and wicked as it was, it prevailed before that great Tribunal when they disclaimed all power to discriminate between lawful votes and returns that they knew, or might know, to be fraudulent, and thus enthroned in the place of power one who had not been elected by the American people!

So the deed was done, and on the 4th of March, 1877, Mr. Hayes was inaugurated President of the United States! His administration was in some respects a marked improvement on that of his predecessor, who, being a soldier, naturally leaned upon the army for support, and kept large garrisons in the Southern cities, as if they were conquered provinces. To withdraw these was one of the first acts of the new administration—a step taken by the advice of the Secretary of State, Mr. Evarts; while the Secretary of the Treasury, Mr. John Sherman, by a wise financial policy, restored the public credit, resumed specie payments, and began to pay off the enormous debt incurred by the war at the rate of a hundred millions a year! In all these signs of returning prosperity no one rejoiced more than Mr. Field. But even this might be too dearly paid for by the sacrifice of the national honor. As he looked over the country, and saw the cities alive with the activity of business, and the fields waving with abundance, there was one blight on the smiling landscape—that we were under a government, or at least an administration, that had no right to exist; that there was in the chair of President one who was not placed there by the people's will. As to personal qualifications half the country might prefer Mr. Hayes to Mr. Tilden. But that had nothing to do with the case. The question was not which was the better man, but *whom did the people elect?* *He* was the Lord's anointed, and no one else could take the crown without sacrilege. The assumption of authority by another was as flagrant an usurpation as if General Grant had surrounded the Capitol with troops, and declared that he would hold possession. The right of the people to choose their own rulers was the highest token of sovereignty, and it had never been disputed. The country had just celebrated the centenary of its independence, and in all that hundred years there was never a question of right to the succession. Were we to begin now, and follow after the South American republics, where power can be grasped by any pretender, if he has the army behind him? So reasoned Mr. Field, in whose view this seizure of the Presidency was the greatest of crimes; even though the country, with its immense vitality, might survive the shock, and still flourish under it, or in spite of it. No glittering prosperity could ever blot out the memory of this stupendous wrong.

CHAPTER XIX.

JOY AND SORROW. THE DEATH OF HIS SON. VISIT TO HIS DAUGHTER IN JAMAICA.

Even the most intrepid traveller is not likely to make more than one grand tour around the world. Mr. Field had gone to the ends of the earth to see his child, and now it seemed as if the ends of the earth were coming to him, when, in the regular course of promotion in the English service, Sir Anthony Musgrave, after five years in South Australia, was transferred in 1877 to the island of Jamaica, of which he was Governor for five years. This was within a week's sail from New York, and brought those dearest to the father and grandfather very near home. As he sat alone on the night of February 12th, 1878, he wrote: "The last hours of seventy-two years are nearly run out. I have had in the main a happy and a prosperous year. My vigor, bodily and mental, is unimpaired. The great event of the past year in my domestic life has been the visit of my daughter, son-in-law, and grandchildren, which gave me unspeakable happiness"; to which he adds, as if it were from the overflow of a heart too full to be restrained, that he had decided to build a church tower in Stockbridge, with a peal of bells, in the name of his grandchildren, living and dead, to be called the Children's Chimes. "It will be a memorial of those who are enshrined in my heart, while the ringing of the chimes at sunset I trust will give pleasure to all whose good fortune it is to live in this peaceful valley." The generous purpose was carried out that very year. The modest campanile was erected on the green in front of the church, and bears an inscription which tells us that

THIS MEMORIAL TOWER
MARKS THE SPOT WHERE STOOD
THE LITTLE CHURCH IN THE WILDERNESS
IN WHICH JOHN SERGEANT
PREACHED TO THE STOCKBRIDGE INDIANS
IN 1739.

But Sergeant was not the only missionary in the wilderness. In his footsteps came Jonathan Edwards, who, though he was the philosopher of his age, preached not only to the handful of white settlers, but, by an interpreter, to the Indians, till in 1758 he was called to be President of the College at Princeton, where he died; after whom Stephen West was the pastor for sixty years. The associations of three such saintly men may well make the place holy ground.

The autumn of that year (1878) brought Mr. Field's usual pilgrimage abroad, where he spent his time chiefly on the Continent, going directly from Liverpool to Frankfort-on-the-Main to attend a meeting of the International Association, which was made delightful by the hospitality of the warm-hearted Germans, who gave them a public dinner and an excursion to Homburg, courtesies which certainly contributed to the cause of peace and good will.

After the meeting he went on to Munich, and thence through Augsburg, Ulm, Stuttgart and Carlsbad to Strasburg and Metz, from which he visited the field of Gravelotte, where (as he thought) the French *ought* to have been victorious, and apparently would have been but for the incompetence of Bazaine. From Metz he went to Luxemburg, and drove about the town, through the park built on the site of the old fortifications and along the deep ravines, which form a moat round the beautiful city. If this did not rouse in him the war spirit, it did the historical spirit, and so he must needs make a pilgrimage to Sedan, and go over the battle field, and visit the house where Napoleon the Third surrendered to King William of Prussia! From these warlike memories he came to Paris on a more peaceful errand, to attend the meeting of the Institute of International Law, where he met an old friend, Mr. Groesbeck, of Cincinnati, and the representatives, not only of different countries of Europe, but also of Asia, in the Chinese and Japanese Ministers. One evening that he dined with the former, it was amusing to observe the diversity of languages. Neither of these Ministers spoke any language but his own, but each had a secretary who could speak French, so that when the Chinese Minister gave a toast, his secretary translated it into French to the Japanese secretary, who translated it into Japanese to the Japanese Minister ! It was well that the sentiment that was to pass through three languages was one of peace and prosperity to all.

These visits to Europe were not unfrequently returned in America. The same autumn Dean Stanley crossed the sea, accompanied by his friend Mr. (now Sir) George Grove and Dr. Harper, who were all guests of Mr. Cyrus Field in New York and at his place on the Hudson. Then, wishing to show them a little of the scenery of New England, he brought them up to the Berkshire Hills, and after taking them to Williams College, came with them to Stockbridge, where they were for several days the guests of our oldest brother. It was delightful to see the enthusiasm of the Dean as he looked down from the hill top into the valley, through which the Housatonic winds its way, and exclaimed in surprise, "Why did you not tell me of all this?" As we drove him to Lenox, the Stockbridge Bowl, set in the bosom of the hills, reminded him of the lake scenery of England. On Sunday he preached in the Episcopal church, and (recalling the historical associations which he had learned only the previous day, how Ephraim Williams of Stockbridge, as he was to go out to the field in the old French war, made the bequest that was the foundation of the College which bears his name,) thus alluded to the young hero who had fallen in battle a hundred and twenty-three years before : "Had the forefathers of this great nation not struggled to reclaim the wilderness, and convert the savage, and build up the Church of God by river and by forest ; had there not been men like the gallant soldiers who guarded these frontiers, to catch, in the intervals of war and bloodshed, visions of a happy and peaceful future, and lay the foundations on which learning and religion might freely flourish and abound—this nation would never have been born, this empire would never have arisen."

From the church he came to our cottage on the hill and spent the afternoon. My brother had told me that his delight was, not to see our cities, so much as the interior of American homes. I can see him now as he sat upon a low chair before the open fire, (for which there was an excuse in a touch of frostiness in the October air,) more interested to ask questions about the country and its local history, than to speak of aught which concerned himself or England. When at last we walked across the lawn as the sun was going down in the West, his gentle face seemed to reflect the peace and calm of the day, as he said, "I would not have missed this for anything." In return for our little courtesy he hoped to welcome us to Westminster Abbey, where he could have the pleasure of going with us over the ancient pile, pointing out the historic names of many generations ; but alas ! before we crossed the sea again, he too was laid to rest in the shadow of the great Abbey which he had done so much to make known to the world.

Thus in the midst of life we are in death, a warning that was soon to come home to us nearer still.

The year 1880 should be marked with a cross, in token of a great sorrow, the death of Mr. Field's only son, which came without a warning. It was midsummer, and the city was deserted, as all who could get away had fled to the seashore or the mountains. Our family was divided in its country homes, Cyrus having a place at Dobbs Ferry, and "Young Dudley" (as we sometimes called him to distinguish him from his father) at Hastings—both on the Hudson. But wherever we were, Stockbridge was the paternal home, where our father and mother had lived and died, and were buried, and where the eldest and the youngest of the brothers spent their summers, and here we had planned our family meeting. Mr. Field, who was at the moment at Long Branch, was to come up to welcome his brother the Justice and his wife from Washington. His daughter-in-law had come in advance, while his son, who was very fond of coaching, would drive four-in-hand across the country. A more beautiful excursion could hardly be found in Old England itself than that from the Hudson to the Housatonic. It is all hill and valley, with roads winding hither and thither through the woods or along the course of streams, and when he took his seat on the box, with no companion but the faithful "Michael," and cracked his whip, they started at full speed, and went up hill and down dale. Not the slightest incident marred the delight of the journey, till, as the sun was setting over the Western hills, he drove up to his father's door. Here were all the conditions of a delightful family union, when in a few hours all was changed. After the long drive of the day he slept soundly, but woke in the morning and spoke to his attendant in his usual cheerful tone, when suddenly the heart stopped beating, the golden bowl was broken, and life came to an end. It was but a few minutes before we, who were near neighbors, were on the spot. But one glance at the marble face was enough, and all that could be done was to soothe the distracted wife. A message was sent immediately to his uncle Cyrus to be communicated to his father, and the next morning brought both to the home that was now turned into a house of mourning.

On the afternoon of the same day, August 10, 1880, The Evening Post announced the sad event:

"Mr. Dudley Field, the only son and the partner of the eminent lawyer David Dudley Field, died suddenly this morning. He left Hastings-on-the-Hudson last Friday morning to drive to Stockbridge, Mass., and was at that time in excellent health. He had made arrangements to meet all his uncles at Stockbridge this week, and Judge Field and the Rev. Dr. Field had already joined him and were with him at six o'clock this morning, when he died very suddenly of disease of the heart.

"Mr. Field was forty-nine years old, and was very well known in this city both as counsel and advocate, although his professional reputation was necessarily overshadowed by that of his father. He was very popular in the profession, being a man of pleasing address and genial temperament, and his death will be sincerely mourned by a very large circle of acquaintances."

The shock was all the greater because it was wholly unexpected. It was the sudden close of a life that was still in the prime of vigorous manhood, and that promised so much. From his very boyhood he seemed to have every gift of fortune. From College he went abroad, and spent a year in Europe and the East. But the greatest of his opportunities was to sit at the feet of a master of the law, and to enter upon practice with the prestige of his father's name. Thus the world had opened all its gates to him for a brilliant career. On such a prospect the curtain now fell.

It was a sad day when the old home, known for its hospitality, saw a gathering for another purpose, indicated by the flag at half-mast. A note in his father's diary gives the incidents of the last farewell:

"August 12. To-day my son was buried. The sky was lowering, but there was no rain. The funeral services were very simple. At five o'clock our nearest friends came to the house, where a prayer was said and a few verses of Scripture read, and then the carriages wound slowly down the hill, following the remains to the Episcopal church, where the full service was read, the anthem chanted and the hymn 'Abide with me' sung. Then the body was borne to the grave by the workmen in my service, assisted by a few others, the pall-bearers, relatives and assemblage following on foot. At the grave the coffin, covered with flowers, was placed in a cedar cover, and the whole lowered into a vault made of brick at the bottom and sides, and covered with heavy slabs of marble. On the turf which covered the ground I placed an anchor of flowers at the foot, and a broken shaft of flowers at the head. Mournful chimes were then played a few minutes, and we left the grave and the cemetery. By this time the moon, half full, had taken the sun's place, and a soft light shone upon us as we returned to our home. I could but think that it was a merciful providence which had brought my son to die under his father's roof, and to be borne to his last resting-place by his father's servants."

So ended a career whose possibilities seemed but half fulfilled when he was cut down in the midst of his days. But if the brilliant promise of his early life fades in the distance, we cannot forget the warmth of a heart that never grew cold. He had a great love of children, and the early death of his only child was a blow from which he never recovered. Perhaps none have a better opportunity to know the heart of a young man than his classmates in College. Living in daily intercourse, they know one another more intimately and more truly than in the great outside world. And therefore it has been so grateful to us to hear those who knew him then tell us that there was no one to whom they could go more freely for any act of kindness; and that all felt that they had lost a friend when they heard that he had gone to the grave. They will keep his memory green.*

* In 1883 his father placed a memorial window of his only son in St. Paul's Church in Stockbridge, and one also in the hall of the Kappa Alpha Society in Williamstown.

A heavy heart is not made light by a change of place. But it is a relief to the burden of sorrow to turn from dwelling only on one who is "loved and lost" to another not less dear who still remains. So long as there is yet one to love, a stricken father is not quite desolate, mourning as one who will not be comforted. To find such a change of scene and association Mr. Field left New York at the close of autumn for Jamaica, of which Sir Anthony Musgrave was the colonial governor. A few notes from his diary will keep track of the voyage and the visit :

"November 25, 1880. Started in the ship Atlas, bound to Jamaica, on a visit to my daughter and her family. A snowstorm had come in the night, and the streets, the ship and the shores of the bay were all white as we steamed out to sea. It was very cold, and I had to wrap myself in my warmest. But the sea was not ruffled, the snow and rain had ceased, and the night was fine. After a day or two the repose of the voyage gave me relief from the constant strain of work, with the added burden of so much sorrow. When I came on board I was nearly worn out; but the quiet of the ship, the absence of care, and the softly murmuring sea soothed my nerves. Nobody importuned me, nobody called me. I was alone with myself, with a small ship's company, and with nature, the sea, the winds, the clouds and the stars.

"November 28. Dudley's birthday. As I sat upon the deck all the morning, I thought of the bright day when he was born, in a front chamber on Murray Street, looking out upon the green of Columbia College, and a canary singing in his cage over the coming of the child. I ran along the years of his life till he died. How my heart was bound up in him! Then I thought of what was left to me in my daughter and her children, to whom I am going."

As they were sailing Southward, each day brought a milder climate, and all the passengers were on deck, enjoying the softer air, while he was for the most part sitting in his sea-chair with a book. He had taken with him the recently published "History of Our Times," by his old friend Justin McCarthy, and very interesting he found it. It set him to thinking whether government was really made much better by the long discussions in Parliament or in Congress, apropos of which he recalled an observation of Lord Normanby, whom he had met six years before in Queensland, that in all his life in Parliament he had never heard but two speeches that changed the vote in the House of Commons: one was a speech of Lord Palmerston on the famous Don Pacifico case; and the other a speech of Macaulay on the exclusion of the Master of the Rolls from the privilege of sitting in Parliament. So difficult was it to move the government. Sir Rowland Hill told him of his experience in getting his plan of cheap postage introduced. He argued and argued, but made little impression till one day the Duke of Wellington sent for him to explain it, and getting interested, told him he would take it up. As the Iron Duke could speak in a tone of command, soon everybody discovered that cheap postage was one of the greatest blessings ever bestowed upon the people of England !

"November 30. The last day of autumn. About nine last evening we passed Wattings Island, 1,000 miles due south from New York and 470 from Kingston, and Bird Island at four this morning, and at six stopped at Fortune Island and took on board negro workmen for service on the ship and in port till her return. From this we passed Castle Island and then struck out straight for Cape Maysi, the eastern end of Cuba.

"December 2. Kingston. We anchored off the harbor in the night, and steamed up to town by seven o'clock this morning. The Governor's carriage was waiting for me, and I was driven to King's House, where I found myself at eight o'clock surrounded by my daughter and her husband and their children.

"December 6. At three in the afternoon we left King's House in a landau and drove five miles to Gordon-Town, at the foot of the Port Royal Mountain. There taking the horses, which had been sent on before, we followed a bridle-path, said to have been laid out by the Spaniards, for an hour and a half, when we drew up before a low cottage, 4,000 feet above the sea. This is Flamstead, where Jeanie and her family have passed three summers. It is said to be eighty years old, and is embowered in flowers and vines. Kingston, city and harbor, is at our feet, and the highest range of the Blue Mountains, 8,000 feet, fills the horizon to the north and east. When Columbus was asked by Isabella what Jamaica looked like, he crumpled a sheet of paper, and then opening it half way, said that the surface was like that! It was a good illustration. I never saw a mass of mountains of so many shapes and so sharply cut. The thermometer now, at eleven o'clock, stands at 71, and a gentle breeze stirs the foliage about me as I write. Church, the artist, resided for a while in these hills, at a cottage a mile or so to the southeast of Flamstead, and he thinks the climate the best he has ever known. The quiet is complete; there is no neighbor within fifteen minutes' walk.

"December 8. Yesterday at three P. M. we had a shower of rain, lasting half an hour. When it ceased, we started on a ride among the mountains—Jeanie, Anthony, an orderly, a servant on foot and myself, in single file, along steep mountains and among stunted trees. We passed the spot where Jeanie was thrown over the hillside from a runaway horse. It is a frightful place, and it was a miracle that she was not killed. Our path lay along Mount Elizabeth, to the southern end. The views were grand. We did little more than walk our horses, now and then starting into a gentle trot. Coming down from the mountain one day, we saw a phenomenon I had never seen before. It had been raining, and instead of a rainbow there was a circle, an aureole, around the head of each of the riders as he rode, mirrored in the mist on the opposite side of the ravine.

"December 20. Yesterday afternoon at five I went with the Governor to the camp of the West-Indies Regiment to hear the band. The musicians were all black except the leader. The privates of the regiment are black, but the officers are white. I am told that there is not a black officer, high or low, in the British Army.

"December 28. In the afternoon the Governor, Mr. Baden Powell and myself, made a visit to the Commodore at Port Royal. We were taken over to the tomb of a person who was swallowed up in the great earthquake, thrown out again, and lived afterward thirty years!

"In Jamaica I learned two lessons. One was how completely one phase of life and occupancy could be blotted out by another. We are apt to think with amazement of the changes in Europe which the Northern barbarians effected when they came down upon the Roman Empire. The example of Jamaica explains it fully. The Spaniards colonized the island and inhabited it for two hundred years, until it was taken from them by the English. There is not now, however, so far as I could learn, a vestige of Spanish rule remaining, except the broken walls of a convent on the north side of the island ; the names of three or four small streams emptying into the sea, also on that side ; and the corruption of a name constantly used on the south side. Near Kingston is a small river which rushes rapidly through a ledge of rocks. This is now called 'Bog Walk,' a corruption, no doubt, of Boca d' Agua.

"The other lesson was the impossibility of either a social or political admixture of the Aryan and the Negro races. The population of Jamaica is roughly estimated at 500,000, of whom 50,000 are whites, 100,000 *browns*, and the rest blacks. The negroes live in comfortable huts, and the green lanes of their villages are often charming. On market days there are crowds of men and women buying and selling. The white dresses and the headgear of the women make a picturesque scene. But in spite of all this, and though they are as free as the whites, and have been so for seventy years, there is no mingling of the races. The browns hold themselves aloof from the negroes, and the whites from both."

It is a far cry from Jamaica to the Alps, and yet there was Mr. Field in the following autumn. On the last day of summer he left St. Moritz at seven o'clock, drove up the Engadine to the Malaya Pass, and descended by a very long and steep zigzag to the valley, a road that is wonderful for its scenery. At Casteregno he passed the boundary between Switzerland and Italy. Here the chestnut trees begin to cover the sides of the valley. Having taken the extra post, he travelled rapidly to Lake Como, where a steamer was waiting, and at six o'clock he was in the Grand Hotel at Bellagio. A day or two after he had one of the surprises that make the delight of travel :

"September 2. At the wharf this morning, as I was about to go on the steamer for Como, I met my brother Stephen and his wife, who had been at the Hotel Grande Bretagne all day yesterday, neither of us knowing that the other was at Bellagio. We went together to Como, and there I left them at the station to go on to Milan, where I am to meet them on Monday. Around the lake the houses, gardens, boat-houses, fountains, winding walks, and the dark green foliage, with the variety of trees, shrubs and vines, make scenes of indescribable beauty. The charm of the Italian lakes lies in the grandeur of the mountains that surround them, the frequency of bays and inlets, the windings of the lakes, and the softness of the climate, not to mention the numberless villas which in the course of generations have been built upon the shores.

"September 5. Milan. The town is full of visitors to the Italian Exposition. I have visited it with great interest, considering what advances Italy has made since her unity has been established. Of all the European nations, she is to me the most interesting, from the progress she has made since she was freed from the rule of Austria, Naples and the Pope, and of the petty sovereigns who divided and enslaved her, and has become one united kingdom from the Alps to the Adriatic. Milan is a bright and cheerful city. The people are better looking than the French or Swiss ; the profiles and bearing of both men and women are finer.

"September 22. Went to Mentone, where the house of most

interest to me was the Pension Anglo-Americana, in which my grandchildren stayed in 1879. Arrived at Monte Carlo at five and took lodgings for the night at the Hotel de Paris, opposite the Casino. The day was wintry and the breakers dashed hard against the shore. The road was either alongside the breakers or above them, giving the most picturesque views of land and sea ; a succession of headlands jutting out into the deep, with bays between ; from which rose slopes covered with vineyards and orange-trees, and dotted with churches and villas, and behind all a glorious background of mountains. Strange that all this beauty and sublimity should be profaned by the vices of men, but here at Monte Carlo is the greatest gambling house in Europe. After dinner we paid a visit to the famous (or infamous) Casino, where we were required to present our cards, and received in exchange tickets of admission to the Cercle des Etrangers, and passed into a large hall, a sort of reception room, where men and women were walking up and down, and then into the gambling room, where were four tables, three for roulette and one for faro, and all crowded with players, among whom were a number of women ! Another entrance opened into a reading-room, furnished with more papers than I have seen together since I came abroad. Into this I strayed, and was met with the ghastly news of Garfield's death ! I had no heart to think of anything else, and came straight back to the hotel.

"Returning to Paris shortly after, I attended a memorial service for the martyred President in the Protestant Church of the Oratoire. No death since that of Lincoln has created such a sensation throughout Europe as that of Garfield."

This year the Social Science Congress met in Dublin, which Mr. Field had not visited before, and in his first walk round the town he "found the streets as dirty as in New York" [happily our streets are better now], and there was a great deal of squalid poverty, but these unfavorable impressions were soon dispelled by Lord O'Hagan, the Irish Lord Chancellor, who invited him to be his guest at "Woodlands" and with true Irish hospitality gave a dinner in his honor, at which thirty sat down at the table, among whom were Archbishop McCabe and Mr. W. E. Forster, the Chief Secretary for Ireland, with whom he dined the next evening at the Vice-regal Lodge in Phenix Park. Mrs. Forster is a daughter of the famous Dr. Arnold.

But, with true American curiosity, the one spot in Dublin that Mr. Field wished to see was the place where Robert Emmet was executed, one of the saddest tragedies in history, with which every American is familiar. The pathetic story of his secret engagement to the daughter of Curran, as told by Washington Irving,* and his courage in the face of death, have thrown a romantic association over his name, which was increased by the emigration of his brother, Thomas Addis Emmet, with other illustrious exiles, to the New World, where Mr. Field had seen them in his early days, and it was

---

*The picture by Irving in his "Broken Heart" receives its last touch from the lines of Moore ending:

Oh! make her a grave where the sunbeams rest,
  When they promise a glorious morrow;
They'll shine o'er her sleep, like a smile from the West,
  From her own loved island of sorrow!

a sad interest to stand on the very spot where perished the youthful martyr of Irish independence.

It had become such a habit of Mr. Field to spend part of his summer vacation abroad, that it is enough to say that the next year (1882) he followed his usual course, with only this change, that, as the place of meeting of the Association for the Reform and Codification of the Law of Nations was in Liverpool, he had no necessity to cross the Channel. Nor was this a hardship or privation, for though he had friends in France, Germany, and Italy, yet next to his own country, there was no spot on earth where he felt so much at home, and so much in love with the country and the people, as in dear old England, where he spent two delightful months, returning in October.

CHAPTER XX.

THE AFTERNOON OF LIFE. THE QUEEN'S JUBILEE. DEATH OF SIR ANTHONY MUSGRAVE.

The happiest part of a man's life is when he has come to "the land where it is always afternoon." The struggles of life are over ; the battles fought, the victories won. Not that he has ceased to be an actor in the world's affairs, but he has reached a higher elevation, where he breathes a serener air. Into that broad upland Mr. Field had now come. Though he was approaching his eightieth year, his eye was not dimmed, nor his natural force abated. His form was as erect and his step as quick and firm as ever. But there was a little softening of the inner man. Old contests, if not forgotten, were subdued. The combative element in him was not quite so strong, perhaps because the victorious can afford to be magnanimous. Or was it rather that the sun had crossed the meridian, and that life, if not quite so stirring as in the midday of battle, was full of quiet thoughts, of cheering memories, and still more cheering anticipations. With the years, as they had come and gone, there had been a more general recognition at home and abroad of the immense service that he had rendered in his reform of the law, in sweeping away the technicalities of legal procedure, which, from once being sacred, had now become matters of ridicule and contempt. In 1883 Lord Coleridge made a visit to this country and was received everywhere by bench and bar with the respect due to the Lord Chief Justice of England. On the eve of his departure New York did him honor in a great array of the legal profession at the Academy of Music, which he addressed with a frankness that disarmed all criticism. He did not assume to speak for England, as he held a somewhat isolated position in the politics of that country. "I have never shrunk," he said, "from calling myself a radical, who, while greatly admiring Mr. Gladstone, find myself more heartily in accord with Mr. Bright than with any other living Englishman." A most happy introduction this, which sounded as if the Lord Chief Justice of England were almost a republican! At any rate he sympathized with liberty wherever he found it, and saw more to admire than to criticize, and was more ready to learn than to teach. In this spirit he referred to our systems of jurisprudence, "some of which he confessed he had not been successful in mastering"—a gentle suggestion that even here there were a few things that might be improved in the administration of the law! He had been told that the English courts despatched business more rapidly than ours, and "he could not express the pleasure he felt to think that anything in England was done faster than here—even a lawsuit!" He had been told also that the English judges take the liberty of assuming the direction of affairs more than the practice of some of our States would permit. From his point of view he could not help thinking that the English were right; and yet from our point of view, so different were the circumstances, that we might be right too.

But better than all was the lesson of England's experience. He said: "As the result of ten years of labor by a committee of which he was the chairman, the English judges had recommended certain changes in the methods of procedure, to simplify proceedings. *It was high time that something was done.* A distinguished practitioner once said that he did not think the world or England would be the worse if every case in 'Meeson and Welsby' had been decided the other way!" But this conservatism was not confined to England, for he had been told that in one of our States these old methods of practice shone as bright as ever! To such worshippers of the past he suggested that, "as we had in the Yellowstone Park a collection of the prodigies and monstrosities of nature, so the lovers of these old forms should set up a park for quaint pleadings, where the *absque hocs* and *surrebutters* might be preserved to gratify future curiosity"—to all which Mr. Field listened with a quiet satisfaction that he had lived to see the day when England and America were united in the work of Law Reform.

But—to turn from the professional to the personal—as our eldest brother was the head of the family, it was a part of our household traditions to remember his birthday. With the death of his only son, and the absence of his only daughter, his three brothers were his nearest kindred, and it would have been a sort of sacrilege—at least towards our household gods—if we had not all come together. We must meet somewhere: if it could not be in New York, then in Washington, in the well-known house on Capitol Hill, which has been famous for thirty years for its generous hospitality. Here we met on his birthday in 1884. Of course it added to our pleasure that others should share in our admiration for one so dear to us, as when the Justices of the Supreme Court of the United States came in a body to pay their respects; and at dinner the government was represented by President Arthur and his Secretary of State, Mr. Frelinghuysen; Chief Justice Waite, and Judges Harlan, Blatchford, and Gray; Senators Edmunds, Bayard, and Gibson; Mr. Carlisle, Speaker of the House; with Representatives Randall, Tucker, Hewitt, and Dorsheimer; to whom was added a representative from the Antipodes in Sir Henry Parke, whom Mr. Field had met on the other side of the globe, at Sydney, where he was Prime Minister of New South Wales. With his large stature and white hair he was a striking figure, such as became one of the founders of the new empire of the Southern seas.

The next birthday (1885) rounded out his eightieth year, when his brother Cyrus gave a reception, at which were not only representatives of his own profession, lawyers and judges, but men of science and learning, Professors in Columbia College and in the University of New York ; and men of affairs, merchants and bankers—all of whom came together to do honor to one who had done as much as any man of his day to establish the foundations of the Commonwealth.

In the month of April he was invited to Halifax, Nova Scotia, to make an address at the Dalhousie University, where he was received with the greatest courtesy by the bench and the bar. A number of the judges went to the station to meet him and bid him welcome. The Academy of Music was crowded to hear his address on the Comparative Jurisprudence of the English-speaking peoples. Of the impression made by this visit I have heard from several quarters, but from no one who was more enthusiastic than the late Sir John Thompson, whom I met at the Bering Sea Arbitration in Paris, and again at Ottawa, when he was the Prime Minister of Canada, and made for himself such a reputation across the sea as led to his appointment as one of the Privy Council, for which he was called to England to be sworn into office, and had gone with the Ministers to Windsor for that purpose, where he died suddenly in the Castle, to the great grief of the Queen. The English government paid an honor to his memory such as had never been given to any one on this side of the ocean except to George Peabody, in sending a ship-of-war to take his remains to Halifax, where he was buried with all the funereal pomp of a great military parade with reversed arms and folded banners. He was one of the men who could hardly find words to express his admiration of David Dudley Field.

The year 1887 was an *annus mirabilis*, as it was the year of the Queen's Jubilee, an anticipation of what we have had ten years later. As it was to be in early summer, Mr. Field sailed for England on the 1st of June, and on the 21st, the great day of the feast, was in his place in Westminster Abbey, in the Diplomatic Gallery, where he and Mr. Phelps were the only ones in plain dress, a stern simplicity which republicans might regard as a distinction, (as it was for Franklin in Paris,) in contrast with the rich costumes and decorations of the European Ambassadors. The scene was one of the greatest brilliancy, but of course all eyes were fixed upon the central figure, eyes that were wet with tears, when the Queen seemed to be lost in the mother, as she kissed her children and grandchildren.

That was a time of general rejoicing in London, a pleasant episode of which followed two days after in a dinner given by the Association of Foreign Consuls, in which forty nations were represented : indeed every nation that had diplomatic relations with England, except China. As they came in one by one, and their names were announced, now the Consul of Germany, and now the Consul of Brazil, etc., etc., it seemed as if indeed the ends of the earth were coming together, and that this was a sign and token of the time when

> "The war-drum throbs no longer, and the battle flags are furled
> In the Parliament of man, the Federation of the world."

But no Parliament could keep a grandfather long away from his grandsons, the eldest of whom, who bore his own name, was at Dartmouth, on board the training ship Britannia; while the two younger were in Scotland, pursuing their studies under the watchful care of Mrs. Drummond, a friend and kinswoman of Dean Stanley. They lived in a castle, an old building of irregular shape, once the scene of conflicts between the Highlands and the Lowlands in their border feuds. The grounds were charming, full of old trees and pleasant walks. From the castle Mr. Field drove to the school where were Arthur and Herbert, when he had to confess that it was impossible to describe his emotion as the dear boys opened the door and rushed into his arms.

Returning from Scotland, he had a few days to spare, and thinking it a good time to see "how they do things on this side of the sea," he went down to Durham to attend the Assizes. There were two judges, one a Protestant and the other a Catholic, both of whom went to church before they went to court. Mr. Field attended the service in the Cathedral, where he had a seat in the chancel, and observed the judge, as he came in wig and gown with an escort of the sheriff, chaplain and policeman, after which there was a sermon ! The two judges had apartments in the old palace of the bishops. At eleven o'clock they came to the court house in a stage coach, preceded by trumpeters. This was preserving the majesty of justice ! Mr. Field went first to the criminal court with the judge and sat beside him all the morning. He charged the grand jury, who stood in a side balcony a few feet higher than the judge. Then he waited for them to act on the indictments presented, while he read the depositions of the committing magistrate. After half an hour two of the grand-jurors came into the balcony and the officer in charge passed down to the clerk of the assize, in a net bag fastened to the end of a pole, two indictments, and withdrew. The person indicted was brought in and put on trial. In one case two defendants were tried for highway robbery ; one was acquitted, the other found guilty and sentenced to penal servitude. A woman was put on trial for concealing the birth of a dead child. She had no counsel, but the judge was very lenient, and when the jury found her guilty, with a strong recommendation to mercy, he let her off with only a week's imprisonment. Mr. Field then went over to the civil court, where Judge Matthew was sitting, and in the evening dined with the judges at the Castle.

Two old customs he found still kept up at Durham: one, for the judges to receive on leaving each a *jacobus*, to help them procure protection on their forward journey; the other, to be entertained by the Dean, where as they dine a hymn is chanted, and at the end the Dean gives them his blessing and a shilling!

From Durham he went to Bath, the great resort of English fashion a hundred years ago, and still famous from its association with the distinguished figures of a former generation. Here lived Lord Chatham and Gibbon the historian; Fielding, the novelist; Lady Huntington, the friend of Wesley; Napier, the author of the Peninsular War; and Walter Savage Landor.

Leaving these memories behind, Mr. Field was next to witness a demonstration of the present greatness of England in the naval review at Portsmouth, where he was a guest on board of one of the troop ships and followed the Queen's yacht through the whole squadron, a display of "sea-power" such as the world never saw before, nor since till ten years afterward (1897), when it was eclipsed, but only by England herself, and in the same waters.

From the Isle of Wight he came back to London to attend the Peace Conference at Guildhall, where they were welcomed by the Lord Mayor, and in the evening a great banquet was given at the Mansion House, at which there were three hundred guests, and Mr. Field had to respond for his countrymen.

That summer (of 1887) seemed to be devoted to fêtes and celebrations. But after the sunshine come the shadows: and the next year he was called to England on a sadder errand. He was spending the summer at his seaside home on the Sound. The 9th of October was the birthday of his daughter, and his thoughts were flying over the seas to her, when a message from his brother Cyrus was put into his hand, telling him that her husband, Sir Anthony Musgrave, had died at Brisbane, the capital of Queensland, the day before, after an illness of but five hours! The shock was the more terrible in that it was wholly unexpected. He was in the full vigor of manhood, and never more active or more useful. Brought up in the service of his country, he was an admirable type of that class of men who, trained for their high positions, have done so much for the glory of England. With his long experience in different parts of the world, he may have well looked forward to many years of usefulness and honor. His death was therefore a great public loss. But the most agonizing reflection to Mr. Field was that his only child was a widow, and far away on the other side of the globe. But, thanks to the ocean telegraph, it was possible to communicate with her, and with his message of sympathy went the assurance that he would meet her in England, to which he assumed that she would immediately return; and he sailed the next month. He met her at Plymouth, which was her first port, and came with her to London. After a week or two they went to Scotland, to see her youngest son, Herbert. To a stricken mother no sympathy could be so tender as that of one who had shared her great sorrow. He was still there at school near the picturesque old castle, whose occupants were as venerable as its ancient walls.

Returning to London, it was necessary to make plans for the winter. It was too late to return to America, and the winter in England would be bleak and cold. And so, after some deliberation, Mr. Field decided to go with a party of friends to Egypt, where they spent the winter, going up the Nile, and did not return to England till the spring, and reached America in May.

After nearly a year's absence from his country he was glad of a quiet summer in Stockbridge. Nothing was so restful to him as nature, and he was more than willing to exchange the ceaseless roar of London for the stillness of the Berkshire Hills. The last of June brought the day of Commencement at Williams College, and we drove up through the county together. With the beauty of the season were the associations of other days, as we passed over the same old roads, through the woods, and by lake and stream, that we had travelled many times when life was young.

At Williamstown he missed his life-long friend Mark Hopkins, to whom it had been his sad privilege to pay his tribute of love and admiration the year before. There were a few old veterans wandering about the grounds, as if looking for some familiar face that they should see no more. At the meeting of the alumni Mr. Field was the most conspicuous figure, and when he entered the dining hall, the whole company rose and greeted him with cheers. Grateful as all this was, it was a constant reminder that he belonged to a generation that was rapidly disappearing.

The summer was passing quietly when there came a shock to us all. On the 14th of August the telegraph brought the astounding news that that very day there had been an attempt upon the life of our brother Stephen by the notorious Terry, who had threatened to kill him because of a decision which he had given on the bench—a threat which might have been treated with contempt had it not been that he was a man of blood (he had killed Senator Broderick in a duel many years before), which led the government to detail an officer to accompany the Judge on his visit to California to hold court—a precaution that proved to be very timely, as the bully, who was a giant in stature, followed him from place to place to carry out his threat, and finally approached him at a table and struck a blow, and raised his arm for another, which would probably have been fatal, if the officer had not shot him dead on the spot! The tragedy created great excitement in California and all over the country. Although the issue was a relief, we could not feel that our brother was quite safe till he had crossed the Continent and we had him under our own roof.

JUSTICE DAVID J. BREWER

[*Though two Presidents of the United States had been assassinated, the attack on Justice Field was the first on a Justice of its Supreme Court. Had he fallen in the discharge of his duty, he would have been succeeded soon after by one of his own blood. Justice Brewer is the nephew of Justice Field and of David Dudley Field, whose Christian name he bears, and in whose office he began the study of law, and inherited the courage of both his uncles, as well as their clear head and determined will.*]

The season closed with more grateful associations. Mr. Field, in addition to the duties imposed upon him by his connection with societies at home and abroad, was also the President of the American Bar Association, which met this year (1889) at Chicago. It was not the first time that he had been in that city on a similar errand. Thirty years before it had been his fortune to deliver an address at the opening of the Law School of the University of Chicago on the Magnitude and Importance of Legal Science. The present occasion brought together hundreds of lawyers, not only from the West, but from all parts of the country. In his opening address he reviewed the changes in statute law in the States and by Congress during the preceding year. The sessions continued for three days, and were closed, in the usual American style, by a dinner, at which he presided "with a dignity and grace," says one who was present, "that gave a peculiar charm to the occasion." It was a lesson in courage, and an inspiration and example to the young men of the profession, to see so many of the most distinguished members of the bar gather round this old warrior, who had fought the battle of law reform for half a century.

CHAPTER XXI.

THE PEACE CONGRESS IN LONDON.

The summer of 1890 found Mr. Field once more in England, so regular was the swing of the pendulum from one side of the ocean to the other, from the land of his fathers to the home of his children. His daughter, after the death of Sir Anthony Musgrave, had taken a house at Harrow for the education of her sons at the famous school founded more than three hundred years ago, from which have come many who have added to the glory of England in arms; in literature and science ; in the pulpit and at the bar.

To be with those so dear to him was to Mr. Field the chief attraction to England, but he had also this summer a special engagement, to preside at a Peace Congress, to be held in London, that would bring together representatives from many countries, who were enlisted one and all in the common cause of promoting the peace of the world.

As it was necessary for him to be in London, or very near to it, no suburb could be more convenient than Harrow, which is only ten miles away, and from its elevation (for it is "Harrow-on-the-Hill") one can almost see the dome of St. Paul's, so that while he was far enough from the great city to be out of its rush and roar, yet he was so near that he could be whirled into it in half an hour, and be brought back again at any hour of day or night.

As the meeting of the Congress was not to be until July Mr. Field had several weeks to enjoy the society that gathers only in a great capital. At a lawn party at Mr. Gladstone's he met Lord Ripon, whom he had last seen at a reception in New York, on his return from Washington, where he had led the way for the Alabama arbitration. As he was afterward the Governor-General of India, he had represented England in two hemispheres. With Lords and Commons were well-known writers, among whom were Mrs. Humphrey Ward and Mr. James Bryce, who has made our part of the English race known to our kinsmen across the sea by his "American Commonwealth." But the chief charm of all was Mr. Gladstone himself, moving about among his guests, enlivening all by the animated conversation of one of the greatest of living men.

From the Prime Minister who had ruled England for so many years, it was but a step to the present Prime Minister, Lord Salisbury, and the members of his cabinet, whom Mr. Field met at St. James's Palace, where the Prince of Wales received in place of the Queen, with his brothers, the Duke of Edinburgh and the Duke of Connaught.

From Palace to Parliament was an easy transition. That very evening he had an appointment at the House of Commons, where he heard an animated debate on the Irish question between Mr. Balfour, Mr. Gladstone, Sir George Trevelyan and others, after which he dined with Sir Richard Webster in the crypt below, where may be seen every evening when Parliament is in session some of the most famous men of England. With Sir Richard were two of his sisters, and Sir William Hart Dyke and his wife, with the Solicitor-General and Mr. Henry Moskelyne.

Turning from Parliament, which has centuries of history behind it, Mr. Field found that England was not so old as to be above trying new experiments in government, the most notable of which was the London County Council, that had been introduced to take the place of the old "vestries," which, antiquated and cumbrous as they were, were yet so rooted in the very soil of England, like the oaks which had stood the storms of a thousand years, that it seemed that they could not be removed. Yet the Reformers did achieve the impossible in framing an ideal city government, which is almost as difficult as to frame that of a kingdom. To govern Paris is to govern France. It would be too much to say that to govern London is to govern England : but certainly a wise and just government of the greatest city in the world would be an "object lesson" to all cities and all countries.

Mr. Field was curious to see this new departure in city government, and Mr. Frederic Harrison, who was a member of the Council, took him to it, and introduced him to the President, Sir John Lubbock, who had succeeded Lord Rosebery. He found it to be composed of men of all ranks and conditions, from the Duke of Norfolk, the first Duke of the realm, to John Burns, the representative of the working classes. In one point it extended its membership further than any American body, as it had at least one member of the other sex, Miss Cobden, a daughter of the famous Richard Cobden. Whether it was that her gentle presence imposed a restraint upon the other members, the proceedings were as quiet and orderly as if they had been in a church. There was none of the hurly burly and confusion that one sees in the Chamber of Deputies in Paris or in our House of Representatives in Washington. Everything was conducted so purely with a single eye to business, that, if Mr. Field had been asked his opinion, and his pride as an American had not forbidden, I am afraid that he would have answered that London had the best municipal government in the world; while New York, with its Board of Aldermen, largely composed of Irish bar keepers, had the worst! Whether it will be better under the constitution of the Greater New York remains to be seen.

It was full midsummer when the Peace Congress opened. It had been organized only the year before in

Paris, where it had its first meeting, and now crossed the Channel, carrying out what in war might be called a strategic movement, recognizing the principle that to reach the people of a country, the most direct way is to advance on the capital, the centre of population. As became a country in which the Christian religion is recognized as the most potent influence for peace among men, its sessions were prefaced by a special service on the preceding Sunday in St. Paul's Cathedral, where seats were reserved for the delegates, and Canon H. Scott Holland preached a sermon on the text, "They shall beat their swords into ploughshares and their spears into pruning hooks."

On Monday morning the delegates assembled at the Westminster Town Hall, where they were met by the Organizing Committee, of which Mr. Hodgson Pratt was chairman and Mr. W. Evans Darby secretary. Nothing could be more grateful than the hearty English welcome. If they could only have had the presence of two of their old leaders! But Lord Shaftesbury, who had been the friend of Mr. Field for many years, and was foremost in every good cause, had gone to the grave; and the mighty voice of John Bright was forever silent. But the love of liberty, of justice, and of peace, which they had kindled in the hearts of their countrymen, remained behind them. It was also an inspiration to those who came from the Continent. France was represented by a Member of the Institute,

M. Frederic Passy, who took a very active part in the discussions, as did also Dr. Charles Richet, of the University of Paris, M. l'Abbé Defourny, and others, who read papers and made speeches in French. Whether it was the presence of the Gauls that kept away the Germans or not, there were but three representatives from Germany, one of whom was a resident of London, and another a lady, the widow of a German pastor, who had lived there; while the third, Mr. Gustav Meier, was a prominent citizen of Frankfort-on-the-Main, but too progressive and radical in opinion for the German authorities. He removed later to Switzerland. There were representatives from Italy and Spàin; Belgium and Holland; Denmark and Sweden; Austria and Servia; and even from Asia Minor and India.

In his welcome the Chairman had said: "We have desired to mark our international character by appointing a president who is not an Englishman, but a citizen of a friendly nation, on the other side of the Atlantic," and in the afternoon the Congress was formally opened by Mr. Field, who as he rose to speak, looked round on an audience such as is rarely assembled in London, or in any European capital. Of course, it was largely one of Englishmen, with a strong element of Americans, but with them were many of other countries who, if they spoke in different tongues, recognized one another as kindred in a common humanity.

Mr. Field began by disclaiming for the Congress any official character. "We are here," he said, "to do our part in influencing public opinion to promote the peace of nations. We have no authority from any government. We appeal—as we only can appeal—to the reason and the conscience of our fellow men." Then advancing immediately to his subject: the two great conditions of peace were Disarmament and Arbitration. The first was more of an European than an American question, as our army was so small that it would hardly serve for the smallest European State. Though our country spread across a continent, and our population was over sixty-four millions, yet our "standing army" numbered but twenty-five thousand soldiers! But it should be said in explanation that we really had no enemies: that our vast dominion was bounded, not by rival kingdoms, but by two oceans; so that we needed but two or three dozen regiments, which were distributed from the Atlantic to the Pacific; a regiment here and there holding a fort that guarded one of our great commercial cities, and that might, on occasion, serve as an aid to the police in case of mobs or riots; while other regiments were distributed on the border to protect the settlers against the Indians. As to the cost of our army, it was utterly insignificant for a nation so rich as ours.

But the moment we crossed the ocean all was changed. Here were great empires crowding one another, whose armies had swelled to hundreds of thousands, till the whole continent trembled under their mighty tread. The mere existence of such countless hosts, drawn up in battle array, was itself a provocation to war. And then the fearful cost! Even England, the richest nation in the world, felt the drain upon her vast resources. Said Mr. Field:

"The burdens of the warlike establishments of the Continental States are already grievous to be borne. Yet the German Emperor has just called for more batteries of artillery to be added to his vast army, that he may be able to cope with the ever-increasing armaments of France; and even in England—impregnable England—it seems to be a political maxim that her navy must always be kept on a level with any two navies in the world. In the admirable address of Mr. Charles Roundell, on the progress of the working classes of England during the present reign, it is stated that a calculation has been made for the purpose of showing how each pound of the national taxes has been spent during the present century. The calculation is, that there has been spent out of each pound:

	s.	d.
On war and preparations for war...........	16	3½
On all expenses of civil government........	3	8½

For all these wastes and woes there was but one remedy, an agreement between nations that, in case of difference, instead of rushing into war, the questions in dispute should be submitted to the impartial judgment of outside parties, that were not enemies to either, but friends to both! This was not a new thing under the sun. "Arbitration between States," said Mr. Field, "is as old as civilization."

"Two of the Grecian States, when Greece was in her glory, had a long-standing dispute about an island off their coast. They finally agreed to submit the dispute to arbiters, and the award was religiously kept. Since then the world has been deluged in blood, but now and then during the tempest a voice has been heard crying for the arbitrament of reason to replace the arbitrament of the sword. Henry of Navarre was one of those who cried for it, and the Papacy has more than once offered its mediation. Finally, when the Temple of Janus was closed in 1815, men turned their thoughts more than before to the means of preventing the reopening of the gates. If the means adopted have not been altogether successful, they have prevented some wars, and even one prevented is worth all the trouble that the friends of peace have ever taken.

Of this arbitration our two English-speaking countries had given a noble illustration. After our Civil War we were in anything but a friendly mood. A sense of wrong kept up a constant irritation, a feeling of bitterness, that might have continued to this day, if we had not agreed to submit our differences to an outside, and therefore an impartial, tribunal.

The Alabama arbitration was a lesson to the whole world. But the Americans had bettered the instruction by going one step further still in what we may call preventive arbitration, as it anticipates danger in case of any incident that excites the public, and prevents an explosion by the assurance that the matter will be fairly met, and fully explained, if not directly between the parties themselves, yet by reference to other countries that are friends of both. Only the year before the Congress in London, there had been an "International Conference" in Washington, composed of representatives of all the Republics of North, Central, and South America, which, after some weeks of deliberation, adopted arbitration as the principle of American International Law for the settlement of differences, disputes, or controversies that might arise between them! At the close of this conference Mr. Blaine, Secretary of State, bidding adieu to the delegates, said: "If in this closing hour the Conference had but one deed to celebrate, we should call the world's attention to the deliberate, confident, and solemn dedication of two great continents to peace. We hold up this new Magna Charta, which abolishes war, and substitutes arbitration between the American Republics, as the first and great fruit of the International American Conference."

The summer of 1890 may well be called a golden summer, as the very air seemed to be filled with peace:

> No war nor battle's sound
> Was heard the world around."

The whole earth was at rest and quiet. Hardly had the Peace Congress adjourned before it was followed by another assemblage, kindred but not the same, an

"Inter-Parliamentary Conference," composed of members of the Parliaments of different countries, who in meeting face to face came to that full understanding, which is the best assurance of peace. When their deliberations were over, they all sat down together at a feast of good will, at which Mr. Field was a guest, and when called upon for his word of cheer, answered briefly:

"My Lords and Gentlemen, I am going to preach you a very short sermon upon the text proposed by Mr. Shaw-Lefevre—an International Parliamentary movement. Last week I had the honor of being present at an unofficial Congress, composed of private individuals of many nations, earnestly bent on doing what they might to further the cause of international arbitration. To-night I am proud to address a body of Parliamentary representatives inspired by the same lofty ideal.

"I hear people declare us enthusiasts, dreamers, unpractical folk chasing a phantom. But stop a moment! Think a moment! Is it true that we are unpractical? What is that prayer we hear Sunday after Sunday, 'Give peace in our time, O Lord.' What does that mean? It means that we have the consciences of the world with us. Things change as time rolls on. Suppose the common people in the time of the Plantagenets and Tudors had claimed the right to manage the affairs of the nation. What would the nobles have said? But what do the nobles say now?

"We are called unpractical, but when the German Emperor demands more battalions for his armies, and a representative of the groaning German people rises in the Reichstag and asks with whose blood and whose money those battalions are to be paid for—is that unpractical? And when the statistician tells you Englishmen that during the whole of this century, for every pound of public money raised, 16*s.* $3\frac{1}{2}$*d.* have been spent for war—is that unpractical? And when you learn that to-day out of six hundred and seventy members of the House of Commons there are two hundred and thirty-four ready to vote for an arbitration treaty, and that if only one hundred more members will join us, the problem is solved—is that unpractical?

No! we are not visionaries in fighting the battle of civilization. The contest may be long, but the victory is sure. We may not see it in our day, but our children will, when the church bells shall ring all over the world for the coming of universal peace."

And was this gathering of the nations merely pomp and show, signifying nothing? On the contrary it was more sacred and binding than any treaty. From the hour when the Americans were taken into the hearts and homes of England, they could not help feeling that they were no more "aliens from the commonwealth of Israel," but fellow-heirs in the great inheritance of learning, of liberty, and of religion.

After the strain of this continued excitement Mr. Field felt the need of rest, and with his daughter and her two younger cadets (the eldest was on board his ship in the Mediterranean), took flight to the Continent. They had engaged rooms at Heidelburg, which had especial attractions to young students in its ancient university, as well as in its beautiful scenery on the Neckar. Leaving them in these picturesque surroundings Mr. Field went to Homburg, to which Americans flock not only for its waters, but for the great number of visitors from all parts of Europe, among whom are always some notable personalities.

A striking figure this summer was the old Duke of Cambridge, so long the commander in Chief of the English army, in which he succeeded the Duke of Wellington, to whom Mr. Field was introduced, and although watering-place acquaintances do not ordinarily amount to much, there seems to have been an attraction between these two old veterans. Again, a stranger of such commanding presence that he might have been a soldier, introduced himself as Sir Charles Russell. The two men were at once drawn to each other by the common interests of professional life, and by the relations of their two countries, and were soon plunged in a long conversation about the English bar and English politics. This first interview gave Mr. Field a very high opinion of his new acquaintance, so that it was no surprise, on the death of Lord Coleridge, to see Sir Charles Russell named at once for the succession as the Lord Chief Justice of England.

From these restful days Mr. Field was recalled to England to take part in another "Association" of which he was a member, and might almost be called the founder—that "for the Reform and Codification of the Law of Nations," which met this year at Liverpool.

Returning to London, he joined some American friends, with whom he had been invited to pay a visit to Winstead Abbey, the home of Byron, an invitation which appealed to one who could well remember when Byron was the idol of the youth of America, not only for his poetry, that will live as long as the English tongue, but for his romantic career, dying in Greece, where he had gone to join in the struggle for liberty.

Accepting the invitation, they left London for Newstead Station, where the carriage of Mr. Webb, the proprietor of the estate, was waiting for them. The Abbey is a mile and a half distant, to which they were driven between rows of trees to where a turn brought them in sight of the Abbey, the arch of the chapel standing in the gloaming naked against the sky. The rest of the old pile remains or has been restored.

They were welcomed with true English hospitality and introduced to whatever there was that had any association with the poet. Here was Byron's own room, with the bed on which he slept, and the old hall, where he had his revels with his friends. The room assigned to Mr. Field was the one occupied by Washington Irving when he visited the Abbey, to take in its features for the description in his Sketch Book. From the Abbey they were driven to Hocknall church, where the poet sleeps after his stormy life: and the evening was spent in looking over his manuscripts.

From this old Abbey Mr. Field and his friends flew away to Scotland to visit American friends on Loch Lomond, and then, returning to Liverpool, embarked for their home beyond the sea.

CHAPTER XXII.

VISIT FROM HIS DAUGHTER AND HER SONS—THE DEATH OF HIS BROTHER CYRUS.

To spend a season in London, in a constant round of public meetings and social engagements, may be very delightful, but would hardly be prescribed by a physician to a man in his eighty-sixth year. Mr. Field had an iron frame that could bear any amount of fatigue, but when he had crossed the sea he felt the reaction, and found it wise to reserve his remaining strength by going into winter quarters.

But to a man who never wanted for occupation the months were not long nor lonely, and he celebrated his eighty-sixth birthday with his brothers and nephews and nieces around him. In the evening General Sherman came in to offer his congratulations. They were warm friends, and found great pleasure in recalling their memories of former years. But the warrior's work was done. The next week he was taken ill and died in a few days. The funeral pageant was such as had not been seen in New York since that of General Grant, and was a warning to many of the veterans who followed him to the grave, among whom was Mr.

Field. The warning came none too soon, for in another week he, too, was in the hands of the doctor, who, after a careful examination, told him that his stout old heart did not beat quite so firm and strong as when he was in the full swing of lusty life. Its irregular beating was a danger signal. As he could not go abroad to see his dear ones, they must come to him. He took a house at Dobbs Ferry, where he was soon joined by his daughter and her two youngest sons, as the oldest was on board his ship. Thus the family that had been at Harrow the year before was established on the banks of the Hudson and passed a happy summer together.

It was not till the beginning of September that they took their leave. As Mr. Field's brother Cyrus had a yacht, which was always at the service of coming and departing guests, they all went on board for their last sail. It was a perfect day. The woods were beginning to be touched with their autumn hues, while light clouds were floating in the deep blue sky. In an hour or two the boat drew up at the Cunard dock, from which the voyagers waved their adieus to those on board the yacht as it turned and steamed up the river.

Mr. Field lingered in the country for some weeks to enjoy the beauty of the autumn, coming into town on the 12th of October. He was still under the doctor's care, but went out on the 3d of November to cast his vote for the first time under the new ballot, formed after the Australian model.

The next day saw him in a novel court. Though he had been all his life arguing cases at the bar, he had never been present at an ecclesiastical tribunal! Professor Briggs, of the Union Theological Seminary, was accused of heresy before the Presbytery of which I was a member, and I invited my brother to accompany me to hear his defence. It was written out in full, and the reading took two hours and a half. But Mr. Field, who was always interested in a subtle argument, sat to the end, though I am afraid that he did not go away with increased respect for our church courts, when he saw an eminent scholar arraigned because of his interpretation of some passages in the Old Testament. But he was not much concerned about the issue, for he was sure that, sooner or later, truth would make its way. He was content to say with Galileo, "The world does move!"

The winter was a very quiet one, as the rigors of the season kept him within doors, but even then there was an exhilaration in looking out through the frosted panes at the flying snow. Though shut up among his books, he was not without company in the great minds that spoke to him from the printed page, while he was still an interested observer of the events of the passing time. His friends, too, felt it to be a privilege to spend an hour in conversation with him, so that he was never lonely, and when he completed his eighty-seventh year, looking backward on the life that was nearly ended, and forward to the longer life that was soon to begin, he thus moralized with himself:

What is it *now* to live? It is to breathe
The air of heaven, behold the pleasant earth,
The shining rivers, the inconstant sea,
Sublimity of mountains, wealth of clouds,
And radiance o'er all of countless stars.
It is to sit before the cheerful hearth
With groups of friends and kindred, store of books,
  Rich heritage from ages past;
  Hold sweet communion soul with soul,
On things now past, or present or to come,
Or muse alone upon my earlier days,
  Unbind the scroll whereon is writ
  The story of my busy life,
Mistakes too often, but successes more,
And consciousness of duty done.
It is to see with laughing eyes the play
  Of children sporting on the lawn,
  Or mark the eager strifes of men
  And nations, seeking each and all,
  Belike advantage to obtain
  Above their fellows; such is man!
It is to feel the pulses quicken, as I hear
  Of great achievements near or far
    Whereon may turn perchance
The fate of generations ages hence.
It is to rest with folded arms betimes,
  And so surrounded, so sustained,
  Ponder on what may yet befall
  In that unknown mysterious realm

Which lies beyond the range of mortal ken,
Where souls immortal do forever dwell,
Think of the loved ones who await me there,
And without murmuring or inward grief,
With mind unbroken and no fear,
Calmly await the coming of the Lord.

With such serenity he contemplated the future. But he could not be insensible to the sorrow of one so dear to him as his brother Cyrus, whose life had been not only one of great activity and distinction, but of complete domestic happiness. Married at the age of twenty-one, he had lived with the wife of his youth for half a century. Only a few months before they had celebrated their golden wedding, with congratulations from both sides of the ocean. But the next summer, when they had removed to their beautiful home on the Hudson, she was taken ill, and died at the close of autumn, to be followed in a few months by their eldest daughter, which, with other sorrows, quite broke his heart.

From that moment he lost his interest in life. He had no heart to go anywhere, but once came with Dudley to us on my birthday. It seemed to comfort him to be with his brothers, and we tried all our gentle arts to cheer him. He brightened a little and once or twice a smile passed over his sad face. But his heart was in the grave, and we could not repress the foreboding that this family meeting might be our last, and so it proved. In June he went to the country, and there in midsummer the end came. In the diary which Dudley kept, he recalls the final scene :

"July 12th. Our dear brother Cyrus breathed his last this morning. He had been ailing and mourning all the while since our dinner at Henry's, but in June he was moved to his country seat at Dobbs Ferry, where he hoped he might revive, and he did a little, but it was only a flush of life from the country air, and so he lingered, sometimes better, sometimes worse. Stephen arrived from Washington a week before, and Henry from Stockbridge, and both remained at the house and were with him constantly. I went two or three times a day from Hastings, where Laura [the wife of Dudley, Jr.] was occupying her old home. This morning Stephen and Henry sent for me to hasten to Cyrus's bedside. I knew what the message meant, and went at once. I found him unconscious, but breathing still ; we watched him closely, sitting by his bedside, the three brothers, Mrs. Judson and her two sons. Hemorrhage from the lungs set in, and at 9:50 his lips ceased to move. His busy life was ended.

"A simple religious service was held at his house on Thursday afternoon, and the next morning we went in a funeral train to Stockbridge, where we rode slowly through the village street, so beautiful with its long avenue of maples and elms, to the old Congregational

Church, in which our father had preached for so many years, and the beloved form was laid in the aisle before the pulpit. The service was very simple: only a prayer, with reading of the Scriptures and the singing of one or two favorite hymns; and the procession formed again, and moved across the green to the burying ground where our father and mother lay, and where his wife had been laid but a few weeks before. There, in the sweet summer afternoon, we laid him to rest in a bed of ferns and pine boughs and covered with flowers. Peacefully now he sleeps where he so often said he wished to sleep, by the side of his wife and close to his father and mother, his sister and his oldest son. Long as any of us survive, shall we cherish the memory of our beloved brother."

ARTOTYPE. E. BIERSTADT, N. Y.

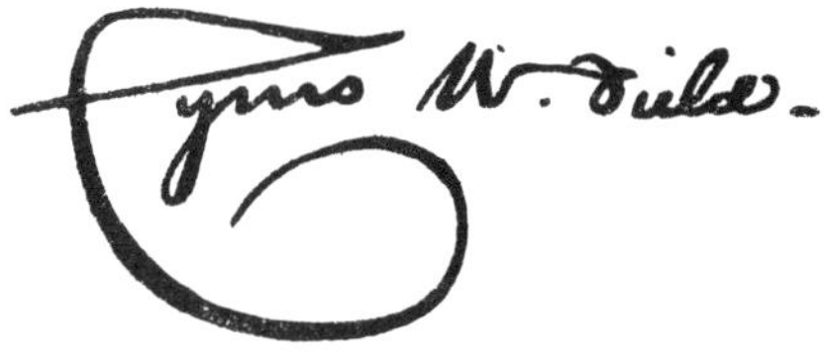

PHOTO. BY SARONY

CHAPTER XXIII.

THE LAST SUMMER AMONG THE HILLS.

The summer of 1893 Mr. Field did not spend abroad. One year before we had laid our dear Cyrus to rest beside his kindred, among the hills where he was born, and his eldest brother could not but choose to pass the following summer—the last, as it proved, that he was to spend on earth—in the quiet valley so dear to us all from its associations with the living and the dead.

As Mr. Field's house on the hill top in Stockbridge was much too large for his diminished household, he took up his home for the summer in the village, in "Laurel Cottage," that was full of pleasant memories as it had belonged to his second wife.*

It is in a quiet nook, embowered among the trees,

---

*Mr. Field was three times married, first to Jane Lucinda Hopkins, of Stockbridge, who was the mother of his children, who died in 1836; second to Mrs. Harriet Davidson, the widow of James Davidson, who died in 1864: and third to Mrs. Mary Elizabeth Carr, the widow of Dr. Samuel J. Carr, a physician of Baltimore, who died in 1876. "Laurel Cottage" has since been made familiar to the public by the delightful letters of Matthew Arnold, who occupied it in the summer of 1886.

with a background on one side of the rocky knoll of Laurel Hill, at the foot of which the Housatonic flows gently under the willows. Mr. Field's room was on the second floor, in the rear, looking South, so that it was full of sunshine, while from the window he looked down the green slope to the river, beyond which rose the wooded side of Bear Mountain, so named from the bears that were once as numerous among the rocks and trees as were the Indians who built their wigwams in the valley below.*

And if there was sunshine without there was sunshine within. He was always sitting at his table, reading or writing, but ready to lay down book or pen to talk on the topics of the day, on which he gave his

---

*Possibly his interest was increased because of a feeling almost of reverence for the primeval forest. The sound of the woodman's axe had no music to his ears, and he was almost indignant at the farmers, who swept acres upon acres, leaving the earth naked and bare. This he looked upon as a kind of desecration, and from time to time bought large tracts to save the forests, so that at last he found himself the owner of a whole mountain side. Of this he gave to the town fifty-eight acres, including the Ice Glen, a deep gorge in the mountain (which had apparently been rent asunder by an earthquake), that for its wildness is a favorite resort of the young people, who come at night, when the darkness is lighted up by flaming torches, which but magnify the surrounding gloom and perchance give a creeping chill to the young men and maidens, that is only removed as they emerge by a dance on the green !

opinions freely, and was no less ready to listen to mine, however little they might be worth, from which we wandered off to graver subjects, for his mind was so active that he was ready to talk on the law or the Gospel, on politics or religion.

It may surprise some who did not know the man to be told that our conversations were often on the gravest subjects—of the supernatural and the life to come. He did not talk of these things with everybody. As he did not intrude into the opinions of others, no stranger would presume to catechise him as to his belief or unbelief. But, like every thoughtful man, he was not without his questionings about the great mysteries of life, and when he was with an old friend, like Mark Hopkins, he talked freely. But now that friend was gone, and he had his own silent, solitary thoughts. As he rode over the hills, and saw the sun going down in the west, he could but reflect how soon he would sink below the horizon. And then what? Was it all a blank? or was there another life that was to begin? Man's breath goeth forth from his nostrils. But is the soul only a breath? Is thought only the vibration of particles of the brain, as the strings of an instrument give forth sound? When the instrument is broken the music is gone. Why may not the last sigh of the departing soul be the utter going out of life, growing fainter and fainter till it is lost in the eternal silence?

All these questions hung on the greater one of the existence of God. Mr. Field had in his college days studied Butler's Analogy and Paley's Natural Theology, and accepted their conclusions. But with his logical mind he was always open to argument, and was not afraid to look any proofs squarely in the face, even if they led him to annihilation! Such a man could not be indifferent to the scientific speculations of the day, supported as they were by new discoveries. Darwin had made a great stir in the scientific world by his work entitled "Origin of Species by Means of Natural Selection," followed up by "The Descent of Man," in which he attempts to trace it to a development from a lower order of animal life. Indeed he did not hesitate to picture the ancestor of the human race, saying that "Man is descended from a hairy quadruped, furnished with a tail and pointed ears, probably arboreal in its habits!" This was an ancestry that was not very flattering to our pride, but the theory was caught up by the atheists of the Continent as doing away with the need of an Author of all things. But in America there was at least one man of science, Louis Agassiz, who was not carried away by this assumption of superior knowledge: as I once heard him declare in the ringing voice that bespoke a conviction which nothing could shake, that the adaptation of means to an end, which runs through nature, is the infallible token of *mind*, the proof of an intelligent Creator.

Another great authority was equally positive. In the year 1884 the British Association for the Promotion of Science met for the first time on this side of the Atlantic, in Montreal, and among the distinguished men who came to it was Sir William Thomson, now Lord Kelvin. As he had been closely associated with our brother Cyrus in the laying of the Atlantic cable, the latter claimed him as his guest as soon as he landed in America. On his way to Montreal, he came to us in our country home, and spent a few days in the Berkshire Hills. Of course I could not lose the opportunity of questioning such an authority on the relation of science and religion—questions which he met with the coolness of a philosopher, to whom nothing was sacred but truth. He thought that the much vaunted theory of natural selection had had its day. Cold and cheerless as it was, he would not shrink from it, if it was supported by evidence. But it was, to use the form of a Scotch verdict, "unproven." "But what," I asked, "do you say to the bold prediction of Tyndall that 'in matter will yet be found the promise and the potency of all life?'" to which he answered with a smile, "I do not think Tyndall would say that *now;*" and then he told me how Pasteur had exploded the theory of spontaneous generation ; and gave me his own opinion that the argument from design in the material world, as wrought out in what he called "that excellent old book, Paley's Natural Theology," was *unanswerable !*

All these points I talked over with my brother for hours, and he assented to the conclusions, but never argued about it, for the questions were too awful to be discussed like a point of law. Sometimes he sat silent, leaning his head upon his hand, with a far-away look, as if he was peering into the distant and unknown. A photograph taken, I know not where, perhaps on the other side of the globe, shows him in these thoughtful moods, as I have seen him a thousand times.

But happy as he was this last summer in riding about the Berkshire Hills, yet as the season drew on, and the autumn leaves began to fall, I perceived a yearning for the dear ones beyond the sea, and he said, "I want to see my daughter once more, and my boys," as he always called his grandsons, even when they were nearly grown to manhood. Indeed the eldest, who bore his grandfather's name of Dudley, had just reached his majority, and it was partly to celebrate this event that he wished to spend the coming Christmas in England. If he could but once more be with that beloved group, he could die happy. The doctors shook their heads, for he had not yet fully recovered from the illness of three years before. But love carried it over prudence and that last satisfaction was given him. Leaving home late in the autumn, in two weeks he was sitting before the open fire at the home of his daughter in East Grinstead, in Sussex, about thirty miles from London, to which Lady Musgrave had removed after her sons had finished their studies at Harrow. Here they were all gathered round him. Dudley was already a midshipman in the navy, but fortunately his ship was now in an English port, so that he was able almost every Sunday to visit his mother and grandfather. Arthur was in the military school at Woolwich, while the youngest, Herbert, had made his studies for the same profession, and had gone through his examinations, but had not yet heard the result, for which he was waiting with no small anxiety, as there were four hundred candidates, and only fifty appointments. But one morning The Times brought the full report, from which it appeared that he was, not only one of the fifty, but the second on the list! This was, of course, immensely gratifying to the young soldier, and to his mother and brothers, but perhaps most of all to his grandfather, in whom the paternal instinct was very strong. It did one's heart good to see the mixture of pride and affection that glowed in his face as he looked round the little circle of those who had his blood in their veins. If he was ambitious for his grandsons, it was only that as they grew in years they should develop a manliness that gave promise of an honorable career. In a pamphlet of "Personal Recollections" which he had prepared for his grandchildren, he closes with this tender farewell to those who should come after him:

"Here, in the middle of my eighty-eighth year, I

close what are hardly worthy to be called 'Reminiscences,' since they are little more than a succession of dates, with names of persons and places. But even these have their use. The dates of the years as they pass are so many milestones to mark the successive stages of our life's journey : while the names of places far apart on the face of the globe, tell of the goings to and fro : and as a background for the personalities that appear as actors on the stage, they recall the varied scenes and occupations of a long and laborious life. These guide posts will be of service at least to my grandchildren, who from these 'Notes' may turn back to the 'Diaries,' where all is detailed with greater fullness, from which they may know what manner of man their grandfather was. To them he leaves this brief story of his life, only reminding them that, on whichever side of the ocean their lot may be cast, the elements of true manhood are the same ; and bequeathing to them, as their best inheritance, the love of freedom, the spirit of independence ; fidelity in every position, private or public ; and the traditions of truth, justice and honor."

CHAPTER XXIV.

HOMEWARD BOUND—THE GOING DOWN OF THE SUN.

Delightful as are the homes of England, the country is not quite the same in December as in May. It is now as when Keats wrote the exquisite lines:

> "St. Agnes' eve! ah, bitter chill it was;
> The owl with all his feathers was a' cold."

Although Sussex is in the south, and its chalk hills rise up like the cliffs of Dover, as if to protect the land from the sea, yet the winds sweep over the South Downs, and howl round castle and cottage. Mr. Field, accustomed to the blazing fires of America, had to wrap himself up very warmly, and still felt that the climate of England in winter was not quite suited to one of his age; and after the Christmas holidays were over, and the grandfather's heart was filled with joy and pride, he bade adieu to the household so dear to him, and accompanied only by his faithful valet, Watson, who had been with him for years, he crossed the Channel to Paris, where he found his "nice and warm apartment waiting for him" at his old quarters in the Hotel Bristol. Though it was mid-winter Paris was as gay as ever. But he was so eager to get into a warmer climate that he left the same night for Cannes, though he missed the luxury of travel to which he had been accustomed in America. "The *train de luxe*," he said, "is a misnomer: there is no luxury in it!" But any feeling of discomfort vanished as he reached Marseilles, and looked out on the glittering Mediterranean.

Nice was bathed in sunshine. His hotel was on the quay, and even in mid-winter, January 15th, he reports: "The sun is shining all glorious this morning." His letters seem to breathe the warmth of the atmosphere. He writes to his daughter:

"Of course I greatly miss your companionship, and that of my dear boys, but I am better off in this climate. The sun has shone brightly the five days that I have been on the Riviera, and I am perfectly comfortable. My faithful Watson guards me. I took a walk with him before lunch along the boulevard, which skirts the bay for a mile or so. The scene was a gay one, such as only France can exhibit: all sorts of people and all sorts of vehicles, and I might add all sorts of amusements. The French are an amiable and volatile people, with a streak of the tiger in them!"

And now the sea itself took on a new interest, when a letter from England informed him that his oldest grandson, who was a midshipman in the navy, and had been waiting orders, had been ordered to the East India squadron. He answered at once:

"This is good news if the station is healthy. I suppose that on board the ship one is protected from disease more than on land. God prosper the dear fellow! How fortunate it is that I came over as I did, and could see all my brave boys and you together. Give Dudley my warmest love and wish him every good fortune. Keep up your heart, my darling!"

Writing again, he asked about the ship and her commander, and was gratified to get the best reports, not only of the superior officers, but of his fellow midshipmen. A few days later he writes: "Before this my dear Dudley is off on his way to his duty in the service to which he has devoted himself for life. What a dear brave fellow he is! He will yet do us all credit, I firmly believe."

Happy dreams of a proud grandfather, which warmed his heart every time he thought of "his boy" on his way to India to the brilliant career which had been pictured for him. Happy in his anticipations, he was happy also that he did not live to suffer the bitterness of disappointment. But only a few months after his own death in America, came the tidings that the grandson who bore his name and had given such promise for the future, had died on the other side of the globe, in the harbor of Bombay.

From Nice Mr. Field took his journey by easy stages: resting a couple of days at Monte Carlo; and again at Mentone, where a daughter of his brother Cyrus, Mrs. Andrews, had lived for many years.

When he reached Genoa, he laid out his plan for the rest of the winter. He had six weeks to spend in Italy, and dividing the time so as to get the most out of it, he thought it wiser, instead of going direct to Florence and Rome and Naples, to reverse the order and sail from Genoa to Naples, so as to be at once in the warmest climate, where he might spend a couple of weeks, and then come north slowly, so as to be in Rome for the Holy Week, and wind up with Florence, from which it would be an easy day's journey back to Genoa, from which he was to sail for America.

This was an excellent division of time, which he carried out with a military precision, and with a success beyond his anticipations. He wrote from Naples, "The weather is so mild that I do not need a fire. I have no sensation of cold; and being careful to keep out of the night air, I feel as safe as if I were in Stockbridge or Gramercy Park." And then, looking out upon the Mediterranean, he adds: "Dudley is by this time far on his way to Port Said. I can imagine the dear fellow sailing past Naples in this 'great and wide sea.' God bless him and you all!" One day he spent in an excursion to Pompeii, and found the excavations greatly extended since his visit fifty-seven years before! Looking back through all those years it was like recalling a past existence to sit in the Grand Hotel du Vesuve, and look out upon the bay that never loses its beauty, and see the smoke of Vesuvius ascending as he had seen it in the long ago of more than half a century.

Yet with all the attractions of Naples those of Rome were greater. The very next morning after his arrival he was in St. Peter's, and "To-morrow," he writes, "I intend to visit the Coliseum, and other monuments of old Rome. But I restrain myself to two or three hours a day." He had reason to be on his guard, for nothing is more wearying than sight-seeing. In his younger days he had explored them all, going day after day to the Forum and the Capitol; seeking out the spot where "great Cæsar fell;" and riding along the Appian Way, where he could almost hear the tramp of the Roman legions, returning from the wars,

> "Bringing many captives home to Rome,
> Whose ransom did the public coffers fill."

If he had not now the strength for such fatiguing excursions, it was something still "to breathe that haunted air."

But modern Rome, if it be not quite so imposing to the imagination as ancient Rome, is still the Capital, and combines more to attract the stranger than any other Italian city. He found the climate but little changed from that of Naples. There it had been almost too warm for an overcoat; while in Rome the air was a little crisp, but all the more bracing. He writes to his daughter: "If you could see me basking in the full light of an Italian sun, you would think me well off. All is cheerful about me. Our hotel (the Quirinal) is excellent, the city is clean, the streets are full of people, all seeming interested in something; life is in its best estate as far as outward appearances go."

With so many attractions, it is not surprising that Rome should bring together, more than any other city in Europe except Paris, a very miscellaneous society, as it is from many countries; and a very charming one, as it includes artists and authors and scholars studying ancient history; and notable public men: French deputies or English Members of Parliament; who, to prolong the Christmas holidays, find no winter resort so full of interest as the "Eternal City."

Rome has also a large American colony. The hotel was full of Americans, who appeared at a reception given by Mrs. John Hay in numbers equal to the weekly reception of the American Minister. In this goodly company no one was more welcome than Mr. Field himself. Wherever he went he was surrounded by friends and admirers, who were all delighted with the youthfulness of one who seemed to belong to another generation. Those who had known him in former years said they had never seen him more full of life; at once enjoying more and contributing more to the enjoyment of others.

Those whom he had known in his earlier visits were

few, but it was good to look into their faces again. The oldest of these was the American artist Terry, who had lived in Rome half a century, and his charming wife, whose first husband was the famous sculptor Crawford, and who was the mother of the popular author, Marion Crawford. As Mr. Field's birthday (February 13th) was at hand, they would have him to dine with them. He felt it to be hardly prudent to be out in the evening, but could not deny himself the pleasure of sitting down at luncheon with such dear old friends. The same day he wrote to his daughter in a tone of grateful satisfaction with the past and calm contemplation of the future: "I am stronger than I was a year ago, when I passed my birthday with the Judge in Washington. The voyage and the sea and the journey since have done me good, and above all the visit to you and the sight of my boys has created a soul under the ribs of death." But in his last words there is a tone of sadness that is almost prophetic: "What may be in store for us in the year now entered upon God only knows. I only know that we must keep brave hearts, prepared for any event, and seeking to do our duty whatever may befall."

Next to Rome in its attraction to those who come over the sea, is Florence, where every winter brings together a large foreign population, in which are hundreds of English and American visitors: and here, as at Rome, Mr. Field's countrymen gave him a hearty welcome. Among the resident Americans no one is better known than Professor Fiske, of Cornell University, who has lived here for years, which he has devoted to collecting rare books. His early editions of Petrarch are of such value that he keeps them locked up in cases as he would precious jewels. Another treasure is a collection of Icelandic literature! Most of us hardly know that Iceland ever had a literature. It would seem as if the intense cold would freeze the very blood and brains of the inhabitants. But the long evenings have been favorable to reading and to writing also. Here is a Bible centuries older than Luther's, and a collection of other volumes which show that there was a dawn of letters in this far away island, almost in the Arctic circle, long before the Renaissance came in Central and Southern Europe.

Among the well-known virtues of our American professor is that of hospitality to his countrymen, which he shows in the most delightful way. He would come in his carriage to take Mr. Field to a drive to the Tower of Galileo, or to some other of the beautiful points of view around Florence; and next bring the codifier of America face to face at his table with one of the most distinguished of jurists and statesmen of Italy; and again give him a reception at which he could meet the best representatives of Italian society as well as the English and American residents. These courtesies made his visit so pleasant that he could say truly, "My days are passing serenely in Florence."

But such days always come to an end, and he took his way to Genoa, from which on the 28th of March he writes to his daughter:

"It is now eleven o'clock and we go on board at four. So these are my last words before reaching my own beloved land. We leave Genoa at ten to-morrow, and go first to Naples, touch at Gibraltar, and through the Azores direct to New York, where our arrival is promised for the 9th of April.

"Ever lovingly

"Your father,

"DAVID DUDLEY FIELD."

With this last message of affection to the one he loved most on earth, he embarked the next morning from the birthplace of Columbus, for the new world that Columbus discovered, and on a ship that bore the name of Columbia!

Looking, as we were somewhat anxiously, for his safe return, we counted the days from the time that the good ship passed the Straits of Gibraltar. Although it was April, the voyage was so tempestuous that most of the passengers kept snugly in their berths. But no storm could drive him below. He was so superior to the weakness of others that he hardly showed the proper degree of sympathy. I always told him that such indifference was from the absence of the sensibilities which belong to our poor human nature, which only provoked his amusement, for nothing in nature thrilled him in every nerve like a storm at sea.* The rough weather did not abate till they were in sight of our coast, and indeed the Columbia entered our harbor in what Americans would call a blizzard! As soon as she was reported to be coming up the bay, I set off for the pier of the Hamburg American Line, in Hoboken. The ship was at the dock, and Mr. Field had just driven away. Following to Gramercy Park, I found him not at all the worse for his voyage. As soon as he heard my voice he called to me, and as I entered the room, he was standing with his back to a blazing fire, and threw his arms around me, saying, "I was never better in my life!" That brotherly embrace I shall never forget:

"Ah, little thought we 'twas our last!"

Even now, as I think of him those arms are round me still.

Going up to his library, we spent an hour in ex-

---

* The Rev. Dr. Van Dyke, of New York, who was his fellow passenger, wrote afterwards that "on the voyage he was so happy, so energetic, and such an inspiring companion, that in spite of his great age he seemed young. Those days on the sea were pleasant to him; and he increased the pleasure of others. I shall always be glad to think that I was his fellow-traveller and privileged to listen to his wise and cheerful conversation."

changing the experiences of the winter. He had much to tell of England, France and Italy, while I could only supply the domestic incidents of which he wished to hear. But no matter what was the subject, he entered into it and gave his opinion with all his old-time freedom. Recalling it since, I have asked myself if there was any trace of feebleness or mental decrepitude, and I cannot recall the slightest. Although he was in his ninetieth year, there was no confusion of thought or language. He was within a few hours of the end of life, and yet his mind was as clear, and his conversation as fresh and vigorous, as if he were but seventy or fifty. Whatever weakness might touch his stalwart frame, his intellect never grew old!

I came again in the afternoon, but a reporter was with him, and our conversation was deferred till the next day. We never looked into each other's eyes again. That very night, about three o'clock, he awoke with a chill and rang for his valet, who was so well trained and experienced that he was competent to act as nurse and almost as doctor, who did everything to relieve him. But as soon as his physician could be called, he found that the chill was the forerunner of pneumonia. Watson said that there had been some delay at the pier after the ship reached it, and that Mr. Field went suddenly from the warm cabin into the cold air on the dock. His old heart trouble, from which the doctor said he had probably not been entirely free any time during the last twenty or twenty-five years, reappeared, and he sank from hour to hour. I saw him that afternoon, and calling his name, there was a faint sign of recognition, but he did not speak. After a consultation, the physicians thought he still might rally, and that I could safely go home. But at three o'clock in the morning the nurse called the doctor, who saw at a glance that, as one expressed it, "the great lawyer was going before the greatest Judge," and in half an hour, without a tremor, a motion or a sigh, the heart stood still.

Coming so suddenly, the shock to us was terrible. But when we recovered our self-possession, we could not but reflect on what might have been: that he might have died on the other side of the ocean, in a foreign country, surrounded by strangers; or on the voyage, in which case we should have had sorrow upon sorrow. But he had reached his country, and died under his own roof, among his kindred. Nor could the summons have come more gently. The footsteps of death had been as soft as the footsteps of angels. As long as he was conscious of anything, it was of home, and of the love and the tenderness here and beyond the sea.

And, after all, the work to which he had devoted his life was done. He had but one remaining ambition (to be sure it was a pretty large one), that his codes should be adopted all over the world! He said:

"They are written and published. It is only a question of time when they will be accepted." He was going up into the Berkshire Hills (for which he waited only till the apple blossoms should appear), where he would spend the summer, not only in the scenes most dear to him, but in an occupation to which he had looked forward with eager interest. It was to put on record the story of his long and somewhat stormy life, that would be a history of the great battle for Law Reform, in which he had been foremost for more than half a century. Thus he was twice happy in the past and the future; in his memories and his anticipations; when he closed his eyes for the last time and sank to his rest.

As only the day before the city papers had announced his arrival from Europe in robust health, few knew even of his illness, so that the announcement of his death was a surprise. One of the first to whom word was sent was Mr. Choate, who had been for years his neighbor in Stockbridge. He came immediately, and, as he looked upon the marble brow of one who was but a few hours before so full of life, he said that he had never seen anything so majestic in death; that

> "He lay like a warrior taking his rest,
> With his martial cloak around him."

As soon as the bulletins announced the sad event, there was a general feeling among the people to whom his form and figure had been familiar for half a century, that a great personality had disappeared, whose like they should not see again. Every public tribute was paid to his memory. The flag upon the City Hall was hung at half-mast. The courts adjourned, with appropriate words from the bench. The Legislature was then in session and, to quote the report from Albany, "the news of the death of this great man wakened a feeling of profound regret." The speaker, who announced it in the Senate, said: "He died crowned with honor. His life was a lesson and an inspiration." Both houses adjourned in respect to his memory, and appointed committees to attend his funeral.

The last service was on Sunday afternoon in Calvary church, where he had attended for forty years, which was crowded by representatives of the old families of New York, and a large deputation from Williams College, with the President at their head. The pall-bearers were : Chief Justice Fuller, of the Supreme Court of the United States ; Charles Butler, who was over ninety years of age ; William M. Evarts, Joseph H. Choate, John Bigelow and Abram S. Hewitt ; Judges Charles Andrews and A. R. Lawrence and ex-Judge Charles A. Peabody ; Chancellor MacCracken, Robert E. Deyo, H. H. Anderson and Robert M. Gallaway.

The services were, as he would have wished, very simple, with no eulogy. It was enough to hear in the arches above the echo of the voice that has sounded through all the centuries, "I am the Resurrection and the Life, saith the Lord: he that believeth in Me, though he were dead, yet shall he live!"

The next morning we bore him away to the Hills, to which his eyes had been turned, and laid him down under a weeping willow, whose long tresses drooped over his place of rest, beside the graves of those he loved.

When we came back from that visit to the house prepared for all the living, a great element had gone out of our lives, and the world seemed emptier than before. But if public applause could make up for the loneliness of grief, we had it in an abundance that was quite overwhelming. The tributes from the press were such as I have never seen at the death of any one except our martyred Presidents, or the heroes of the war. This took me by surprise, for with all my love for him, I could not but remember that he had been a man of war from his youth, and I looked for some sharp criticisms, but every voice was hushed, and all recognized the immense service which he had rendered to his country. One editor indeed, who is second to none of his brethren in America, placed him high among the lawgivers of history, and as such among the benefactors of mankind.

When a man who has been so long in the public eye passes away, the first question that will arise in some minds is as to the benefactions that he left behind him. These were things which Mr. Field never spoke of. His codes were his best legacies. But, as to the minor point, although it is something which does not concern the public, I may dismiss it in a few words which will be quite sufficient. As some thought of Mr. Field as of a cold temperament, absorbed in his own affairs, now that he is gone, we may lift the veil of privacy, and show him as he was.

Certainly he was not of the number of those who throw away money right and left, where it might do as much harm as good. His gifts were prompted by personal attachments. He had the feeling of a child towards the place where he was born. Our parents, to whom we owed everything, were married in 1803, so that 1878 measured off three-quarters of a century, and on the very wedding day, the last day of October, the four brothers who were living, went up to the old home in Haddam, Conn., to dedicate two small parks which they gave for the recreation of the inhabitants, one on the site of the old meeting-house, where our father preached for years, and the other on "Isinglass Hill," a bold, rocky eminence rising behind the village, where the older brothers used to play. There was a large gathering of the people, who seemed much pleased with this remembrance of the old town. Some years after, when our eldest brother died, it was found that in his will he had given $5,000 to Haddam, that the parks might be laid out with taste by the planting of trees, with open lawns between, that they should be an inheritance to the people forever. The same home feeling had led him to give $10,000 for the tower in Stockbridge, to which he added in his will $5,000 for the ringing of the chimes at sunset. Of public objects the first in his eye was Williams College, to which he gave first and last $40,000.

But there was one act of beneficence, done in secret, that was still more characteristic. When Chief Justice Taney died he left two daughters who were literally penniless, and had to support themselves by writing in the departments. When this came to be known, there was a general feeling that it was not quite to the honor of the profession that the daughters of the Chief Justice of the Supreme Court of the United States should be left to want. At a meeting in Washington the case was stated delicately, and it was assumed that the bar would deem it not only its duty but its pleasure to look after the family. But the sympathy did not go beyond the stage of oratory. Chagrined at this failure to pay what he regarded as a debt of honor, Mr. Field gave to the clerk of the Supreme Court his bond to remit to one of the daughters $500 a year during her life, which he paid from 1873 till her death in 1891, thus contributing $9,000 to save the credit of the bar. This he did when he had never seen the daughters, nor the Chief Justice himself, except on the bench, and though his decision in the Dred Scott case was very repulsive to him. The incident is enough to show that, if he was careful as to whom he gave, when his heart was touched he was a very generous man.

But the gift of money is the least of all gifts, for if given unwisely, it will only make the poor poorer, and more dependent than before. It is not charity that men want, but justice. If it be a good deed to step forward to defend a poor man in the courts, it is better still to give him a law by which he can protect himself. Teach him his rights, and he can stand on his feet, calling no man master. When he is on the same level as the rich man he is lifted up with a feeling of self-respect. He is as good as anybody. There is one law for all men. No man is so high as to be above its power: and none so low as not to be under its protection.

But how far have the reforms of the law introduced by Mr. Field extended? Are they not limited to a few States, so that in point of fact but a small portion of the American people share in these benefits, real or imagined? This is not a question for argument, but for statistics, for which I do not trust to any knowledge of my own, but to the authority of one who is as well informed as any man in the country. To my inquiry how far the new codes have been adopted in the United States he replies as follows:

"NEW YORK, January 12, 1898.

"DEAR DR. FIELD:

"Your brother's codes, with such modifications as were deemed necessary to accommodate them to each locality, were adopted in whole or in part in Twenty-seven States and Territories.

"But, in addition to this, the principles of your brother's Code of Civil Procedure, and especially its fundamental doctrine of fusion of law and equity, have made their way in so many other States, that I do not know of any, outside of New England, Delaware, Kentucky, Louisiana, Maryland, New Jersey, Pennsylvania and Tennessee, which have not been seriously affected by the influence of his codes. As to these, Louisiana is still governed practically by the French law; Pennsylvania had united law and equity long before the codes were framed; and there was really not so much occasion for reforms in that direction in New England as in other parts of the country. Even in the excepted States, the old common law practice hardly exists, outside of New Jersey, Delaware and Pennsylvania. In fact, the principal difference between States which have adopted the codes and those which have not is that in the latter the process of reform has been carried out by cutting away useless forms instead of by positive constructive work.

"THOMAS G. SHEARMAN."

This was an extraordinary statement, but it only

whetted my appetite for something still more exact. States and territories are indefinite quantities, ranging from forty thousand inhabitants in Nevada to six millions in the State of New York. The total result would be more satisfactory if the separate statements could be transmuted into the aggregate population, for which I applied to the same high authority, and received the following answer :

"NEW YORK, January 18, 1898.

MY DEAR DR. FIELD :

"In reply to your inquiry I have made a hasty calculation, from which I judge that, assuming our population in 1890 to have been 63,000,000, 38,000,000 of those resided in States where your brother's codes of practice have been in substance adopted. But the fundamental principle of those codes—that is, the fusion of law and equity, and the administration of justice in a single court, instead of being divided between a court of law and a court of chancery—have been adopted in States containing much more than nine-tenths of all the population. Of course, some of these, such as Pennsylvania, had adopted this principle long before the date of your brother's codes ; but for the most part, this change is a result of the codes.

"THOMAS G. SHEARMAN."

This is simply astounding. It is a revolution. The computation of thirty-eight millions is made on the basis of the census of 1890. But Mr. Field lived till

1894, and the natural increase of these four years would be at least two millions, making a total of forty millions!

But can such sweeping changes be permanent? Those who were opposed to the codes from the beginning, have explained their success as a craze for reform, which had swept over the country as a tidal wave, but which would be followed by a reaction, and pass away as swiftly as it came. This is indeed possible, but is it probable? We can only judge of the future by the past. So far we have yet to learn of a single State or Territory that, having adopted these codes, has gone back to the "beggarly elements" of the old, tedious and roundabout way of obtaining justice. "Revolutions do not go backward," at least peaceful revolutions that are in the line of human progress. If the new laws are better than the old why should they not stand till they are superseded by codes that are better still? But this is a free country, and we are not responsible for what may be done by a future generation. We read in the Bible that once the sun went backward, but we hardly expect to see the miracle repeated in our day.

Accustomed as we are to see our legislatures meeting from year to year, and enacting new provisions of law, we are apt to think of laws as transitory things, which change with the ever-shifting popular will. But they are the oldest creations of man—as old as civilization, or as history itself. To trace the genealogy of our laws, we should not stop at King Alfred, nor the Code of Justinian, but go back to the laws of Moses, which, though given three thousand years ago, have been flowing on through all these centuries, like the waters of the Nile. When our Pilgrim fathers crossed the sea they formed in the cabin of the Mayflower a constitution for their little State, which they tried to frame after the pattern given in the Mount. Traces of that code still remain. The setting apart of one day in seven as a day of rest, dates from Mount Sinai, while the sacredness of marriage received its sacrament of baptism in the Garden of Eden.

As laws are the oldest of human institutions so are they the most enduring. A good law does not weaken by time, but grows stronger and stronger. Men do not get tired of justice, but cling to it, and hand it down as a sacred heritage to their children. The legislator who has framed but one such law has planted in the earth an acorn that may grow to be an oak, with trunk so strong, and arms so wide, that many generations shall sit under its shade. It may even grow to the stature of the cedars of Lebanon, whose mighty trunks have stood the storms of three thousand years! The sturdy growths of law become knarled and knotted by time, till they become a part of the very constitution of human society, to endure as long as society itself.

And well is it that it is so, for law is the only thing that holds the world together; and holds it not for evil, but for good; not to make men slaves, but to make them free.

A thought that was never out of Mr. Field's mind was the moral effect of laws that commend themselves to the plain and sober sense of common people. He believed that nothing was so demoralizing as injustice, as it destroys the sense of right and wrong. On the other hand a simple maxim of law, that was an echo of common sense and common justice, was an education in righteousness, and the constant pressure of a code so framed was a powerful influence upon national character—an influence that was not only perpetuated but increased from generation to generation.

"Let me make the songs of a people, and I care not who makes its laws," is a very pretty saying that lacks nothing but truth. A song of home or country may indeed send a thrill to the heart of an exile from the land of his birth. But laws are not meant to thrill us with transient sensations, but to rule our lives, grasping us like the forces of nature, surrounding us like the atmosphere, and holding us fast like gravitation.

Does this put us in the remorseless gripe of nature; under the crushing weight of laws to which there is no relief of sunshine or of song? I answer that in the last analysis law *is* harmony. "Law has her seat in the bosom of God, and her voice is the harmony of the world." Gentle manners are the offspring of an authority that is firm but kindly. When there is one law for all men, high and low, rich and poor, then will come the day of the great reconciliation. But it is in the order of things that law should go before, and songs and rejoicings should follow after.

If it be a question of the fame that shall live, as between the lawgiver and the conqueror, we have the final judgment of one who was both. When Napoleon was in exile at St. Helena, he found that Europe was not perpetuating his name by celebrating his victories, and that they would give him but a poor hold on the gratitude of the world that he was leaving behind. But there was another and better title to the remembrance of future generations: "I shall go down to posterity with the Code in my right hand!" Was there ever a nobler claim for immortality? Napoleon is dead, but the Code Napoleon still lives and may live as long as the nation for which it was made exists. But is he the only one that has followed this path to glory? On the morning when the flag was drooping at half-mast over the City Hall, a judge sitting on the bench adjourned his court, saying that the words of Napoleon might have been spoken with far more truth of an American jurist who had just breathed his last.* May not the tribute of honor which we gladly pay to the sovereign who served his country by his laws more

* If the benefit of laws be measured by the myriads they rule, the population of the States and Territories which adopted the codes, was greater than the whole population of France.

than by his wars, be claimed also for one who devoted his life to the laws of another country in another hemisphere?

Here, at the end of my story, I recur to my text on the title page: "It was the boast of Augustus that he found Rome of brick and left it of marble. But how much nobler shall be the sovereign's boast, when he shall have it to say that he found law dear and left it cheap; found it a sealed book, left it a living letter; found it the patrimony of the rich, left it the inheritance of the poor; found it the two-edged sword of craft and oppression, left it the staff of honesty and the shield of innocence."

Our American reformer was no sovereign and had no power to establish law by a decree, but standing alone—with but one purpose before him, that inscribed upon his tomb:

"*To bring justice within the reach of all men*"—

he pursued it for half a century, against an opposition that would have crushed most men, till before he closed his eyes in death he had given law to forty millions of his countrymen. Surely he who has left such a record to those who come after him, will have a name in history, as one who did as much as any man of his generation, to bring in the better time—which prophets have foretold—of the universal reign of righteousness and peace.